Memoirs of a Muppets Writer

(You mean somebody actually writes that stuff?)

by Joseph A. Bailey

Walnut Press

New York
www.WalnutPress.com

Dedicated to my beautiful wife, Gail Frank Bailey,
the first producer to believe I could write anything more
complicated than a beer commercial.

With special thanks to my dear friends
Gary Apple, Steve Gilford and Jack Heiszer
for their help and encouragement.

Published in New York, New York, by Walnut Press.
Cover and book designed by Angélica Yunuhén Sánchez
www.angelicayunuhen.com

Acknowledgments

Essentially, what you are about to read are my own personal "war stories" from 20 years of writing for the Muppets. So, these stories are about the people who were closest to me. However, there are many other *Sesame Street*, Muppet and production people, not mentioned in this book, who contributed mightily to whatever success my Muppet writing might have achieved. It's only right to acknowledge them here.

The Henson Family: Cheryl; Heather; Lisa; Brian; John and Mrs. Jane Henson.

The Sesame Street Cast: There's an old acting adage that goes, Never work with children or animals. These very talented artists not only worked with hundreds of children but also frogs, bears, pigs, penguins, assorted fruits and vegetables, and many other beings of undetermined origin. The cast members during my years on *Sesame Street* were: Linda Bove (Linda); Northern Calloway (David); Emilio Delgado (Luis); Will Lee (Mr. Hooper); Loretta Long (Susan); Sonia Manzano (Maria); Bob McGrath (Bob); Roscoe Orman (Gordon); and Alaina Reed (Olivia).

Sesame Street Writers: Judy Freuberg; Tony Geiss; Emily Pearl Kingsley; David Korr; Ray Sipherd; and Norman Styles.

Additional Puppeteers: Cheryl Blalock; Fran Brill; Louise Gold; Brian Muehl; Martin Robinson; and Caroly Wilcox.

Additional Puppet Designers and Builders: Cheryl Blalock; Bonnie Erickson; "Faz" Fazakas; Michael K. Frith; Larry Jameson; Mari Kaestle; Rollin Krewson; John Lovelady; Amy Van Gilder and Caroly Wilcox.

Production Staffers: Ozzie Alfonso; Martin Baker; Dr. Lewis Bernstein; Chris Cerf; Dave Conner; Victor DiNapoli; Blake Norton; Bob Emerick; Danny Epstein; Sharon Goode; Richard Holloway; Cher Jung; Lynn Klugman; Dick Maitland; Nat Mongioi; Thelma Moses; Bob Myhrum; Blake Norton; Mercedes Polanco; Tish Rabe; Arlene Sherman; Lisa Simon; and Emily Squires.

My sincere apologies to anyone I've omitted – It's been a while.

To
MARION —
KEEP THOSE
BALLS COMING
WEST
Love
Joe

AMEN CUM IN VIDICI CAEN

Sam Beaulieu, 1939 – 2008

Chapter 1
The Muppet Show

It was February 1977 and I was soaking up the sun on the idyllic Caribbean island of Antigua. I was also out of work.

During the fall of 1976, I was half way through my fourth season on the *Sesame Street* writing staff. After a hundred or so scripts, I felt I needed a break from the show. So, one day over lunch during the writers' hiatus, I told Jon Stone, *Sesame Street's* Executive Producer, that I would be leaving the show after the second half of the writing season.

Jon, understandably, was not happy about it. But, he understood and wished me luck. Shortly afterwards, it suddenly occurred to me that for the first time in four years, I had to find a job. I was "on the beach" now in more ways than one.

After four seasons together with Jim Henson on *Sesame Street*, I felt I knew him pretty well. So, I wrote him the following letter:

October 12, 1976

> *Dear Jim Henson (wherever you are):*

> *Since I picture you these days as a body constantly in motion, I've decided to put typewriter to paper rather than attempt a phone call.*

> *At the end of January 1977, my current contract with CTW will expire, and I've decided to leave Sesame Street at that time. After four seasons with the show, I feel I've expired all my possibilities of presenting the alphabet in new and different ways. So, after my present batch of scripts is finished, I'll be free to go on to other projects.*

Sometime in the future, when you've had a chance to catch your breath, I have several ideas I'd like to discuss with you. A Muppet Christmas Special and a feature length Muppet film are among them.

By the way, I told Jon Stone about my decision about a month ago, so now I consider myself a free agent, open and aboveboard.

Please give me a call when you have a chance.

Regards,

Sometime in early January 1977, I received a call from Jim's secretary setting up a meeting for the following week. At the appointed time, I went down to the converted carriage house on East 67th Street that was then Muppet Headquarters.

Jim and I had a lovely, amicable, half-hour chat about my leaving *Sesame Street* after four seasons, and *The Muppet Show,* which had started airing the past September and was more successful than either of us could have imagined. Jim then suggested I might want to write some audition pieces for the show. I said I would and left.

For the next two weeks I slaved over a *Muppet Show* script. These were the days before VCRs, but I had made audio cassettes of several episodes of the show. So, I was able to break it down on paper for structure and balance and get a flavor of some of the characters, who, with the exception of Kermit, were completely different from the *Sesame Street* cast and, therefore, new to me.

With the exception of the guest star material, on January 19, 1977, I messengered a complete *Muppet Show* script, to Jim on 67th Street. It had 24 separate scenes, which was about right. The regular *Muppet Show* had about 27 pieces, including introductions, quick sight gags, musical numbers, and a four-scene backstage story line. The guest star usually got two production numbers and a one-on-one interview with Kermit.

My script had a backstage story line built around the cast going on strike and refusing to do the show unless Kermit paid them. Kermit, as usual, was broke. Eventually Scooter's uncle, the unseen tyrant who owned the *Muppet Show* theater, agreed to make the payroll if the show produced his favorite form of entertainment. The uncle's favorite entertainment turned out to be lady wrestling.

Because Kermit was unable to find a second lady wrestler in time, the show ended with a wrestling match between Piggy, wrestling as *The Princess*, and Kermit, in drag, as the *Masked Crusader*. The piece ends with Piggy throwing Kermit out of the ring and into the box with Statler and Waldorf, the two elderly hecklers.

When Statler suggests, *I think you'd better give it up, Frog!*, Kermit replies with the oldest (and corniest) vaudeville joke: *What? And leave show business?*

Now that the script was finished and in Jim's hands, there was nothing to do but to wait for his reaction. I paced the floor for about two weeks before I finally called Jim's secretary and asked, "Well? Did he laugh?"

She called back later to make an appointment for me to see Jim.

In his low key way, Jim told me he liked my material and we discussed the show for a while. When the conversation came to a close, he said to me, "Well, what are you going to do now?"

I told him that my wife and I were leaving soon for a two-week vacation on the Caribbean Island of Antigua. He said he hoped we'd have a good time and the meeting ended with no further discussion.

So, my wife, Gail, and I went to Antigua to spend two weeks lying in the sun. When the two weeks were up, we were having such a good time we decided to stay a few more days. At the time, Gail, was a free-lance producer/director with no current commitments. And I, of course, was jobless. So there was really no reason for us to go back to frigid New York. Because of reservation limitations, we were forced to change hotels, not an undue hardship, to spend another few winter days in the Caribbean sun.

After several days at the new hotel, we returned from the beach on a late Sunday afternoon. The desk clerk handed me a telephone message. That was very unusual. No one ever called us on vacation. In fact, beside the weather, one of the reasons we liked vacationing on small Caribbean islands was how difficult it was to reach us. So, for a moment, I was afraid of a family crisis.

Instead, the message read, "Call Jim Henson immediately." Somehow, Jim had tracked me down in the middle of the Caribbean, even though I had changed hotels. I got on the phone to the Muppet offices and soon had Jim on the other end.

"Where are you?", he asked. "We're having a writers' meeting for the opening show of the new season. Why aren't you here?"

"Well, Jim, you see, nobody hired me."

"Oh. (Pause) Well, how soon can you get here?"

This was my first indication that behind the scenes, The Muppet Show was very much like, well, behind the scenes of The Muppet Show, only with people.

I told Jim I'd call him right back. I hung up the phone and called the airport.

"I've got to get to New York immediately. What have you got going to New York tonight?"

"Sorry, sir. We can't help you.", the pleasant voice with the West Indian lilt replied on the other end.

"Why not?"

"The airport is closed, sir."

"Closed!?"

"Yes, sir. You know, locks on the door, gates chained up. That sort of thing."

The Antiguan airport was not the hub of international travel of, say, O'Hare in Chicago. I confirmed our reservations to New York for the following Tuesday night and called Jim back.

"Tuesday night is the earliest I can get to New York, unless you want to send a plane for me.", I reported.

"Wednesday morning will be fine."

That night, my wife and I had a first class dinner to celebrate the fact that I was again gainfully employed.

We returned to New York on Tuesday night. When we got home, our apartment sitter had left a note saying that I was expected at a breakfast meeting the next day with Jim Henson and Jerry Juhl, *The Muppet Show* head writer, at the Regency Hotel on Park Avenue.

Wednesday came with temperatures in the mid-20s. After three weeks in the Caribbean, it felt like the Arctic Circle. I dressed in slacks and my warmest turtleneck sweater against the cold. At that time I owned a three-quarter length sheepskin coat with a long, curly, dark brown lambskin lining and cuffs. I put that on over the turtleneck.

I arrived at the hotel and met Jim and Jerry in the lobby. As we were about to enter the dining room, the maitre'd told me that I wouldn't be admitted because I wasn't wearing a jacket. I asked the coat check attendant for a waiter's jacket, which was usually the solution to that problem. But I was told they didn't have any.

"Well, you'll just have to wear your coat.", Jim said with an impish grin.

So, the three of us entered the dining room and took a table. The room was full of well dressed, high-powered executives taking "power breakfasts," and here was I, soaked in sweat, trying unsuccessfully to keep my lambskin cuffs out of the eggs benedict.

Attempting to look professional, I took out a pad and pencil and muttered something about taking notes.

"Well. We have to give him something to write down.", Jim said to Jerry, thoroughly enjoying my discomfort.

"We'll be going to Los Angeles in about a week. Can you make that?" I assured Jim that I could. "And, we'll be sailing for England on the QE-2 on May 8th. Okay?"

I've often been asked how we wound up producing *The Muppet Show* in England in the first place. In 1975, there was no cable TV and only three American television networks: ABC; CBS; and NBC. Incredible as it sounds, all three of them turned down the show after seeing the pilot. Puppets, they believed, were only for children.

In Europe, it was just the opposite. Europeans were used to sophisticated puppetry. In the 17th, 18th and 19th centuries, Punch and Judy were used for political satire. After the traditional opening lines, the puppeteer was free to do whatever he liked. So, Punch and Judy regularly ridiculed regents and governments. Sometimes they were the only political criticism allowed. After all, a king could behead a political opponent, but he'd look pretty silly beheading a puppet.

I've also seen European puppet productions that featured singing and dancing body parts. I'll leave it to your imagination to figure out exactly which body parts they were.

So, it was Lord Lew Grade, the flamboyant British impresario, who believed in and backed *The Muppet Show*. Lord Grade owned A.T.V. Studios outside of London. So, that's where the show was produced. Lord Grade also secured a spot for The Muppet Show on English television, where it was as big, if not a bigger, hit than it was in the United States.

At the start of the show's premier season, 1976, the Muppet gang went to England on the QE-2, mostly because Jim and his wife, Jane, wanted to take a sea voyage. The only way that Jim, who was always pressed for time, could do it, was to take the company with him. It was becoming a tradition for the Muppets to sail to England on the Elizabeth at the start of every new season.

Jim, Jerry and I finished breakfast and left the Regency's dining room. In the lobby, Jim excused himself to do a press interview and Jerry and I agreed to continue our conversation in his room. He and I were standing at the elevators and Jim was striding quickly on his long legs toward the door on the other side of the lobby when suddenly I had a realization.

"Hey, Jim!", I shouted across the lobby, "Who do I talk to about money!?"

"Al Gottesman!", Jim yelled back before disappearing out the door.

Jerry and I went up to his room to continue our conversation. I had known Jerry through the Muppet pieces he contributed to *Sesame Street* . But I had never met him in person. So, this was the start of a friendship that lasted until his untimely death in 2005.

That afternoon, I called the Muppet offices to set up an appointment with Al Gottesman, who was the head of the Muppet legal department. "Sorry, I was told, "Mr. Gottesman just left for a two-week Caribbean vacation."

So, for the next two weeks I reveled in the fact that I was going to write the hottest show on television, while at the same time not knowing how long the job would last or how much money I would be making. Life with the Muppets was like that sometimes.

Chapter 2
First, A Little Background

It was the best of times. It was the best of times. To begin with, it was all a marvelous fluke. At thirty years of age, I got to run away and join the circus. The adventure lasted for 20 years. And, the only adverse effect was an acute case of Muppetitis, an incurable disease caused by overexposure to Muppets in close quarters. Its most serious symptom is an uncontrollable urge to speak in strange voices at inopportune times.

Maybe it had something to do with being born on April Fool's Day (minutes old and a joke already!). That's as good an explanation as any, because I certainly never saw myself as the literary type. I'm not even sure if writing for the Muppets actually qualifies me as a true member of the literati. I was not one of those kids who was reading Chaucer and Shakespeare under the covers with a flash light. My undercover flashlight reading ran more to Marvel Comics and the occasional *Playboy*.

Neither did I come from a literary family. Both my parents came from the immigrant ghetto of early 20th Century Hell's Kitchen. My father was an Irish-American saloon keeper who left school in the eighth grade to go to work when his parents died. My mother, the *intelligencia* of the family, had a high school degree. The closest my family ever got to the literati were the sports writers my father hung out with at the track. I could imagine myself many things: jet pilot; cowboy; fireman; Archbishop of Boston; but never a writer.

Nor did I grow up in a literary atmosphere. I was born in Brooklyn, New York, but grew up in Boston. Not the Beacon Hill, Symphony Orchestra, Harvard's-across-the-River, Cabots and Lodges Boston. I grew up in the shot-and-a-beer, "How about them Bruins" Boston.

My first memories are of living in a small, two room, hotel suite in Boston's notorious tenderloin known as the *Combat Zone*. The Brigham Hotel was located directly over the Silver Dollar Bar. The Silver Dollar, then known worldwide as *The Poor Man's Stork Club*, was one of, if not, the world's biggest saloons. The main room boasted the longest bar in the world: 130 feet.

Behind the main room was a good sized night club called, *The Blue Room*. *The Blue Room* required jackets and ties. Ladies had to be escorted. It had an orchestra, dance floor and full kitchen. It attracted Boston's elite. The Silver Dollar Bar catered to every class: upper; middle; lower; and no.

Since my father owned both the Brigham Hotel and the Silver Dollar Bar, life was like a never-ending performance of *Guys* and *Dolls*. My world was filled with bartenders, waiters, waitresses, chefs, musicians, horse players, cops, saloon keepers, and the occasional wise guy.

The most read document in my universe was the *Morning Telegraph*. I thought sitting at a bar all day, handicapping horses, was a respectable way to make a living. I even knew a few guys who did make a living at it.

Until I went to boarding school at five and a half, and saw another kid, I thought I was a midget. That's because my father had hired a midget bartender, called, (naturally) "Charlie McCarthy." He did it just to see the expression on patrons faces when, after a couple of drinks an ethereal voice would ask, "How about another?" Then two hands would appear from behind the bar, take the empty glass and replace it with a full one.

I couldn't understand why Charlie was allowed to stay up late, smoke Chesterfields, drink rye and play the horses. I wasn't.

The boarding school, Saint Joseph's Academy in Wellesley Hills, Massachusetts, run by the Sisters of Charity from Halifax, Nova Scotia, was a bit of a change from the Silver Dollar Bar. For one thing, there were real kids, not midgets. There were about 30 of us five-and-a-half and six-year-olds, sitting around on steamer trunks full of underwear with our names sewn into the waistbands. This may sound strange to you. But we didn't know anything else. We just figured when you were five and a half, you shipped out.

In retrospect, my eight years at Saint Joseph's may have stimulated my sense of creativity. Since we were a large group of boys who ate, slept, washed, and studied together, and usually walked everywhere two abreast in line, it was easy enough for us to create fantasies about being recruits in an army camp or the crew of a battleship. Some of them lasted for days.

After Saint Joseph's, I went to Boston College High School. There, the Jesuits taught me History, Theology, Math, English, Latin and Ancient Greek, all under pain of death and/or dismemberment.

As you might imagine, my mother and father were not the type of parents to whom you announced one day, "I've made a career decision: I'm going to dedicate my life to writing funny things for frogs and pigs to say to children."

My father, the Irish saloon keeper, had told me, for as long as I could remember, "Go to law school. Go to law school. Go to law school!"

When I finally asked him, "Why?", he told me, "Look, you go to law school. You graduate. You pass the bar. Then we bribe someone and make you a judge. That's a lifetime job, and all you have to worry about is where the 'juice' is coming from." This actually made perfect sense in 1950s Boston, where corruption was right up there with banking and fishing as a major municipal industry.

Next to the priesthood, my mother, an Italian-American housewife, thought that Nirvana was a civil service job with a pension after 30 years of clerking in the Department of Motor Vehicles.

But then fate lent a well-manicured hand. In college, I joined the campus newspaper, but not because of any burning literary bent. My girlfriend at the time was on the newspaper staff and we used the newspaper office for day time trysts between classes.

We were getting strange looks when we came out of the office together. So, she decided I should join the newspaper staff to protect whatever was left of her reputation.

She was really good looking, so I ran right down to the newspaper and volunteered. But it wasn't until my first newspaper meeting that I realized people actually wrote stuff in the newspaper office, and soon, I was expected to do likewise.

At the meeting, the paper's editor explained that they always needed fillers to finish out the last three inches of a column. Having always had a quick mouth, but no love for composition or spelling, I figured the easiest thing I could write was a humor column that could be cut to fill out the bottom three inches of the short columns. Without thinking, I suggested we call it, *Bailey's Three Inches*, an inopportune idea which supplied the college's sororities with endless entertainment for the rest of the semester. We finally just called it, *J.B.*

It was then that I discovered how naive I really was to think I could just write comedy. When the great actor Edmund Booth was dying, a friend asked if dying was hard. "No.", replied Booth. "Dying is easy. Comedy is hard." I quickly discovered how right he was. Mostly, I plagiarized material from *Tonight Show* monologs and cleaned up *Playboy* Party Jokes. Mercifully, all copies of *J.B.* were suspiciously destroyed years ago.

In February 1962, the middle of my sophomore year, due to a family crisis, college and I parted ways by mutual consent. (In truth, it was probably a little more mutual on their part.)

Part of my mustering out of college was an exit interview with my student advisor. He asked me if I had any thoughts of my future. I told him my master plan was to get a job, probably pumping gas, save my money all winter, and in the spring, buy a motorcycle, ride it to Sausalito, and chase girls.

I had never been to Sausalito but I liked the sound of it, and I understood there were a lot of girls there to be chased. (Eventually, I did motorcycle to Sausalito 30 years later. There were still plenty of girls to chase. But my wife, who is usually pretty broad-minded about my motorcycle escapades, drew the line on that one.)

My advisor brought up my newspaper column and a little satire I had written on the sophomore English Lit. reading list called, *Death of an Enemy of Major Barbara's Ghosts in the Rye*. He said I had a flare for writing and suggested that I try to get a job writing advertising. Having read Sloan Wilson's, *The Man in the Grey Flannel Suit*, my only impression of advertising at the time was martinis, wall-to-wall carpeting and girls. So, it seemed like a pretty good alternative to pumping gas through the long Massachusetts winter.

(The only other talent I had exhibited so far was tending bar. Since that's done standing up, and writing is done sitting down, my career decision was easy. Although, as I've often said, I met a better class of people tending bar.)

I put together a portfolio of my college columns and some ads I had created for my high school year book. Then, I ran a newspaper ad next to the advertising column of the Boston Globe which read:

HELP!
Talented young man needs position
in advertising or public relations.
(Phone Number)

A wonderfully adventurous man by the name of Edwin F. Hall, who ran a one-man P.R. and advertising agency, took a gamble and hired me for the princely sum of $50.00 a week. Ed ran the business from the attic of his home in Sharon, Massachusetts. Since Sharon was some 35 miles distant from my home, with no public transportation, I used the job as an excuse to buy my first motorcycle. My parents were less than enthusiastic.

Chapter 3
Mad Man

E d Hall's clientele were among the industrial research and development firms located along Route 128, the electronic golden girdle around greater Boston that sprang up because of the close proximity to the Massachusetts Institute of Technology. My first assignment was to write a short speech for an executive of an electronics firm.

Now that I had landed a job as a professional writer, and gotten my first assignment, I immediately came down with a severe case of writers' block. I sat frozen at the typewriter.

After an hour or so, Ed, a very patient man, told me to write the Lord's Prayer.

"Sorry, I'm not very religious.", I told him.

"Write it anyway."

So, I began to type, "Our Father, Who art in heaven . . ."
When I finished, Ed said to me, "Is that what you want to say?"

"No.", I told him. "Instead of 'Our Father', I was thinking more along the lines of, 'Good evening, ladies and gentlemen. It's a great pleasure to be here tonight."

"Well, scratch out the first line and write that in its place."

I did.

"What about, 'Who are in heaven'"?, Ed asked.

"I think, 'I want to speak to you about something very important to our industry.' might be more appropriate?"

See?", Ed told me. Now you're re-writing. Re-writing is always easier than writing."

And so, I had my first lesson in big-time, professional writing: All writing is re-writing.

My first advertising assignment was to create an ad for an industrial glassblower. One of Ed's clients had hired a glassblower to make one-of-a-kind lab glassware to the specifications of their research staff. They had set him up with his own shop. The thought was that other R & D firms in the area might also need his services.

Before I wrote the ad, I spent an afternoon with the glassblower watching him work. It was fascinating. One of the great things about writing advertising is that it was really a liberal education. Every new client was a new industry, product or process and market to be studied and mastered.

Under Ed's tutelage, I wrote space ads, brochures, press releases and magazine articles for his industrial and corporate clients.

But, after six months or so, Ed lost a major account and could no longer afford my $50 a week. So, he had to lay me off with a glowing letter of recommendation. Getting laid off, I was soon to find out, was an occupational hazard in the advertising business.

My next job was writing for the catalog division of a large engineering firm. I spent my days singing the literary praises of industrial fire alarm systems and hospital nurse call systems - heady stuff.

The owner of the firm was a big aficionado of world class yacht racing. He spent millions building a racing boat for that year's America's Cup Race. When the boat failed to qualify, most of my division got laid off. Hands down, that's the classiest reason I've ever gotten for being canned – *So sorry. The yacht didn't make it to the America's Cup. Have to let you go. Ta.*

For the next few years, I worked steadily in several advertising agencies and advertising departments in Boston and Providence, R.I. I created ads for such subjects of extraordinary fascination as textile chemicals, water expansion tanks, knitting machines, office furniture, high vacuum equipment and paint.

Jack Drummey, The Creative Director of deGarmo-Boston Advertising Agency, was well known around town as a larger-than life personality. He was the Man of The Year and President of everything, including the Boston Advertising Club. Jack had his own radio show and later had political cartoons published in the Wall Street Journal. He was also my boss.

Jack really taught me the craft of writing creative advertising copy. He taught me how to make it interesting and keep it that way. He was one of the most naturally creative men I've ever met.

Several months after I joined deGarmo-Boston, they started to actively pursue new business. And so, we started a series of new account presentations. Once we had a foot in the door, we would dream up a creative campaign while the account- and media-guys would draw up plans of their own.

The pitch crew consisted of the account executive, who would cover the business end, Jack, who was very theatrical, would do the creative presentation. There was also an art director, and a copywriter, me. But, we said very little. The art guy was there to look arty. And, I was there to look, I guess, *writer-ly*.

After two presentations or so, Jack decided I would look more *writer-ly* if I wore horn-rimmed glasses. My then girl friend, who worked summers for an optometrist, took me in for a pair of plain lens glasses. She picked out a very nice tortoise shell, late Cary Grant pair of horn rims for me. Jack insisted I wear them to presentations. I may have even wrangled a raise.

The next two presentations were successful. And after the third, Jack attributed our victories to my glasses. He became intrigued with the whole let's-dress-the-copywriter-up-funny thing. I could see his mind at work. Finally it came to him. I should grow a beard! I guess he'd seen something about bearded creative types in *Advertising Age*. I flatly refused at first. But Jack kept at me.

Then came the agency's Christmas party. My girlfriend, the afore mentioned summer time optometrist's assistant, was also in her senior year at Emerson College, studying for her degree in Theatre. As a gag, she took some spirit gum and crepe hair and put a false beard on me for the party.

That did it. Jack insisted I grow a beard. I did and the business grew, too. Most of the people who grew beards in the '60s did so to protest the war in Vietnam. Not me. I grew mine for the lofty purpose of increasing bottom line revenues.

In June 1967, my girlfriend, the retired optometrist's assistant and now actress, was awarded her degree in Speech and Theatre Arts from Emerson College. Modeling for walking around money, she spent six months, in vain, looking for acting work in Boston.

Finally, she sat me down and said, "Look. I'm an actress and you're a copywriter. New York is the center of theatre and advertising. What the hell are we doing in Boston? Let's move to New York."

I didn't need much convincing. My whole family was in New York except my parents. Thanks to them, I even had a New York accent. And my girlfriend had grown up right across the Hudson River in Union City, New Jersey. Her parents still lived there. So, we decided to put together a grub stake and move to New York. She went after modeling and movie extra work, and I went to work writing for the Radio Shack.

The Radio Shack, which then boasted 11 stores, nationwide, was perfect for me. Whenever they produced catalogs and fliers, they hired a staff of copywriters and art directors. We got paid by the hour – probably about $2.00. The copywriter received a layout of a catalog page. From it, he could tell how many letters he had for a headline and how much copy he could write. When he finished, he would "spec" the copy - indicating font, size, spacing and width – and sent it off to the typesetter.

To stretch the job out, I took up photography to continue working after the copy was all written. I even talked them into letting me take the printing mechanicals to the airport on my motorcycle to ship them to the New Hampshire printer. On those trips, I got my hourly rate *plus* 15 cents a mile for the bike. I think at the time, gas was around 20 cents a gallon. The bike got 60 miles to a gallon of gas.

When the publications were finished, Radio Shack let everybody go. So, during the hiatuses, I traveled to New York, slept on friends' couches, and looked for a copywriting job. I picked up some free-lance work from E.J. Korvettes department store and the men's department of Lane Bryant, a department store that specialized in big and tall men..

Finally, I got a permanent copywriting job in a division of J.C. Penney. Once I had steady work, my girlfriend and I moved to a tiny apartment over The Press Box, a celebrity steak house on East 45th Street in Manhattan.

Ironically, my girlfriend never pursued her acting career. As soon as we got into town, she landed a job as an assistant film editor. One production job let to another and another, and now she's a very successful television producer, married to a very fine actor.

Although J.C. Penney was a permanent job, I still had free-lance status there. It seems that Penney's had a company policy against their "associates" having facial hair. And I had a beard, thanks to Jack Drummey. So they could only hire me on a free-lance basis.

At the end of the week, I billed Penney's for five days of writing at a day rate of probably $50.00 a day. I was a vendor, not an employee or, "associate" as Penney called them. There was only one other guy at Penney's who was free-lance, an art director who insisted on wearing gaudy suspenders festooned with naked women.

The division of J.C. Penney for which I worked was called Treasure Island. It was a group of nine department stores located in Madison, Wisconsin and Atlanta, Georgia. Penney used them to experiment with new marketing and merchandising techniques.

Working for Treasure Island was a real writing apprenticeship. All day long, I wrote newspaper ads for cameras, sports equipment, stereos, household appliances, tires, motor oil, linens, lawn furniture, power tools, men's fashion, camping equipment, televisions, toys, lawn tractors, lighting, school supplies and home furnishings – another education.

I eventually moved on to real advertising agencies and got to write my share of real fun consumer stuff like SAAB automobiles, Beefeater Gin, and Heineken Beer. I was learning the techniques I would use later to "sell" the alphabet to kids on Sesame Street, years later.

And, I was a real Mad Man. I had a office on Madison Avenue. I had a closet full of tailored suits. I hung out in the *Mad Men* places: P.J. Clark's, The Roosevelt Hotel, and Toots Shor's. I was 26. I was making about $400.00 a week. Guys making $300.00 a week were buying houses on Long Island. Life was good.

Then Madison Avenue started to loosen up. This was the 1960s and the "creative revolution" was in full swing. Volkswagen was encouraging everybody to "Think Small." Noxzema Shave Cream had a sexy Swedish blonde urging men to "Take it all off."

Nehru suits and turtlenecks were replacing grey flannel. Hair got longer and longer and the mini skirts got shorter and shorter. However, the two-hour, three martini, expense account lunch was still a hallowed institution.

The first cold day of winter, I threw caution to the wind and decided to wear a turtleneck instead of a shirt and tie, I went to work and discovered half the agency had done the same thing. I was in a meeting with two other creative types and we were all wearing turtlenecks. An account executive stuck his head in the door and announced that we looked like a convention of U-boat commanders.

Loopy things happened in New York in the 60s. One Christmas, I got to lead a kilt-y band! A sketch artist at the agency where I worked was a kilt-y band aficionado. He and a few of his piper buddies had been asked to entertain at the office Christmas Party. They decided they needed a drum major and since I was tall and bearded, they offered me the job.

On the day of the party, I formed up with the rest of the band at the artist's East Side apartment. There I donned the kilt, the tartan knee sox, major's hat, and then topped it off with a sporn (fur pouch) and a smee (dagger). Then we headed downtown to the office.

On the Lexington Avenue subway, a guy stood up and gave me his seat. The band tells me this happens a lot when you wear a kilt in public. The joke gets old fast.

When we left the subway, the band formed up behind me. I banged my ten-foot baton on the sidewalk. "To the right! Hard! March!", I commanded. And with the skirl of bagpipes and a rattle of drums, I marched my little four man kilt-y band into our office building, through its lobby and into an elevator. The music continued all the way up to the 36th Floor. We were a big hit at the office party.

Then, someone got word to us that MacGregor Sportswear had their head quarters several floors below in our building. They had gotten wind of a kilt-y band in the building, and invited us to *their* Christmas party, which was in full swing. We were an even bigger hit at MacGregor, who plied us with another well-known product of Scotland.

At MacGregor, we were told that our presence would really be appreciated around the corner at Al Italia. Their reservations phone operators occupied two floors in a neighboring office tower. Even though it was Christmas Eve, they were chained to their phones. Entertaining two floors of lonely Italian women seemed a most Christian thing to do in the spirit of the holiday.

So, I fired up the band, marched it out of MacGregor, to much applause, into the elevator, through the lobby and down Fifth Avenue. Most people cheered us on. But, you'd be surprised how many people on the street ignored us. We marched into the *Al Italia* building and elevated to the phone banks.

We serenaded the signorinas, who were also very appreciative. But I must tell you, in the elevator, some of those Italian girls tried to slip a hand up my skirt.

In the mid 60s, business was booming on Madison Avenue. People were jetting off to exotic locations to film commercials. The business was looser. Creative was king.

At one point I had two jobs at the same time. I had heard my agency was about to lose an account. So, I jumped the gun and got my old job back at Penney's. When I turned in my resignation, the agency head told me the account wasn't leaving. He then amazed me by telling me to take the job at Penney's but remain on salary at the agency, too. It didn't last very long. Eventually the client did leave. But, I got a new motorcycle out of the deal – my first B.M.W.

On another occasion, I was working for the ad agency that handled Beefeater Gin. I had scheduled a week's vacation in London and I suggested to the agency president that since we were Beefeater's American agency, maybe I should stop by the Beefeater distillery and show the flag. He thought it was such a good idea that he volunteered to have the agency pay my hotel bill.

When I got to London, I called the marketing manager at Beefeater and introduced myself. "Advertising people bore me," he told me with a hint of British humor. "But come on Thursday. We're having a meeting of advertising blokes from England, Ireland and Scotland. So, you can all bore each other." That night, I received a warm letter of welcome, directions to the distillery, and a bottle of their very fine product.

Thursday started out disastrously. I had been out much too late the night before with a gang of Australians. If you wanted a cold beer in England in those days, you had to find an Aussie first.

So, I overslept and discovered I had no film for my camera. I figured I had to bring back some pictures to justify my hotel bill. Without so much as a cup of coffee, I left the hotel and ran around London looking for Minox camera film, not the easiest film to find.

I just barely made my 10:00 a.m. appointment at the distillery. The first thing my host said to me was, "Well, how about a drink?" What was I to do? The fact was I didn't even like gin, having misplaced a rather large, four-door DeSoto sedan during a martini drenched evening some years before. But, this was an important client. "I'll have a martini," I replied bravely.

"I know how you Yanks like them.", He explained, as he built me a double.

I took a tentative sip.

"Drink up. Drink up! You have to take the tour before lunch."

"Breakfast of Champions" went through my mind as I downed the double martini in one gulp.

I was then introduced to Nigel, my distillery guide. Nigel was from somewhere in the Midlands, so I could barely understand a word he said.

The distillery was a bit of a disappointment. Since gin isn't aged, there were no old oaken casks in dusty cellars. Everything was stainless steel and glass. It looked more like a Chevrolet plant than a venerable old distillery. I took copious pictures of everything anyway.

It did have one feature that a Chevy plant didn't. I guess because of WW. II and the fear of air raids, the distillery seemed to have a bar every hundred feet or so on the assembly line. Of course, Nigel insisted we stop at every one of them. After the second or third stop, Nigel became completely incomprehensible. By the time we finished, I was a little incomprehensible myself.

Back in the conference room, about a dozen or so international versions of me had gathered and, of course, opened the bar. They were playing a game. I never did get the name of it. But, it involved (How can I put this delicately?) holding large coins between the cheeks of one's butt and trying to drop them into a glass on the floor from a standing position. I wasn't very good at it. I guess when it comes to sophisticated entertainment, we Americans will never catch up with Europeans.

After the winner was announced, and properly toasted, we left for lunch. There was a fleet of limousines waiting for us. On the way to the cars, my host said to me, "Sorry about the flag."

"What's wrong with the flag?", I asked.

"It only has 49 stars."

I turned and looked. There, atop the Beefeater distillery, in my honor, brilliant against a cloudless blue sky, flew a 49-star Stars and Stripes. I think I muttered something about not mentioning it to President Nixon.

We arrived at a very exclusive French restaurant. At the bar, I tried to slow down by ordering a Bloody Mary. Meanwhile, my host was deep in conversation with the sommelier about which wines would accompany which courses at lunch.

My memory is a little hazy but I do remember at the end of the very elaborate meal a very attractive woman, who turned out to be the restaurant's owner, going around the table pouring cognac.

"The calf! The calf!", the others were shouting at me. I turned around looking for some sort of bovine.

Then they explained. The idea was that as this woman was filling your glass, you were to rub the back of her calf with your hand. As long as you kept rubbing, she kept pouring. Was there no end to these delightful European traditions!?

After lunch, for some reason, I accompanied the account executive from their London advertising agency back to his office, Since it was Guy Fawkes Day, my new friend invited me to a holiday party in his neighborhood. Guy Fawkes was an English anarchist who attempted to blow up Parliament on November 5, 1605 and failed. Every year on November 5, the Brits burn Guy Fawkes in effigy and set off firecrackers.

So, on the way to the party, we stopped at Harrod's department store to pick up a few tons of fireworks. I remember sitting on a tube train with them in my lap as the rest of the car blithely puffed away on cigarettes and flicked their sparks around me.

The Guy Fawkes Day party turned out to be a rather snooty affair where the conversation ran to, "Basil must be shagging the new nanny. He just bought Gwendolyn a Bentley convertible." The rest of the evening is a complete blur.

I'll admit it. Advertising was fun. It *really* was wall-to-wall carpeting, martinis, and girls (the actress/producer and I having split up amicably a year or so after we moved to New York).

But most importantly, I learned the mechanics of writing. For ten years I earned a living by putting words down on paper, or creating scenarios for industrial films or television commercials.

I've always felt there were two major elements of writing: inspiration and mechanics. Inspiration is something you're born with (or without). There's no way to make Stephen King scary or Dave Barry funny. They just are. But both of them have learned the mechanics of writing. So, when inspiration comes along, they can get it down on paper.

Journalists, novelists, playwrights, copywriters, poets and screen writers all, essentially do the same thing: tell a story. Some of the stories are true. Some are fiction.

There's an old joke about a guy who goes to prison. In the mess hall on his first night, another inmate stands up and says, "14!"

Everybody laughs.

A few minutes later, another inmate stands and says, "34!"

Again, everybody laughs.

Shortly, another con stands and says, "42!"

Cold silence.

The new inmate turns to the guy next to him and asks, "What's going on with the numbers?"

"Well, we've all been in here a long time and we all know the same jokes. So, to save time, we numbered them".

"Then, how come the guys who sad, '14', got a laugh, and the guy who yelled, "34", got one, but nobody laughed at the guy who said, '14'?"

"You know how it is. Some people can tell a joke and . . . "

So, I learned the craft of writing: which words are more effective; which words are more persuasive; how to keep my copy lively; how to think in pictures, and how to cut my work to fit time and space constraints.

Alas, my advertising career came to a crashing halt one Monday morning when I found the front door of my employer padlocked. It was their unique method of informing the staff that they had gone out of business.

Chapter 4
Comin' Thru la Rai

In the early 1970s, the advertising business was in a slump and copywriting jobs were scarce. Fortunately, I had a lot of friends in the New York film industry. So, I paid my rent by working as a free-lance carpenter, stage hand, truck driver, whatever, on television commercials and film shoots around the city. I even acted in one or two. I also worked as a swing bartender in an East Side singles bar.

As part of my film work, I free-lanced pretty steadily for the R.A.I. (Radio Audizioni Italiane), the national Italian television network, traveling around the country as part of their U.S. documentary film crews.

When an R.A.I. producer/director in Rome got an assignment for the States, they came alone, or with one assistant, to New York, where they picked up an American crew through the R.A.I. New York Office. I was recommended to them by a friend of mine who asked me to fill in for him because he was already booked for that day. In free lance, it's either a feast or a famine.

I remember my first R.A.I. job. I was to hold the movie lamp while the producer interviewed Gus Hall, then head of the New York City Communist Party. When we got to Mr. Hall's office, the cameraman got arty and decided to shoot the interview with available light. So, I spent my first day working for Italian television sitting around Communist Party Headquarters and boning up on Lenin.

But, the R.A.I. took a liking to me. I'm pretty sure it's because I let them know as quickly as possible (in really rotten Italian) that my mother's people were from Naples. This was officially my first job in television.

A typical R.A.I. job would start with a phone call. A woman's voice with a heavy Italian accent would ask, *Yawannawork?*

"How many days is the gig?"

Yawannawork?

"Am I going to be traveling?"

Yawannawork?

"Okay. Si. Si!"

Commindaoff.

Hands down, the staff of the New York office of the R.A.I. -- secretaries and assistants to the senior executives -- were the most beautiful, chicest, well-coiffed group of working women I had ever seen. And, I had worked in Madison Avenue ad agencies and production companies.

Unfortunately, their English was very, very limited. But the executives they worked for must have still found them indispensable for some reason, because they brought them all the way to New York, while leaving their wives and kids back in Rome.

Anyway, after I *commindaoff*, one of these beauties would hand me air line tickets and an expense check. That's when I knew where I was going and how many days I'd be on the road -- Look at that. *I'm going Cleveland for three days and then on to Indianapolis.* Since I was going through a fortune on the road in tooth brushes and underwear, I quickly learned how to say, in Italian, *How many days work?* And, *Am I traveling?*, so I could pack accordingly.

I believe the *R.A.I. crew per diem* was $50.00. But, a decent motel room could then be had for $15.00 a night. And most nights, the producer would pick up our dinner bills.

I remember one wonderful guy who, in Baltimore, insisted we go to the best seafood restaurant for dinner and have the best sea food the Atlantic Ocean had to offer. *Because*, tomorrow we were flying to Washington State, and he was planning on going to the best seafood house in Seattle and sampling the best seafood that the Pacific Ocean had to offer. The Italians really lived well on the road.

In truth, most of those dinners were working dinners. But, it was a nice bonus to get home from ten days or so on the road, turn in an invoice for your time, and still have a few hundred dollars in expense money in your pocket. $100.00 went a long way in 1970. My rent was $165.00 a month, utilities included.

So, I traveled the country with the R.A.I. We covered a Barbie factory in Los Angeles. We profiled an out-of-work Boeing aircraft engineer in Seattle. We chased the Mafia from the Waldorf Astoria Hotel on Park Avenue to Arthur Avenue in the Italian Bronx. I interviewed John Kenneth Galbraith – twice.

On weekends, if I was in New York, I had a second job working as a projectionist for an attache' from the Italian Embassy. He had a side line showing the R.A.I.'s Soccer Game of the Week in Italian soccer clubs around New York. On Friday and Saturday nights, we would load an enormous 16-millimeter Sonorex projector into his tiny Ford Pinto and drive to pockets of Italian immigrants in Brooklyn, Queens and the Bronx.

Private Italian soccer clubs are one of those wonderful New York sub-cultures, a side of the city most people never see. Some of them are quite elaborate with beautiful espresso bars and well-equipped function rooms. They not only field a soccer team, they function as a replacement for the cafes back home. A lot of those immigrant neighborhoods are extensions of small Italian villages, peopled with old friends and relatives and local dialects still prevail.

Along with being cranky and unreliable, the Sonorex was also a complicated projector. The sound and the picture ran on separate reels and were difficult to cue up together. Since the audio was in Italian, it was difficult at times to know when sound and picture were in synch. And, since most of the audience spoke limited English, they really couldn't tell me.

"Ay! First, he talks. *Then* he kicks la balla!", was a common complaint.

But, when things went well, I was invited to the club's bar for a drink and an espresso. And, somebody would usually slip me five or ten dollars. One Saturday night, I realized I had invited some people for Sunday pasta and had

35

no wine. New York liquor stores closed on Sundays in those days and it was already past their Saturday night closing hour.

"Who makes the wine?", I asked the bartender in halting Italian. I knew that every one of these clubs had at least one wine maker. The bartender pointed to a guy at the end of the bar.

"Excuse me," (again the rotten Italian) "I understand you're the wine guy around here. And I need a couple of bottles for dinner tomorrow."

Aspeta, he tells me, *wait*, and disappears toward the cellar.

He reappears with two quart *7-Up* bottles filled with red wine and topped off with corks. When I asked him how much, he told me, *niente* - nothing. *Bono appetito!*

Most of the Americans in the New York Office list could speak pretty fluent Italian. I had words I had picked up over the years in a dozen different dialects. So, I muddled along with the Romans in French. But, as I traveled with the R.A.I., my Italian got better. There's no better way to learn a language than to be immersed in it all day, with people talking about what they're doing at the time. Of course, I've forgotten most of it by now.

I gypsied around with the Italians like this from 1970 to 1972. I was paying the rent. Life was interesting. Life was fun. And I was picking up practical production experience. I learned to re-load a camera magazine. I worked with sound men and editors. I drove a camera car. I wrangled equipment. I learned the basics of lighting. I traveled as part of a film crew. All this would come in handy much sooner than I thought.

Chapter 5
TV Writer

One day, I received a call from Gail Frank, a woman I knew from my New York film crowd. (In the spirit of disclosure, I should mention that Gail and I have now been happily married for several decades.)

Because of her background of teaching Creative Dramatics to children, Gail was producing a new children's television show in Boston called, *Jabberwocky*. When the show got rolling, she found herself desperately short of writers. Knowing I was some kind of writer, she called and asked me to do a sample script. At the time, I didn't even know what a script looked like.

This was 1972, the heyday of new, educational children's television, led by *Sesame Street* and other shows like *Zoom!* and *The Electric Company*. Instead of just distracting and entertaining kids, these shows were actually trying to *teach* them something.

Jabberwocky, designed for five-to-ten-year-olds, dealt with affective childhood problems like siblings, fear, competition, and disappointment, as well as some straight educational goals.

The show was situated in a television studio, with the characters working in various studio capacities. It had a puppet character, Dirty Frank, who lived in a chimney and served as our resident "kid". The show also included remote location pieces and creative animation. Among the cast was the well-known character actor, Robert Prosky, and a very young Jobeth Williams.

I sweated my way through the script. I used to write 30-second commercials. Now, I had to fill 30 minutes! Somehow I did, and *Jabberwocky* liked my material. Over the course of production, I wrote about 50 scripts for the show, a valuable learning experience in the craft of television writing.

It was *Jabberwocky* that first led me to *Sesame Street* and the Muppets. When I started on the show, I knew nothing about writing children's television. I relied on my advertising experience to keep the *Jabberwocky* scripts bright and interesting. But except for a few ad campaigns I had never really written comedy.

So, I began every work day with a dose of *Sesame Street*. I analyzed its content, and its presentation. I studied the humor. And, since *Jabberwocky* had a puppet character, I absorbed whatever I could about puppets on television.

Jabberwocky was fortunate enough to win several television awards for local children's programming, including a citation from Action for Children's Television, the first ever given to a commercial television program. But, after several seasons, the show ran its course and went out of production. And, I was out of work, again.

Chapter 6
Let me tell you how I got ...
how I to Sesame Street

It was February 1973 and I was back in New York, contemplating my next career move, otherwise known as looking for a job. I considered returning to advertising. Now that I was an "award winning" children's television writer, I figured I could get a copy job at an advertising agency working on a toy or cereal account. But somehow, after making a positive contribution to children through television, the idea of seducing them into wanting the newest battery-operated plaything or demanding sugar coated breakfast food left me cold.

Not knowing what else to do, I called up the Children's Television Workshop, the company that produced *Sesame Street*. I talked my way past the switchboard and contacted someone on the *Sesame Street* production staff.

"It appears that I'm an awarding winning children's television writer. Maybe we should talk.", I announced. Amazingly, they agreed.

So one freezing cold February morning, I went to the Sesame Street production offices, which were then located directly across Broadway from Lincoln Center. I had an appointment with Bob Cunniff, who was the show's producer.

After exchanging a few pleasantries about our shared Irish ancestry, Bob pointed to the Bert and Ernie puppets behind his desk and asked me how I'd like to try writing for these two guys. And so, I agreed to write four audition pieces for *Sesame Street*, for which I was paid $250.

During my *Jabberwocky* days, I quickly realized that *Sesame Street* was using many of the same techniques I had used in advertising to teach their curriculum – repetition, catchy jingles, demonstration and humor. In fact, it was young children's easy ability to absorb and repeat television commercials that influenced Joan Ganz Cooney's decisions about the format of *Sesame Street* when she originally conceived the show.

Having that insight to *the show*'s teaching methods was extremely helpful in writing the audition pieces. In one, I used Big Bird and his imaginary friend, the mammoth-like Snuffle-upagus, to demonstrate the difference between "wet" and "dry", which was then part of the *Sesame Street* curriculum.

The piece started with Susan, one of *Sesame Street's* adults, and Big Bird just finishing taking laundry off a clothes line. The phone rings, and Susan goes inside to answer it. She calls down from a window and asks Big Bird to take care of the laundry.

It starts to rain and Big Bird starts to take the laundry inside when along comes Mr. Snuffle-upagus. Big Bird tries to keep Snuffy from getting wet and catching cold. Forgetting about the laundry, Big Bird tries to get Snuffy out of the rain under a shed.

The problem is, Snuffy is so big that when his front end is under the shed and dry, his rear end is outside and wet. After coaxing Snuffy to turn around, Big Bird discovers that now that Snuffy's rear end is dry under the roof, his front end is wet!

This process repeats itself several times until the rain stops and with an enormous sneeze, Mr. Snuffle-upagus goes home. Susan comes out to discover her laundry is soaking wet, leaving Big Bird to explain that he was trying to keep Mr. Snuffle-upagus from catching cold.

Another Muppet piece involved Goldilocks and the three bears to explain the word, "bus". After discovering their house had been invaded, the three bears catch Goldilocks raiding their refrigerator. When they demand to know what she is doing, she claims to be waiting for a cross-town bus. There is some general discussion about what a bus is, and how there can't possibly be any buses way out here in the country.

At the appropriate moment, a New York City bus, with Muppet driver and passengers drives into the bears' living room. It stops, and Goldilocks boards. Amid discussions of having the correct change, the bus drives out of the scene.

I sent the four audition pieces to Bob Cunniff and commenced to wait and worry.

Several weeks later, I received a phone call from Brenda Shapiro, Jon Stone's assistant. Jon, I knew from the *Sesame Street* credits, was the show's Executive Producer. The great man wanted to meet me. So, an appointment was set up for the following week.

Wanting to make a good impression on the big boss, I went into my advertising wardrobe and picked out a double breasted, pin striped suit, Gucci loafers, a monogrammed French cuffed shirt and an Italian silk tie.

Jon had also dressed rather formally for the occasion. He was wearing the cardigan sweater with only one elbow gone and his "good" bib overalls. Here was this bear of a man with this Roman nose, halo of white hair and matching beard, who could play Moses, or God for that matter, in any '50s Bible epic. But Moses was dressed in all the satirical splendor of a flannel-shirted Vermont farmer, which he was on weekends. Jon looked like a cross between Zeus and Yogi Bear.

And there was I in my Madison Avenue pinstripes. We looked at each other for a long slow moment in the reception room. It was like the meeting of two alien species. Certainly neither one of us could predict what was to come.

Jon took me back to his small, unimpressive office, which was so comfortably messy it instantly reminded me of Ernie's room, which in some ways it was. He shuffled through the papers on his desk and found my audition material.

He dove in and started telling me exactly how he wanted the four pieces re-written, which was his way of letting me know I was hired. He then directed me to "the sharks down the hall" in the Business Affairs Department to see about salary and contracts. It was then I learned that "creative" people don't discuss business with each other. We have our "people" to do that.

My first contract was for only four shows, so I was still on probation. But when I completed the four scripts, I was signed to a contract for the rest of the season.

And that's how I got - how *I* got to *Sesame Street*.

Chapter 7
Jon Stone

I really can't discuss *Sesame Street* much further without some discussion of Jon Stone.

There were many people who contributed to the creation of *Sesame Street:* Joan Ganz Cooney, who conceived of educational television commercials for children; Jim Henson, who created the wonderful Muppet characters, the puppeteers who performed them, Joe Raposo who wrote all the music, and Jon Stone, the producer who also wrote the show's pilot.

But by the time I joined *Sesame Street* in 1973, the show was in full swing. It had been on the air for three years so the characters had been developed, the kinks had been worked out, and the show ran like a well oiled machine. It had to, in order to maintain its high level of quality over a season of 130 episodes.

In theory, a television show is supposed to be a rigid hierarchy with an executive producer at the top, a producer or producers answering to him, and writers directors and actors answering to the producers. But this pyramid has eroded over the years with writers, directors and actors regularly negotiating Producer, and even Executive Producer credits.

The credit crawl on some shows had become so bloated that a new term has emerged: Show Runner. You won't see it on the crawl. He or she will just be listed in the brigade of executive producers. As unglamourous as it sounds, the Show Runner is the guy who really is the boss and runs the show. If you're looking for a job, you want to talk to the Show Runner.

When I joined *Sesame Street*, Jon Stone was the man who was in complete control of *Sesame Street*. He was the Show Runner. Jon was the Executive

Producer and the Head Writer. He also directed 50% of the daily shows and all of the Muppet inserts. Jon was *Sesame Street* and *Sesame Street* was Jon. Wardrobe people, set designers, prop men, make-up artists, lighting designers, directors, writers, and cast members all answered directly to Jon. Not a word of script or a minute of tape went on the air without Jon's personal okay. The far out, goofy humor, the music, the vaudeville skits, the outrageous puns were all Jon Stone.

Orson Wells once described a film studio as, "the world's greatest set of electric trains." Jon felt the same way about a television studio. The result was a hit show for children and adults and a hugely successful teaching tool.

Jon was one of those rare people who knew what he wanted to do at an early age and then actually did it. Television was in Jon's blood. He once told me that as a kid, he would stand for hours, in a Connecticut winter, watching a small screen, black and white set through a TV store window without sound.

To say that Jon loved television is an understatement. Wherever Jon was, there was a television set and it was on. Once, when he called me from Hong Kong, in the background, I could hear the TV set in his hotel room broadcasting in fluent Cantonese. Jon's daughters, Polly and Kate, had given him a framed cartoon. The sketch showed a beautiful alpine hotel with an incredible mountain view. A man is leaving the office and telling his family in the car, "They didn't have cable, so I told them, 'Forget it.'"

Jon was a graduate of Yale Drama School, and came to New York to pursue an acting career – with very little results. He appeared in a few musical revues. But as Jon explained it, an agent told him it was time to put the "H" back in his name and start over.

So, Jon joined the CBS Training Program and became a writer and producer on the *Captain Kangaroo Show*. During the '60s, he also wrote some Muppet Specials for Jim Henson, which was the beginning of their long relationship.

But at 35, Jon tired of television. He bought a Porsche, moved to Vermont and opened a hardware store.

It was Joan Ganz Cooney who lured Jon out of the woods in 1967 to begin work on her new children's television show. Jon, in turn recruited Jim Henson.

The first year I joined *Sesame Street*, Jon announced it was time to win some Emmys. The opening show of a new *Sesame Street* season was always very special. That season, Jon decided it would be special enough to submit for Emmys.

He commissioned Joe Raposo to write a song for the show's opening that would be the basis of a major musical production number. It would include the entire cast, emphasizing those with singing and dancing talents. And, it would utilize the entire set, including fire escapes and second story windows.

Jon was thinking "Gene Kelly Musical." And, to duplicate those high/low sweeping camera moves, Jon re-invented the Chapman Boom.

The Chapman Boom is that piece of movie equipment you've seen with two guys and a camera at the end of a crane. Its base is a vehicle that can move in any direction and operate on electric power for silence. It allows a camera to pan over great distances and change altitudes at will. But as big as our studio was, a Chapman wouldn't have had room to operate.

Jon's solution was to have a metal plate cut large enough to comfortably hold a camera and cameraman. He then had the plate attached to the fork of a fork lift truck. Once the camera and cameraman were aboard and secured, they could be dollied all around the set while also being raised and lowered as needed. Jon called it the "Ghetto Chapman."

The opening number was wonderful. And that season, the *Muppet* performers and the *Sesame Street* writers won Emmys for Outstanding Individual Achievement in Children's Programming.

Jon was also a stickler for detail. There was no detail too small for his attention. During the first season of *Sesame Street*, the steps of the 123 Sesame Street brownstone were made of wood. The "wooden" sound of people going up and down those steps drove Jon crazy. So the following season, 123 got new steps made out of concrete.

He also fought for years to get real sidewalks on the set, so the cast and the kids could sit on a curb. But that never happened. The sidewalks were, and still are, painted on the studio floor.

Bob Cunniff, the *Sesame Street* producer during the 70s once said, "There was always a slight sense of danger when Jon ran *Sesame Street*." Muppet trains crashed through walls, ceilings fell in and furniture got eaten.

One day, Jon had an idea to illustrate the principles of "open and "closed." It was a classic vaudeville bit which required a small bedroom set with a double bed and working window. The dramatis personae were two of our cast members, Luis and Gordon, dressed up as old men in floor-length night shirts and stocking caps.

Luis and Gordon enter and get into the bed. After a moment, Gordon declares he's hot, gets up, opens the window and returns to bed. Shortly afterwards, Luis declares he's cold, gets up, closes the window and returns to bed. They repeat this two or three times with generous use of the words, "open," and, "close," in the dialogue.

Finally, Luis says he's cold again.

Gordon replies, "You want the window closed?!" He gets up and closes the window.

"Are you happy now?"

"Yes."

"Good."

Gordon then produces a sledge hammer and bashes a man-sized hole in the wall to the outside and returns to bed.

It was this kind of lunacy from the top that inspired the writers to push the creative envelope ever further. Part of the responsibility of writing any show is to come up with ideas that fit it. I always felt my job was to come up with ideas that Jon would have had if he'd had the time. When I wrote for *The Muppet Show*, I tried to write like Jim Henson. The same was true for anyone else for whom I wrote.

There's a well-known writer's nightmare: you're writing for a producer who says, *I don't know what I want. But, I'll know it when I see it.*

But, when you wrote for Jon Stone, you knew exactly what was required of you. Because, Jon *always knew* what he wanted. Jon was a tough taskmaster. He demanded your best. And he got it. Writers dreaded getting re-writes back with Jon's curt notation across the top of a skit, *N.W.I.!* – Not Worth It! Or, halfway through a bit: *S.H.S.!* – Ship Has Sailed!

I knew Jon pretty well. We were writing partners. But our relationship had an added complication: Jon was always the boss. Whenever I was hired to write a *Sesame Street* special, I was hired by Jon Stone, the Executive Producer to be the writing partner of Jon Stone, Writer, to turn out material that would be acceptable to both Jon Stone, Executive Producer and, Jon Stone, Director.

On and off, I worked and traveled with Jon for about two decades. So, let me give you some insight into someone who, if you're in your late 30s or early 40s, probably bent your mind a little bit. And, you're probably glad he did.

As you might imagine, Jon had an impish sense of humor. I have in front of me a postcard he sent me during a research trip for *Big Bird in China*. It's a picture of an empty airplane cockpit with nothing but white showing through the windshield. On the back, Jon wrote:

> *I snapped this of the empty, snow-covered cockpit just after the crash. Out the window, I can see a line of chanting monks approaching to take us to their lamasery. One of them looks like Sam Jaffe. My fifty-first birthday is coming up – why do I feel so young all of a sudden?*

(If you're too young to get it, rent *Lost Horizons*.)

Here's a story Jon once told me about his youth. His father was a doctor and a classic pianist. When his kid sister was three or four, he and his brother, Emerson, would teach her very complicated piano chords. Later on, when Jon's father got home, she would nonchalantly wander over to the piano, hit the chord with both hands, think for a moment and then announce in her little girl's voice, "F flat seventh diminished with an augmented ninth." Until he caught on, Jon's father thought his daughter was a musical genius.

Among Jon's broad panorama of oddities was a penchant for collecting especially ugly postcards. If a card had a swordfish on it, fat women on a beach, or a particularly hideous motel, Jon had a copy. He would then take these horrendous cards with him to exotic places and send them to friends back home. During a research trip that Jon and I took to Ireland, Jon was busily writing postcards. They all featured a glory shot of the Albany, New York Bus Terminal, circa 1958.

On the same trip, while traveling through the town of Limerick, Jon regaled us with one limerick after another, all of which are unprintable here.

Jon, of course, was also a great story teller. Several of his stories were eyewitness accounts of historic moments in television. These are a few of my favorite Jon Stone stories.

In the early '60s, when Jon was a junior staffer on the *Captain Kangaroo Show*, word came down from the CBS brass that on the next day's program they would have to make do with two cameramen instead of the usual three. The network had a corporate assignment that needed a cameraman the following morning.

Two days later, when the cameraman returned, he told the following story:

On the morning of the assignment, William S. Paley, Chairman of CBS, addressed several thousand executives from the CBS affiliate stations around the country. He did it at a breakfast meeting in the main dining room of a mid-town Manhattan hotel. The cameraman's job was to shoot Paley so his image could be projected on TV monitors located throughout the dining room.

After his speech, Paley sat down. *However*, as soon as he did, his speech re-ran on the monitor. Afterward, the cameraman said the entire audience sat in stunned silence, because that *was the first time any of them had ever seen video tape.*

Jon was privy to other early television events. In 1957 he had a low level job at CBS as an Assistant Stage Manager. At the time Elizabeth Taylor was married to Mike Todd. Todd was an impresario of the first order. The year before, he had produced *Around the World in 80 Days* which took the Oscar for Best Picture of the Year. Todd was bigger than life. It's rumored that he's the only man who could handle Elizabeth Taylor.

On any given day Todd could either have ten million dollars in the bank, or be ten million dollars in the hole. It was reported that in 1957, Todd was in the hole, again – big time.

Since Mike Todd needed money, he did what anybody in that situation would do. He rented Madison Square Garden, and threw himself a 48th birthday party complete with circus acts, celebrity performers and 18,000 of his and Elizabeth's closest friends.

He talked CBS into broadcasting it live. CBS then assigned Walter Cronkite to cover it. This was a big deal at CBS. A "remote" in 1957 was rare. The equipment was large, heavy and ungainly. Moving it was a major project.

So, because this enormous remote was being covered at Madison Square Garden, literally all of the CBS executive staff were at Madison Square Garden, "observing" the production from the open bar.

Back at CBS headquarters, the halls and offices were empty. There were only two people holding down the fort. One was Jon Stone and the other was an unknown minor employee whom Jon never named and shall be known herein as the Unnamed Perpetrator.

So, while Mike and Elizabeth were entertaining 18,000 of their closest friends, Jon and the Unknown Perpetrator where sitting around the corporate offices of CBS.

In a moment of boredom, the Unknown Perpetrator said to Jon, "Want to have some fun?" He then picked up a telephone and dialed the United States Submarine Base in Groton, Connecticut. Once he got through, he demanded to speak to a public relations officer.

Unfortunately, some hapless, junior officer answered the phone. Let's call him, "Lieutenant Dupe."

The Unknown Perpetrator said to him, "This is CBS News in Madison Square Garden. Where the hell is the submarine?!"

"What submarine!?", Lt. Dupe replied.

"What submarine?! We're broadcasting live from Madison Square Garden with 18,000 people at a birthday party for Mike Todd, to whom the Secretary of the Navy promised a submarine for the party. THAT SUBMARINE!!! So, where the hell is it?!"

49

"I don't know anything about a submarine!"

"Well, dammit! you better find that submarine and call me right back!"

The Unknown Perpetrator then gave the lieutenant the name and phone number of the CBS executive producer in the Madison Square Garden control room and hung up.

He then called the same executive producer at the Garden.

"This is Lieutenant Dupe of the US Navy Submarine Service here in Groton, Connecticut."

"Yes?"

"Where do you want the submarine, sir?"

"What submarine!?"

"The submarine that the Secretary of the Navy promised Mike Todd. The submarine that was hauled out of the Atlantic Ocean at great expense to the United States government. The submarine that's now on its way by truck from the Navy Base here in Groton Connecticut to Madison Square Garden. Where do you want *that submarine*, sir?"

The Unknown Perpetrator then gave the Executive Producer Lieutenant Dupe's phone number at the sub base.

Meanwhile Mike Todd's Madison Square Garden Celebrity Birthday Party degenerated to an 18,000 person food fight on live, CBS television, which had to be quelled by the local constabulary.

Phone calls flew back and forth between Madison Square Garden and the Groton Connecticut Submarine Base. At the end, it was reported that CBS had 70 stage hands, on overtime, waiting on Eighth Avenue to take possession of a phantom submarine which, of course, never arrived.

Jon had a story about an early children's show that shall remain nameless for reasons soon to be clear. The show had two major puppet characters operated by one puppeteer. One character was easy going and laid back. The other was a nervous perfectionist – a classic Odd Couple.

One year at the show's Christmas party, the puppeteer disappeared behind his stage. The two puppets appeared and joined the party – not unusual in the world of puppetry. Someone put a bottle of scotch on the stage. The laid back puppet immediately grabbed it, disappeared beneath the stage, and reappeared without the scotch.

As the party wore on, the laid back character got gradually drunker, slurring his words and losing his balance. While this is going on, the perfectionist puppet gets more and more irate, castigating the other puppet for drinking too much. Both of the characters are being played by the same guy, who is nipping at a bottle of scotch. At the end of the party, one puppet had passed out and the other was steaming mad until they carried out the puppeteer.

Finally, a short fax that Jon sent me about 15 years ago. It's one of my favorite Jon Stone souvenirs:

> My old friend, Charlie Rosen, Production Designer extra ordinaire, was in town a few weeks ago and we had lunch. Afterwards, we were walking down Columbus Avenue, recollecting what studios, etc. used to be where.

> We paused on the corner of 67th Street and Charlie recalled that there used to be a fly-by-night prop house there, run by two brothers. And now I quote Charlie describing this true incident:

> "I walked in there one morning, looking for some prop or other, and one of the brothers was on the phone:

> 'Sure we do. Of course we do. We got two of them, a big one and a little one. Which one do you want? Well, then come in and check them out and you can choose. When? This afternoon? Three o'clock. We'll be here.'

> He hangs up the phone and yells to his brother at the back of the store, 'Hey Sid! What the hell is a gondola?'

During the creation of *Sesame Street*, coming up with a name for the show became a major problem. Jon said the staff had a running gag about the name. Since it was for children, why not just call it, *The Kiddie Show*. But, since it was for pre-schoolers, someone suggested, *The Itty-Bitty Kiddie Show*. However the show had to appeal to urban ghetto kids, so, *The Inner-City Itty Bitty Kiddie Show* was volunteered. Then Jon got very silly and suggested, *The Dog and Kitty, Inner-City, Itty-Bitty Kiddie Show*.

Fortunately, before it got much worse, someone finally came up with, *Sesame Street*, as the name for the show. Jon admitted he thought was pretty dumb when he first heard it.

Jon and I milked the *Itty-Bitty* title in a sketch for a *Sesame Street* road show. We had a Muppet committee dream up a name for a kids' television show. They finally came up with: *The Dog and Kitty, Pretty-Witty, Nitty-Gritty, Itty Bitty, Kiddie Show.*

Jon actually wrote a song for the sketch which included the phrases: *it's been named by our committee; it'll be the hit of New York City; we think we got a sure-fire hitty; come and join our little ditty; sing along like Conway Twitty; throw away that old self-pity; and dream a dream like Walter Mitty.*

Jon hated offices, bureaucracy, dressing up, Richard Nixon, and committees. He also wasn't big on people with last names for first names. Names like Anderson Cooper made Jon nervous. "How can you trust a guy named McGeorge Bundy?", he would demand.

Jon loved Porches, rebellion, the Marx brothers, Johnny Walker and beautiful women. Over the years, he won 18 Emmys for writing, producing and directing *Sesame Street*. He used them as the base for a large glass coffee table in his living room.

On March 29, 1997, Jon Stone passed away after a long battle with Lou Gehrig's disease. He was the greatest creative influence in my life.

Chapter 8
Writing Sesame Street

I n 1973, The Children's Television Workshop (now Sesame Workshop), the non-profit company that produces *Sesame Street*, was located in a modern office building across Broadway from Lincoln Center, in the ASCAP Building, headquarters of the American Society of Composers, Authors, and Publishers.

Over the years of watching *Sesame Street*, I had romanticized Children's Television Workshop into some kind of intellectual think tank with the emphasis on *Television Workshop*, even though I had no actual idea about what a television workshop might be.

I imagined there would be seminars about the latest video techniques. I expected a guest speaker program with people like Norman Lear and Lorne Michaels addressing the creative and production people. I even thought there might be mini studios for creative experimentation.

Children's Television Workshop was and is a television production company, and a very good one. It gave Jon Stone and Jim Henson their great big sandbox. In 1973 it was producing *Sesame Street* and *The Electric Company*. Having spent two years writing, *Jabberwocky* alone at home, I was looking forward to working in a creative environment.

I enjoyed working in advertising agencies surrounded by other creative people. I assumed a large production company was much like a large advertising agency with corridors of offices full of creative people. And, I assumed the writers more or less kept regular office hours, as ad agency copywriters did.

When I asked Jon Stone about an office, he hemmed and hawed for a few days and finally came up with a windowless little room about the size of a broom closet. It was then that I discovered that Jon avoided going to the office as much as possible. Jon hated going to the office. I soon discovered that the *Sesame Street* writing staff worked at home.

But, I liked the idea of going to an office every day, to sop up some atmosphere. So, I tried it for a while. It turned out my office was next to the educational research department. I got friendly with them and got some good script ideas from our discussions. But, there were no creative people to be found. *The Electric Company* writing staff seemed to like hanging around and writing at the Workshop. But their offices were on another floor. So, I only saw them at lunch.

After a few months, fate pretty much made my decision to work at home when it broke my left ankle while I was moving. On crutches with a cast up to my knee, cabbing across town every day wasn't an option, especially since I really didn't have to be there. My contract guaranteed the show a certain number of scripts. It didn't say where I had to write them. So I was working at home alone again.

The annual *Sesame Street* production schedule was broken into several segments. The writers would write a batch of scripts for about ten or eleven weeks. Then, the show went into the studio to shoot them for about the same amount of time. When the shooting finished, the show would go into hiatus and the writers would go back to work on scripts for the second taping of the season.

Therefore, it was some time after I started writing *Sesame Street* before I got to see my material produced and even longer to see it on television. Scripts were shot as much as two months after they were written. Then, the shows didn't air for another four months.

In those days, *Sesame Street* produced 130 original shows a year. There were five of us on the writing staff: Emily Perl Kingsley; Ray Sipherd; Norman Stiles; Jeff Moss; and myself. Jon Stone also wrote five or six scripts a year. And, Jerry Juhl, for whom I would later work on *The Muppet Show*, contributed Muppet inserts from his home in California.

So, each staff writer was responsible for about 20 scripts a season. Since each script had five to seven scenes of original material, it meant that each writer created about 125 vaudeville skits (for that is, in fact, what they were) a year or about one every three days, including weekends and holidays. That's a lot of funny.

But those early years on *Sesame Street* were when I really learned how to write for the screen. I referred to the show as Stone's Kollege of Komedy, because that's where I learned to find the finish for a bit before starting to write it, how to get to the pay off as quickly as possible and all the other techniques of comedy writing.

Comedy, you see, is very serious business. And when the people who create comedy discuss it, they discuss it very analytically. Once you become one of them, you watch Laurel and Hardy movies and Jay Leno monologues in a very, very different way.

On *Sesame Street*, I quickly learned that pre-schoolers are a very specialized audience because they have a very limited vocabulary and attention span. But, one of the best pieces of advice on writing television for children I ever got came from Dr. Jerome Kagan, a Harvard University professor and child psychologist. Dr. Kagan was our Education Advisor on *Jabberwocky*.

During one of our sessions Dr. Kagan said that when a person is born, he or she is as intelligent as they will ever be. They lack experience and vocabulary but they're not stupid. Inside of every child is a human intelligence with all its brain power intact, and a tremendous curiosity about the immediate world around it.

(My other insight into the mind of a child came from Al Capp, the cartoonist who created Lil' Abner. Capp once described the experience of childhood as being, "half the size of everyone else and having no money.")

So, I began to picture an audience quite different from the cute toddlers in play suits who were squirming in front of the TV and (we hoped) mesmerized by *Sesame Street*. I imagined an alien intelligence out there equal to mine, but with whom I only shared a vocabulary of a few hundred words and, I hoped, a sense of humor. So, whatever I was trying to explain had to be broken down to the simplest of terms and presented as visually as possible. Actually, this is a basic tenet for any kind of screen writing.

Unlike many other shows which are group-written around a table, *Sesame Street* writers were responsible for individual scripts. The writer was assigned a show and was then expected to complete the script to the head writer's satisfaction. After that, the script went into production.

So, material that I had solely written was shepherded through production, set up in the studio, rehearsed, shot and aired. And, I wrote a lot of material. The experience was invaluable. Not only did I see what worked better comedically, but I also got a sense of how my comedic timing worked with real performers. Additionally, I saw how much time actors (and puppets) took to perform certain gestures, as well as how difficult some sketches were to physically produce in the studio.

That point was driven home during my first season on the show. I saw a desert island on a list of available props and scenery – material that had been made or built and used previously, and was now available from storage. So I wrote a skit that took place on the desert island to teach Imagining, another *Sesame Street* educational goal.

It started in the Fix-it Shop with a very busy Luis. The phone rings constantly. Gordon and Susan come in with a TV set that needs- fixing. Ditto David with a radio and Big Bird with a toaster. Finally, he gets a break.

Luis turns to camera and talks about taking a break by imagining that he's somewhere else, like a desert island.

We dissolve to a desert island with Luis relaxing on the beach. But, suddenly, from behind the palm tree, Gordon and Susan appear with their TV, David comes in with his radio, and Big Bird enters with his toaster, all are demanding repairs. David answers a phone from behind the palm tree.

"It's for you.", David says as he hands the phone to Luis.

It was all sort of abstract until the day of the shoot when I got to the studio and saw the crew assembling a 20-foot desert island in the middle of the studio. As two stage hands passed me carrying a 10-foot palm tree, I remember thinking, "This had better be funny!"

The piece worked pretty well and I breathed a sigh of relief when it wrapped. A staff member complimented me on it. And I remember bragging about how economical it was since I used existing scenery.

"Yes," she replied. "But in order to make the actors disappear, we had to build an exact duplicate of half the island and lay it electronically over the original."

Of course, Jon knew this as soon as he read the script. But he liked the idea enough to okay the additional constriction expense.

Educationally, writing *Sesame Street* worked like this: At the beginning of each season, the research department issued a rather dry document entitled, "Statement of Instructional Goals for the (number) Experimental Season of Sesame Street." It varied from year to year, depending on research from the previous season. (*Sesame Street* pieces were constantly tested and rated with age appropriate focus groups.) But, the tried and true stuff, like counting and the alphabet, remained from year to year.

The Statement broke down the educational goals to be covered in the current season. For example:

I. The Child and His World

A. Self

1. Body Parts and Functions - The child can identify, label and state or recognize the function of such body parts as the:

a. head	g. elbow
b. nose	h. hand
c. ear	i. finger
d. eye	j. leg
e. tongue	k. knee
f. arm	l. foot

(Translation: Write pieces that somehow relate to body parts so the child learns the names of those body parts and what their functions are.)

2. The Child and His Powers - the child recognizes that he can act effectively on his own behalf:

    A. By acquisition of skills and knowledge through:
        1. Experimentation
        2. Asking questions
        3. Practice.

B. By making use of previously acquired information (remembering)

C. By anticipating future needs. (planning)

D. By manipulating the environment within his mind. (Imagining)

(Translation: Write pieces that are simple enough for the child to understand that have positive outcomes by incorporating the above.)

And so on through Problem Solving, Emotions, Social Interaction, Natural Environment, Man-Made Environment, Pre-reading skills, Rhyming, Numerical Operation, Cognitive Organization, all the way to Bilingual/Bi-cultural Objectives.

Basically, it was a list of things our audience was capable of comprehending. It was the writer's job to demonstrate the material and make it interesting and entertaining enough to be memorable.

Every *Sesame Street* script started with an assignment sheet. It listed the numbers and the letters of the day, (*Today's show is brought to you by the letter "P," and the number "4"*); the cast members and puppeteers who were assigned to that show; the particular education goals for the show; and a list, by category, of the library Muppet pieces, and live action and animated films that were to be slugged into the show.

The new pieces for the show, which were the writers' responsibility, were divided into two types: Street Pieces, which were shot on the *Sesame Street* set with the live cast and Muppets; and Muppet Inserts, which were all the Muppet bits which were shot in Muppet scenery.

The shows required an opening and closing scene on the Street and a "Street" piece every 12 and a half minutes. This gave the show a solid footing in a "home base" that kept *Sesame Street* from being just a floating montage of cartoons and puppet scenes.

A second rule stipulated that when the show was assembled, there would be two and a half minutes of "something" between the show's Muppet Inserts.

The reason being that puppets, in reality, are an illusion. And if you stay on any illusion too long, it loses its magic.

The final script ran 20 to 25 pages. It listed and numbered every element of the show in order, from the Opening to the Sign Off. The newly written pieces were inserted into their appropriate slots in the script.

The first thing I did when starting a new script was check on the available cast members. Caroll Spinney was always available for "Street" pieces. He's the very talented man who performed Big Bird and Oscar the Grouch. So, Big Bird and Oscar were always around on the Street.

Since Gordon and Susan owned the brownstone at 123 Sesame Street, Luis ran the Fix-it shop with Maria, and Mister Hooper and David kept the corner store, their presence on Sesame Street might suggest a piece based on one of those locations.

Occasionally, puppeteers Frank Oz, Jerry Nelson and Richard Hunt were assigned to a show. That meant that Cookie Monster, Grover, Bert, Herry Monster, The Count, Biff and Sully, the Snuffle-upagus, the Two Headed Monster, and Forgetful Jones were possible characters for "Street" pieces.

Jim Henson insisted that the recognizable Muppets always be performed by the same puppeteers to preserve the purity of the character's personality. For example, Kermit and Ernie were always performed by Jim. Frank always did Bert, Grover and Cookie Monster. And Caroll was Big Bird and Oscar. Jerry Nelson and Richard Hunt would team up as the Snuffle-upagus or the Two-Headed Monster. Jerry was also the man behind (or under) the number-crazed Count Von Count.

A great deal of the Muppets success is due to the creativity of these very talented performers. Over time, they have honed and expanded their characters to make them as memorable as any live character on television.

Writing for the Muppets always involved give and take between the writers and the performers. A writer would write a piece for a certain character. That would inspire the puppeteer to find a new aspect of that character's personality. That, in turn, would inspire the writers to take the character in a new direction.

Strictly speaking, every *Sesame Street* script was supposed to adhere to the teaching curriculum on its run-down sheet. But Jon Stone recognized that it was difficult enough to be entertaining at a consistent level. Being entertaining and covering a specific subject was impossible, especially with the amount of original material we were creating over the course of a season.

So material that covered any subject in the Research Syllabus was acceptable to Jon, as long as it was funny. He felt that the library animation and Muppet pieces contained enough education material for one show and the individual show pieces should keep *Sesame Street* contemporary and entertaining.

If a piece had no recognizable syllabus material in it, we still had a way of getting it in the show. Two rather broad syllabus categories stated that a child could be taught about "Natural Environment" (animals, plants, air, water, etc.) and "Man Made Environment" (appliances, machinery, habitats, etc.) So, if a piece took place outside, it was, "Natural Environment." If it was inside, it was Man Made Environment.

Sesame Street material also had one more condition. At its inception, the show was conceived to reach underprivileged children in poor households. The thought was that those homes only had one television set. So, an effort was made to make the show fresh and entertaining for adults as well as children so there would be less chance of adults changing the channel. It also encouraged the adults to watch with the kids, which was another objective of the show.

Additionally, in the early 70s, more likely than not, poor households had black and white TVs. So, *Sesame Street* writers were forbidden to refer to anything by its color. (I recently had a conversation with a current *Sesame Street* writer. She told me that now, the writers are directed to imagine what their pieces might look like on an I-Phone.)

Finally comes that chilling moment when I have to write five acceptable *Sesame Street* scenes in seven days time. Red Smith, a famous sportswriter once said that writing was easy – you just sat at the typewriter until the blood came out of your forehead.

And I believe it was James Baldwin who equally claimed writing was easy. His theory was if you sat at the typewriter long enough, God would drop by and write it for you. The only problem was that you never knew if God was coming today, next week, next year, or the next millennium.

(A friend of mine once called in the middle of a work day to ask me to stop writing and hang out with him. The day would be fruitless, he maintained, because he had just seen my muse having lunch on the other side of town with a "very talented choreographer,")

All of the above, sadly, are true for me. Some days my forehead was bloodless. And the rest of the time, God was occupied elsewhere. My muse took more time off than a French civil servant. Writing comedy always came hard for me. I spent hours pacing, doodling, and staring into space in search of an idea you could build a "bit" around. But somehow, I turned out something for the first Tuesday morning deadline. (The writers had insisted early on that the weekly script deadline be moved from Monday to Tuesday so they wouldn't ruin their weekends trying to finish a script.)

The second week was more of the same – pace, doodle, day dream. The ideas are slow in coming. This is a way to make a living? I'm working late into the night. I work through the weekend anyway, as well as into Monday night.

Tuesday comes and I go to the office and turn in a script. But now I sit down with Jon for re-writes on last week's script. It's got some problems. Maybe three pieces are okay. Two have problems.

So, this week I have to rewrite or create two pieces for Script Number One and write five new pieces for Script Number Two. The next week, of course, requires a new script, rewrites for Script Number Two and maybe even Script Number One.

In the ensuing weeks, the re-writes seemed to multiply logarithmically.

(Once, I was so frustrated with re-writes that I threw my typewriter across the room and attacked it with a large plumber's wrench. – Another writer told me his solution was to keep a rubber typewriter nearby when he wrote.)

Generally, after 12 or so scripts I wound up working three weeks or so into the writers' hiatus just doing re-writes. Since I made it a point to be in the studio whenever my material was shot, my life boomeranged between the studio and the typewriter with little time left for anything else.

But, it was a terrific learning experience, as they say. I *had* to come up with something to fill all that time. I learned that when you write comedy you look for an ending first before you start to write. Then you work your way backwards like a murder mystery. For example, you can't start by saying, "I think I'll write a piece for Bob and Oscar."

That's the kiss of death. You open on Oscar in his can and Bob enters. And Oscar says . . . Or Bob says . . . No, Oscar starts . . . How about . . . Time is passing and the deadline is approaching.

But, suppose one day you say to yourself, "Wouldn't it be funny if somehow squeaky-clean Bob ended up down in Oscar's trash can?"

BOB IN OSCAR"S CAN (Educational Goal: Differing Perspectives – People do not always agree on everything.)

OPEN TO BOB WALKING DOWN *SESAME STREET*. HE IS WHISTLING HAPPILY. AS BOB PASSES OSCAR'S CAN, OSCAR POPS UP.

OSCAR

All right, Blue Eyes, cut that out!

BOB

What's wrong, Oscar?

OSCAR

Can that racket!

BOB

But I was only whistling.

OSCAR

Yeah? Well it sounds rotten.

BOB

You know, Oscar, everybody's getting a little tired of you coming out of the can and insulting us whenever we go by.

OSCAR

Yeah? So what?

BOB

Well, I think you ought to stop. We don't like it. Put yourself in my place.

OSCAR

No. You put yourself in *my* place.

BOB

What do you mean, Oscar?

OSCAR

C'mon down in the can, Mister Clean.

BOB

What me? Get in the garbage can?

OSCAR

That's right. Put yourself in my place. Come on. See what it's like living in a trash can. Then see if you feel like whistling.

BOB

Well . . . Okay.

OSCAR GOES DOWN IN THE CAN. BOB GETS IN AND STARTS TO LOWER HIMSELF DOWN.

Bob descends completely into the can. For the rest of the piece we hear him navigate through Oscar's in-door swamp, get bitten by Hortense, Oscar's pet dragon, and end up in Oscar's rotten egg collection, breaking several of them.

At the end, Bob exits the trash can much the worse for wear.

In the *Sesame Street* studio I finally saw my work change from the written word into living, breathing television. Whenever anything I wrote was in production, I was on the studio floor talking to carpenters, electricians, stage hands, teamsters, lighting, technical, wardrobe and make-up people while they worked on my material.

All of these people possess unique skills and abilities. I always believed that a good part of being a professional writer was the ability to turn in material that could be produced in the time and with the money allotted for it. So, the technical conversations with the *Sesame Street* production crew added greatly to my professional expertise that started with the R.A.I.

I always found it easier to sell creative material if I had already worked out the production problems ahead of time. So, when the inevitable question came, "How would you produce that?", I could tell them. The more you understand other peoples' problems, the better the writer you become.

The maximum length of any *Sesame Street* piece was three and a half minutes. That was the maximum attention span of our three to five-year-old audience, according to our research. Since the script format we used averaged out to a page a minute, when you put the fourth piece of paper in the typewriter, you knew you had better be bringing the piece to a fast close.

Here's a piece I wrote for Grover's alter ego: Super Grover, the Muppet Super Hero who is absolutely useless.

The education subject was Problem Solving. The message was that you solve problems by trying out a series of solutions until one works.

It was winter time on *Sesame Street*. Snow was everywhere.

OPEN TO A MASTER SHOT OF GORDON'S CAR PARKED IN FRONT OF 123 SESAME STREET. GORDON IS DRIVING. SUSAN IS NEXT TO HIM. MARIA IS IN THE BACK SEAT.

SFX: TIRE SPINNING ON ICE.

THE CAR IS STUCK IN A MOUND OF SNOW.

GORDON

Well, we're stuck.

SUSAN & MARIA

Oh, no!

CUT TO SUPER GROVER FLYING THROUGH THE AIR.

              SUPER GROVER

Stuck? This looks like a job for Super Grover!

INSERT SUPER GROVER INTRO

CUT TO CAR IN STREET. GROVER LANDS WITH A "THUD" IN A SNOW BANK.
GORDON GETS OUT OF THE CAR.

              SUPER GROVER

Never fear, Super Grover is here! Now, what is your problem, sir?

              GORDON

We're stuck.

              SUPER GROVER

Stuck?

              GORDON

Yeah. Stuck

              SUPER GROVER

How do you mean, "stuck?"

              GORDON

The-wheel-is-on-the-ice-the-ice-is-slippery-so-the-wheel-can't-move-and-the-
car-is-stuck . . . stuck.

              SUPER GROVER

(BRIGHTLY) Of, course. Well, I know just what to do. Super Grover to the rescue!

              GORDON

What will we do?

              SUPER GROVER

It is very simple. We will just wait until Spring. Then, the weather will get
warm. The ice will melt and you can drive your car.

GORDON

Grover . . .

SUPER GROVER

Super Grover. *Please*, I am in uniform.

GORDON

We can't wait until spring for the ice to melt. That's months away!

SUPER GROVER

Well, I have another idea.

GORDON

Let's hear it.

(GORDON IS DIGGING AT THE SNOW WITH HIS HAND AND TRYING TO ASCERTAIN THE PROBLEM. HE IS NOT PAYING PARTICULAR ATTENTION TO GROVER.)

SUPER GROVER

I, Super Grover, will blow on the ice with my hot little breath, and that will melt the ice, and you can drive away.

GORDON

You just might have enough hot air to do it.

SUPER GROVER

Stand back! Ahhhhhhhhhh-wheeeeeeeee! (BLOWING ON THE ICE)

GORDON GOES BACK TO THE CAR.

SUPER GROVER

Hmmmmm. My super breath can't melt the ice, either. I know, I'll get something hotter to melt the ice.

EXIT GROVER

MARIA GETS OUT OF THE CAR. SUSAN GETS IN THE DRIVER'S SEAT.

GORDON

Okay. When I count three, you start driving and Maria and I will push the car off the ice. One . . . two . . . three . . .

GORDON AND MARIA PUSH THE CAR OFF THE ICE.

MARIA

Let's go.

GORDON AND MARIA GET INTO THE CAR. SUSAN DRIVES OFF.

ENTER SUPER GROVER PULLING A GIGANTIC FIREPLACE.

SUPER GROVER

There. Now I will build a fire, and the fire will melt the ice, and Gordon can drive away in his car . . . (NOTICES FOR THE FIRST TIME THE CAR IS GONE) . . . It worked! I just brought in the fireplace and at its mere presence, the ice melted and Gordon has driven away already ! No job is too difficult for Super Grover!

ENTER A MUPPET MAN

MAN

Hey! What are you doing with my fireplace!?

SUPER GROVER

Don't bother me now, sir. I, Super Grover, am very busy rescuing people.

MAN

You must be some kind of nut!

SUPER GROVER

But you don't understand, sir. See, my friend has this car and . . .

MAN CHASES GROVER AROUND THE FIREPLACE FOR A RAVE OFF.)

MUSIC BUTTON

FADE

Of course, not everything I wrote saw the light of day. Sometimes even after Jon had okayed a sketch, the Research Department would kill it on educational grounds. I lost a couple of real favorites that way.

In one piece, to teach the various climates in the United States, under the aegis of Natural Environment, I made Cookie Monster a weatherman, complete with a U.S. map and pointer. Cookie explained how it was snowing in Maine and raining in Alabama and very hot in Texas. But then, Cookie's baser nature took over and he started to eat the map.

I guess it was when he proclaimed that, "Chicago is delicious!", that we lost it. Research declared there was a possibility that somewhere some kids would think Cookie really had eaten Chicago, and the piece was bagged. I will admit I spent several days working on a sketch where Cookie really did eat Chicago but to no avail.

However, my all-time favorite *Sesame Street* reject was disqualified over a point of Theoretical Physics.

We had been told by the Research Department that there were two benefits to teaching the alphabet to a two-year-old. Firstly, the alphabet is an essential building block of education. But secondly, the approval and positive feedback that the child receives for reciting the alphabet reinforces his or her's desire to learn.

It was in this light, I created the following: My premise was that if a kid got X amount of approval and reinforcement from reciting the alphabet to adults, imagine what results the following might have.

I started with the idea of creating a new department of *Sesame Street* called, Tips For Tots!. The piece required a corny opening with a theme song and a Tips for Tops logo. Then we cut to Big Bird in front of a blackboard. He is holding a piece of chalk.

BIG BIRD

And, now it's time for Tips for Tots!

(BIG BIRD DRAWS ON THE BLACKBOARD IN COORDINATION WITH HIS DIALOGUE)

BIG BIRD

Okay, tots! You know this! This is the letter, "E," right? "E?" And, these two lines, one on top of the other mean, "equal." Can you say, "Equal?" Equal means, *the same.* And these are your old friends, the letter, "M." And the letter, "C," right? Okay. Let's review. "E" equals, "M," "C." Right? "E" equals "M," "C." Now, we need a number. So, here's the number, "2". But here's another new word, just like, "equals." This little, and it has to be little, number, "2," means, "squared", kind of like the shape with four equal sides. Hey, there's that word, "Equal," again. So, let's review. "E" equals "M," "C," squared. Try it again. "E" equals "M," "C," squared. Once more, "E" equals "M," "C," squared.

I turned this bit in to Jon Stone. Jon loved it and made one brilliant addition. He gave Big Bird the closing line: "And, when anyone asks you where you learned this, you tell them that you learned it on *Sesame Street.*"

As I said, the Research Department rejected the piece, saying I really didn't explain Einstein's Theory of Relativity. I fired off a memo to Research asking them to explain the Theory to me and show me exactly where I went wrong. That was around 1975. I'm still waiting for an answer.

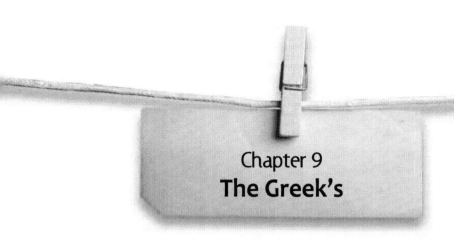

Chapter 9
The Greek's

L incoln Plaza is one of those made-up New York addresses like Avenue of the Americas, which all New Yorkers refer to as Sixth Avenue, its original name. (Hint: If you fly into New York and give a cab driver an address on "Avenue of the Americas," you have a good chance of seeing Newark by moonlight. If you're really unlucky, you could see the sun rise over Philadelphia.)

In reality, Lincoln Plaza is a triangular traffic island/park created where Broadway meets and crosses Columbus Avenue. West 63rd Street forms the third side of the triangle. The ASCAP Building, which housed the *Sesame Street* offices, is on the east, Broadway, side of the Plaza.

On the west side of the triangle is Lincoln Center for the Performing Arts, a 16-acre complex of theaters, performance spaces, rehearsal studios, classrooms and administration facilities that is the home of some of the most prestigious performing arts organizations in the country.

The Metropolitan Opera, the New York City Ballet, the New York Philharmonic Orchestra, The New York City Opera, Juilliard School of Music, the School of American Ballet and many other equally distinguished performing arts companies called Lincoln Center home. Many well known musicians, dancers, conductors and actors worked there on a regular basis.

However, on the south side of the Lincoln Center triangle, bordered by West 63rd Street is the Empire Hotel. Because of its proximity to Lincoln Center, many touring performance arts companies stay at the Empire during their Lincoln Center engagements.

(I once stayed at the Empire for a week while I was in transit from Boston to New York. I was fortunate enough to have an opera company staying there at the same time. In case you're wondering, it's true, opera singers do sing in the shower. So, if you timed your shower right, you could be regally serenaded because their shower singing wafted through the drain pipes into every shower in the hotel.)

On the first floor of the Empire Hotel, across Broadway from the ASCAP Building was an undistinguished bar and restaurant called the Theatre Pub. It was known to its regulars as "The Greek's" due to the nationality of the proprietor.

There were several well-known restaurants in the area like The Gingerman and O'Neil's Balloon, where tourists went in vain search for celebrities. But the Greek's was the local lunch hang out for many of the people who worked in and around Lincoln Center, probably because it had the cheapest martinis in the neighborhood.

It was also a prime location for girl watching. Sooner or later, every female dancer from Lincoln Center passed by the Greek's picture window on her way to Capezio, the dancers' outfitter that was located next door. In fact, every spring the Greek's regulars celebrated Coat Day – the first warm day of the season when the dancers shed their bulky winter coats. (Lest this sound sexist, I can tell you from personal experience that every dancer I've ever met is a shameless exhibitionist.)

George Balanchine, famed choreographer of the New York City Ballet, had a standing reservation every day for lunch. The writing staffs of *The Electric Company* and(when in the office) *Sesame Street* also lunched there. Jon Stone regularly held Sesame Street writers' meetings at the Greek's. So, it was not unusual to have a writer occupying every bar stool in the place.

The first time I lunched at The Greek's and saw this, it occurred to me that in a bar full of comedy writers, if I was going to relate something funny that had happened to me the night before, it had better be *really* funny.

During my first week on the job, I found myself sitting next to Tom Whedon and Jim Thurman, senior writers on *The Electric Company*. Jim was relating a story about playing touch football with Hitler, his 600-pound pet pig. I sat in respectful silence. Eventually, their conversation got around to writing, which

I suspect was strictly for my benefit.

"You know what Jon Stone told me was the most important thing about writing?" Tom asked Jim.

At the sound of Jon's name, my ears immediately pricked up. I sure wanted to hear what Jon Stone thought was the most important thing about writing.

"No," answered Jim. "What did Jon Stone say was the most important thing about writing?"

Now, I'm really listening.

"Well," said Tom, stretching it out, but eventually getting to, "Jon said the most important thing about writing is the "X" key and the "M" key." These, of course, were the days when writers still worked on typewriters.

"Why?", Jim asked.

"Well," said Tom. After another long, drawn out preamble he finally got to the point. "Jon said to me, 'I'll tell you the most important thing about writing. You know when you write a line that you don't like and you want to delete it? Most writers back up and just type XXXXXXX over it. But if you do that sometimes people can *still* read it. However, if you type XMXMXMXM over it they can never make it out."

This writing advice ranks right up there with what Mel Brooks said was the hardest thing about writing. "It's the "M"s and the "N"s. One has two hills and the other has three hills and I can never remember which is which."

Shortly after I joined *Sesame Street*, construction started on a new skyscraper in the neighborhood. When that happened, lunch time at the Greek's was about 50/50 writers and hard hats. Then, a national touring ballet company came to Lincoln Center for a run and the dancers all stayed at the Empire. Now the lunch crowd at the Greek's was made up of equal parts writers, hard hats and ballet dancers.

You might think that this could be an explosive combination of people in the same bar. After all, this was 1973, the Vietnam era. Many of the construction guys sported American flags on their hard hats. Many of the writers, myself included, were bearded long hairs, and some of the male dancers were obviously gay.

But you don't know New York hard hats. After all, this was Lincoln Center, hallowed temple to the performing arts. Let's show a little sensitivity here. These guys may be hard hats, but that doesn't mean they're *gauche*. The point was driven home one day when a gravelly voice with a thick Brooklyn accent inquired from one end of the bar to the other, "Hey Vinny! Did you know that Bruce here danced the second lead in *L'apres midi du Fawn* in Paris last season?"

Chapter 10
The Instigator

O ne of the great techniques that Jon Stone created for *Sesame Street* was taking classic comedy routines from movies and vaudeville and reinterpreting them for our young audience. This time-honored material was perfect for the show. It was broad. It was visual. And, it was universally funny. We scoured old vaudeville and Buster Keaton scripts. And, if there was a Marx Brothers' film on television, whatever the hour, we watched it.

One of the most memorable *Sesame Street* pieces from that era was Sonia Manzano, the fine actress who plays Maria on the show, duplicating the classic mirror scene from the Marx Brothers film, *Duck Soup*. In it, a double tries to convince Groucho that a mirror hasn't been broken by duplicating every move that Groucho makes and *almost* getting away with it. Sonia, in baggy pants, Groucho glasses and moustache, executed it perfectly.

The *Instigator* was inspired by another classic comedy routine.

The only other thing you have to realize about this piece is that in 1974, there was a hot (for *Sesame Street*) romance between teenagers Maria and David.

OPEN TO THE INTERIOR OF HOOPER'S STORE. DAVID IS BEHIND THE COUNTER CLEANING UP. ENTER OSCAR THE GROUCH.

OSCAR

Hiya, Mr. Storekeeper. How about a chocolate sundae with vinegar and a few lemons?

DAVID

Look, Oscar, I can't mess with you right now. I have a date with Maria in a couple of minutes and I'm closing early.

OSCAR

Isn't that cute, a date with Maria.

DAVID

That's right. I got paid today, and I'm going to surprise Maria and take her to the new movie down the street. Now, Maria's going to be here in about five minutes, and I want you to be gone before she does, see?

OSCAR

Aw, what's the hurry? I happen to know that the last three times you had a date with Maria, she was late. Right? Right? Right?

DAVID

Yeah, okay. But . . .

OSCAR

Well, what makes you think she'll be on time today?

DAVID

Don't hassle me.

OSCAR

Me? Hassle you? I wasn't late for our last three dates, was I?

DAVID

No, Oscar.

OSCAR

You know, it's really not very nice to be late for a date, is it?

DAVID

No. It's not, Oscar.

OSCAR

I mean, here you are, right? All duded up with your pay in your pocket, planning to surprise Maria and take her to a movie. And, you know what Maria's probably doing? She's probably sitting around right now, trying to decide how late she's going to be. She's probably sitting around saying, "How late am I going to be for my date with David? Maybe I'll just be an hour late. Or, maybe I'll really zatz him and be two hours late."

DAVID

Oscar, you're being ridiculous. Now, scram.

OSCAR

Ridiculous? She does it to you all the time. She's got a lot of nerve. Especially, after you got Mr. Hooper to let you off early, and then you planned to surprise her and take her to the movies. I'll bet she doesn't even care.

DAVID

Yeah?

OSCAR

Yeah! You know, I'll bet that Maria is at that new movie right now, just so she can ruin your surprise.

DAVID

No!

OSCAR

Yeah!

DAVID

Yeah.

OSCAR

If I were you, man, I'd really be mad.

DAVID

Yeah.

THE INSTIGATOR

OSCAR

She really doesn't care, does she?

DAVID

Not a bit!

OSCAR

I'll bet she's probably seen that new movie two times already, and she probably won't get here 'til next week!

DAVID

I don't even know why I asked her out in the first place! Boy, that makes me mad! In fact, I'll bet she's already seen that movie fifteen times, and she's never gonna get here! I could wait here forever, just getting madder, and madder and MADDER!!!

ENTER MARIA

MARIA

Hi, fellas. Well, David, it's four o'clock. Ready to go?

DAVID

What?! After what you just did to me!!?? Going down to that new movie fifteen times!!! And, ruining my surprise!!! And keeping me waiting here forever!!! I wouldn't take you to the movies if you were the last woman on earth!!!

DAVID STORMS OUT

MARIA

Oscar, what on earth do you suppose is the matter with him!?

OSCAR

(PRIMLY) I'm sure I certainly don't know. However, it appeared to be extremely uncouth, ungentlemanly, and certainly unforgivable behavior . . . Want to go to the movies?

FADE OUT

Since we believe in happy endings on *Sesame Street*, the last scene in the show went like this:

DAVID IS LOCKING UP HOOPER'S STORE AND MARIA IS WITH HIM. SHE HAS HER PURSE AND THEY ARE DRESSED FOR A DATE. AS THE CLOSING CREDITS ROLL, THEY WALK DOWN THE STREET WAVING TO EVERYONE. AS THEY REACH OSCAR'S CAN, MARIA STOPS, REACHES INTO HER PURSE AND TAKES OUT A SMALL SPRAY BOTTLE. SHE LIFTS THE LID ON THE CAN AND SPRAYS INSIDE.

OSCAR

(INSIDE CAN)
AARRRRRRRGAAAAAAAHHHHHH!!!

MARIA

(TO DAVID)
Perfume.

FADE OUT

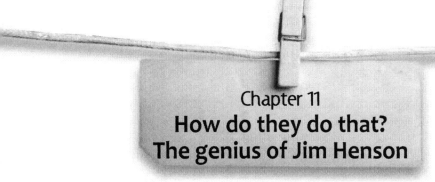

Chapter 11
How do they do that?
The genius of Jim Henson

Before we go much further into my Muppet memories, it's probably a good idea to give you a little insight into Muppet mechanics.

Virtually everyone on earth has seen the performing genius of Jim Henson. Until his death in 1990 from streptococcus pneumonia, Jim, and only Jim, performed Kermit the Frog, Ernie, Dr. Teeth, Waldorf (The round faced old man in the box), Rowlf the Dog, the Swedish Chef, Link Hogthrob, Captain of the Swinetrek and the Muppet Newsman.

But most people never saw Jim's artistic and mechanical abilities, which allowed him to combine puppetry, an ancient art and television, a relatively young art form into a new form of performance art. And, that's the way he wanted it. Jim Henson was a master illusionist. And the last thing an illusionist wants is someone looking behind the curtain.

To begin with, Jim was a devoted fan of Walt Disney. His imagination ran parallel to Disney's, creating fantastic creatures and worlds never seen before. Muppet tradition has it that Muppets only have three fingers and a thumb because it was a Henson tribute to Disney, since Mickey Mouse only has three fingers on a hand. Until the advent of computers, animation was a slow and tedious operation. Each individual cell, or film frame had to be hand drawn and individually photographed. Disney had enormous staffs of artists working on his projects. But Jim had neither the patience nor manpower for that.

In high school, Jim worked at a local TV station making puppets for a children's show. Later, while studying commercial art at the University of Maryland, he took a course in puppet making. It was then that Jim melded his experience in television and puppet making to devise what was really a new, simpler form of animation.

Of course, there have been puppets on television almost since its inception. Howdy Doody, Kukla, Fran and Ollie, and Bil Baird's Marionettes, all preceded the Muppets. (Baird said he dropped the second "L" from his first name because nobody ever pronounced it.) But all of these were just conventional puppets put on television. Jim Henson incorporated television right into the design of the Muppets.

To begin with, Jim did away with the play board, the stage that puppeteers hide behind during the performance. Instead, Jim used the bottom of the television screen for that purpose, "hiding" the puppeteers below it.

He then had the cameras elevated so the bottom of the frame was seven feet over the studio floor. The scenery was raised to the same height. That meant that instead of crouching on the floor, hiding behind props or scenery, the puppeteers could work standing upright. This gave the puppets complete mobility and was also much easier on the puppeteers. It also allowed scenes to be reset faster for a second or third take – in television, time is always money. So, when you see a Muppet scene on *Sesame Street*, or a piece on *The Muppet Show*, it's all done seven feet in the air.

Jim then went on to devise a set of principles for designing puppets specifically for television. To begin with, Muppets are essentially hand puppets. The puppeteer's hand is inside the head. The puppeteer speaks in the character's voice and moves his thumb in sync with the dialogue to animate the puppet.

If you hold your arm straight up in the air and make a "duck head" of your hand, you'll see a puppet's mouth is 16" to 18" above the top of your head. Since the top of the puppeteer's head is the cut-off for the bottom of the TV screen, those 16" to 18" are all the space that's available for the character's body.

Human beings are roughly eight heads high. But, because television is a "close-up" medium, that eight to one ratio would mean the puppet's head would be much too small for a television close-up, not to mention a human hand. So, Muppets are roughly designed on a three to one ratio, one third head and two thirds body.

Since the only support a *Muppet* has is the arm of the puppeteer, weight is always a consideration in puppet design. Imagine working eight or 10 hours a day with your right-hand straight up in the air. So, foam rubber and feathers are the basic *Muppet* building materials. Great care is also taken to make sure that seams and joints don't "read" on camera.

Color also requires a certain amount of attention. Colors change under television lights and some shades just aren't television friendly. They can go dark or muddy. So for example, every Kermit puppet (yes, there are several for practical reasons) is that exact shade of Kermit green.

Big Bird's color is also very crucial. Some yellows can go brown on television. So, Big Bird's feathers are hand dyed that particular shade of yellow that looks so vibrant on color television.

Between takes on *The Muppet Show*, it was not unusual to see a hand appear on camera holding several swatches of material, all different shades of the same color. It was a puppet builder testing to see which shade read the best on camera.

Jim wanted his puppets to be able to gesture and handle props, which most hand puppets of the Punch and Judy variety could not do. So, Jim designed "handed" puppets. Fozzie Bear, Ernie, Oscar the Grouch, the Swedish Chef and Rowlf, the piano playing dog, are "handed" puppets. They have sleeves and gloves which become the puppet's arms and hands.

Usually, the puppeteer puts his right hand into the puppet's head and his left hand into the sleeve and glove. Since the puppeteers are right-handed, "handed" Muppets are all left-handed. The right, or "dead" arm is usually pinned into a permanent position and played away from the camera.

It really gets tricky when the puppet needs to use two hands. When that happens, a second puppeteer is recruited. He or she stands behind the lead puppeteer and slips his or her hand into the puppet's right hand. So, when you see Ernie butter toast, or deal cards, know that each hand is played by a separate puppeteer. The exceptions are the Swedish Chef and Rowlf, the piano playing dog. Both of their hands were "played" by Frank Oz.

The puppets without hands, Kermit: Gonzo; Piggy; and Bert, for example, are called "rod" puppets because their arms are controlled by thin rods, painted to match the scene's background. For these guys to handle props requires the use of television technology.

Let's say, Kermit has to answer a phone back stage at the Muppet Theater. This requires a series of steps. Firstly, when the phone rings, Kermit goes over to the phone and puts his hand on the receiver. Then we stop video taping. Kermit's hand is attached to the receiver and the rod is then removed from his arm and attached to the bottom of the receiver. Then, we resume taping from another angle, say a close up on the phone. The shot widens out as Kermit brings the phone to his ear and the scene continues. When the two shots are spliced together, Kermit will seamlessly answer the phone. The sequence is reversed when Kermit hangs up the phone.

The final piece of the Muppet's success is the television puppeteering technique Jim Henson created for them. Since television, as I said, is a close-up medium, Jim determined that eye contact between puppet and audience was essential. It's the basic reason Muppets appear to be so alive.

Jim accomplished this by having TV monitors around the set so the puppeteers could watch their performances as they were recorded, When a puppet looks the puppeteer in the eye on the monitor, he or she knows that their puppet is looking the viewing audience directly in the eye.

Additionally, Jim discovered that puppets with fixed expressions could appear to change those expressions by changing the angle at which a puppet's head is presented to the camera. For example, Ernie has a permanent happy grin. To make him look baleful or sad, Jim would tilt Ernie's head forward, hiding the mouth and presenting only the eyes to camera. To make Ernie seem to grin, Jim would turn his head slightly sideways.

The most difficult physical aspect of Muppet puppeteering is hand control. Make the "duck head" again with your hand. Then make it go, "quack, quack, quack," very slowly. Notice that your four fingers go up and your thumb goes down. That's the natural movement of the human hand.

However, If you do this with your hand in a puppet, the head will bounce up and down, losing eye contact as well as the illusion that the puppet is alive. When people talk, the jaw moves but the head and the eyes remains steady.

Puppeteers in training work on "talking" with their right hand, moving only the thumb. This is usually done with a puppet, in front of a mirror, reciting the alphabet. The object is to move the puppet's jaw while keeping the head stationary. Try it. Make your "duck head" recite the alphabet moving only your thumb. Not as easy as you thought, is it?

Understanding this Muppet technology is essential to writing for them. It keeps you from writing pieces that are impossible to produce, which is a waste of your time. It also keeps you from writing overly complicated material, which is a waste of everyone else's time.

On the other hand, if you understand the technology, you can make it work for you. I once created an act for the Great Gonzo where he recited the seven-time multiplication table while standing up in a hammock and balancing a grand piano on one finger.

The trick was simplicity itself. We swung a hammock between two posts. Gonzo's feet were attached to the hammock. A Muppet sized grand piano was attached to Gonzo's finger. The piano was then hung, at the appropriate height, with clear plastic, invisible wire. Since the whole thing was rigged in front of a curtain, the puppeteer could slip his hand through a slit in the curtain and into Gonzo's head.

Alas! Gonzo forgot what seven times nine was and got booed off the stage.

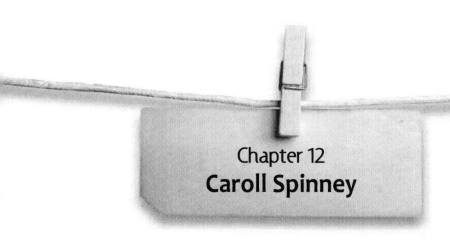

Chapter 12
Caroll Spinney

O f course, the super star, top banana, and good will ambassador of *Sesame Street* is Big Bird, another great Jim Henson creation. In the world of puppetry, Big Bird is a major milestone. His articulated mouth makes him a legitimate puppet. But he's the first puppet to be completely mobile. He needs no play board or camera angles to hide his puppeteer. He's completely self contained.

That's not to say he's easy to operate. The puppeteer's right arm goes up the neck and his hand goes inside the head. And, like other Muppets, his right thumb controls the jaw. His left hand goes into a sleeve and glove to become Big Bird's left hand. Of course, the puppet's right arm is a dummy. But, it is attached to an invisible plastic line that runs up through a loop under the puppet's chin and down to the other hand. This transfers some movement from the operating left hand to the right, which is usually cheated away from the camera.

To add to his height, high heeled boots are concealed inside the legs and feet. The puppet builder, Kermit Love (known in Muppet circles as Kermit the Person), had to go to a transvestite boutique to find high heeled boots big enough to fit a man's foot.

In the earliest versions of Big Bird's designs, Jim tried to work it out so the costume would fit backwards, thereby making its knees work backward like a bird's. That proved impractical. But it's an insight into Jim Henson's sense of design.

Inside the puppet, the puppeteer has to keep his chin almost on his chest so as not to ruin the line of Big Bird's back. Additionally, he wears a leather chest plate which holds his microphone and a one and a half inch wireless television monitor. The monitor is necessary because the puppeteer can't really see out of the suit. Instead, he watches himself on the monitor.

It's kind of like that old joke, put your shoulder to the wheel, and your nose to the grindstone. Now, try and get something done in that position.

The man who actually does work in that position and still does an incredible job of acting is Caroll Spinney. For forty years, Caroll has been the voice and personality of the eight foot, two inch canary. Thanks to Caroll's extraordinary talent, Big Bird sings, dances, roller skates and rides unicycles and motorcycles. He's been to Japan and China and conducted a symphony orchestra in Sydney, Australia.

Caroll, himself, is as fascinating as the character he performs. To begin with, he's a great performer. Imagine trying to perform that universally loveable character under his working conditions. But Caroll is also a fine artist and cartoonist. His Christmas cards are hand drawn works of art. Some years they run two and three pages, comic book style, relating his and Big Bird's adventures of the past year. Other Christmases, they're wonderful illustrations of Caroll, his lovely wife, Debbie, his children, his characters and his home.

Caroll's home is another work of his art. Years ago, he bought a large plot of land in his native New England. He built a Swiss chalet style house on it. And ever since he has been expanding and improving it, adding additions, ponds and landscaping. It's called, Deerhaven after the magnificent creatures that nonchalantly wander around it. Deerhaven is also a wonderful reflection of Caroll's sense of humor and creativity.

It has, thanks to Caroll's design, a sledding course that is about a half mile in length. It takes you down across a couple of frozen ponds and has an A.T.V. at the bottom to tow you back up the hill. But my two favorite features are available all year long.

The first is a feature Caroll's incorporated into the house's original design. When the house was built, Caroll's children were quite young. So, he had a secret door built into his sons' room. It leads to a small balcony over looking the kitchen that is disguised as part of the chalet motif. The reason? Solely so the kids can spy on the grown-ups down in the kitchen.

Secondly, the guest room has a rather unique feature. It overlooks a placid pond. On the other side of the pond, a hill rises, covered by a dense stand of birch trees that Caroll had planted over the years. And, the guest bathroom has the same view. It is possible, while sitting on the commode, to view the bucolic pond and forest.

However! If you know the secret, it gets even better. On the wall, next to the commode is an incongruous light switch. Throwing that switch causes a fully decorated Christmas tree to light up on the other side of the pond. Of course, with Caroll and Debbie it's Christmas almost all year long. It's their favorite holiday. It seems like they put their tree up on Labor Day and take it down on opening of the baseball season.

As I am, Caroll is a motorcycle enthusiast, as are many of his friends. Just after Connecticut passed a motorcycle helmet law, I took my '66 B.M.W. R69S up to Caroll's for a weekend. There were several other bikers there, all raving against the new Connecticut helmet law. One, in particular, told me when I returned to New York City through Connecticut, not to wear a helmet. And, he went on, if a trooper stopped me to say that he said it was okay. His name was Rufus Rose, the puppeteer who had operated Howdy Doody.

I imagined myself being stopped by a Connecticut State Trooper for not wearing my helmet and telling him Howdy Doody said it was okay.

As you know, Caroll also performs Oscar The Grouch. And for some reason, whenever Caroll calls and gets my answering maching. It's always Oscar on the line: *Awright, Bailey, you're not home! Good! I didn't want to talk to ya anyway! G'bye.*

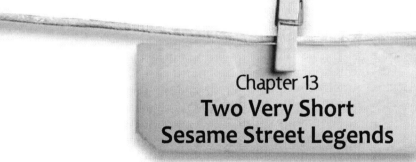

Chapter 13
Two Very Short
Sesame Street Legends

1. Around 3:30 one morning, a little boy came screaming into his parent's bedroom. His parents tried to comfort him. They told him he was just having a bad dream.

"No!", the little boy replied.

"Is it the monsters under the bed, again?", the father asked.

"No. No monsters."

"Well, are you still afraid of the dark?"

"No."

"Well then, what is it?", the parents asked.

"My pillow!", the little boy exclaimed. "It's a rectangle!!!"

2. A little girl who definitely did not want to be zipped into a snow suit explained to her parents, at the top of her lungs, "I cannot co-operate!!!"

Chapter 14
S.R.O.

'm hoping against hope that someone at Sesame Workshop has the foresight to oversee and protect the *Sesame Street* video archives. Over the years, the show has produced some classic television.

One involved teaching the word, "surprise." Jon Stone commissioned a song called, *Surprise!*. The accompanying video, written by Jon, probably involved more pies-in-the-face in three and a half minutes than the Three Stooges threw in a year.

The word, "Surprise" was used liberally throughout the song. Each time it was, some human cast member or Muppet caught a cream pie square in the kisser – always from an unexpected direction or person. Somewhere between 50 and 60 pies were thrown, mostly by Jon Stone, who had a wonderful time directing it.

At the wrap party, the celebration held after the last show of the season is shot, choice pieces from the season were screened. The last one screened was *Surprise!* Predictably, it was a big hit. And, during the applause at its end, Producer Dulce Singer hit Jon Stone square in the face with a cream pie. Somewhere a still shot of that exists – I hope.

Occasionally, *Sesame Street* would do remote shoots in streets around the studio, which was located at Broadway and West 81st Street. At that time, upper Broadway, where the studio was located, was rife with SRO (Single Room Occupancy) Hotels. They were pretty shabby, basically rooming houses for people on small pensions and down-and-outers. A lot of them were named after states, Hotel California, Hotel Carolina, Hotel Nevada.

One afternoon, while the remote crew was waiting around for props or equipment, Jon Stone spotted an SRO hotel across the street from the location. At the time the *Sesame Street* Studio Manager was a wonderful guy named Chet O'Brien. Chet and his identical twin, Snooks, had been a vaudeville dance act back in the 1930s. Chet was an encyclopedia of vaudeville lore and especially classic vaudeville jokes.

Jon said to Chet, "Go inside the Hotel Wisconsin there. And when I say, "Action!" I want you to come out, look at the camera and tell every small hotel room joke you know."

Chet entered the Hotel Wisconsin.

"Action!"

Chet exits the hotel, stops and turns to camera.

"I don't want to say the rooms are small here, but I put my key in the door and broke the window."

"I wouldn't say the rooms are small, but the mice are hunchbacked."

"I don't want to say the rooms are small. It's just the wallpaper's very thick.

"I don't want to say the rooms are small, but I have to go out in the hall to change my mind" . . . And on and on.

I hope that classic piece of video tape is still in existence.

Chapter 15
The White House

I n December 1976, I was asked to write the material for a live *Sesame Street* cast appearance at the White House. Mrs. Gerald Ford was having her annual Christmas party for the children of foreign diplomats. Big Bird and several of the cast members from the Show were going to be the entertainment. Dulce Singer, our producer, was gracious enough to take me and several other staff members along for the ride.

Just for your information, when he flies, Big Bird, the puppet that is, gets his own seat in the passenger compartment, and always first class. Kermit Love, who was Big Bird's builder and dresser, wouldn't let the costume out of his sight. The costume is hidden in a canvas travel bag, which hangs over the seat next to Kermit.

On our flight down to Washington, I sat next to Will Lee, the actor who played Mr. Hooper, owner of the local candy store and soda fountain on *Sesame Street*, until his death in 1982. Although the store has had several proprietors since Will's death, the store is still, and always will be called, "Hooper's," in Will's memory.

During the flight, Will told me that the last time he had been at the White House with the *Sesame Street* cast, Richard Nixon was President.

Will had been blacklisted for five years during the 1950s. At the time, Congressman Richard M. Nixon had a seat on the House Un-American Activities Committee, which determined which actors, writers, directors and producers, including Will, because of supposed communist affiliations, were placed on the blacklist. Blacklisted artists were denied employment for as many as ten years. And many of their careers were completely ruined.

So Will was no fan of President Nixon. He told me that during the reception after the show, he made sure to have a kid in each arm so there would never be a picture of Will Lee shaking hands with Richard Nixon.

We were picked up at Washington National Airport in special White House vans and spirited to the White House. There, we were installed in a very comfortable room with an excellent buffet. While killing time before the performance, Caroll Spinney and I started exploring the halls of the White House.

At one point we encountered a broad stair case with a highly polished banister running down the middle. Caroll couldn't resist. He ran to the top of the stairs and slid all the way down the banister. One of my fondest memories of Caroll is of him sliding down the banister in the White House.

In further wanderings, we encountered the 1,000[th] piano produced by the Steinway Company. A beautiful concert grand, it had been a gift to the White House from the Steinway family. I succumbed to temptation by sitting down and belting out a few bars of boogie woogie on it.

The show took place on the stage of the Gold Room. The kids were seated in rows on the floor. When the entertainment was over, Jon Stone declared the show was a smashing success, evidenced by a small puddle he found on the floor after the kids had left.

Later on, there was a receiving line for us to meet our hostesses, Mrs. Ford and her daughter, Susan. On the line, I succumbed to another temptation. Behind me in the line was Sam Pottle, then *Sesame Street's* Music Director.

Suddenly, I remembered something George Burns had done to Jack Benny on a receiving line to meet the Queen of England. Burns turned to Benny, who was behind him, and said, "Remember! Whatever she says, don't laugh!"

I said the same thing to Sam just before I shook hands with Mrs. Ford. As I moved down the line, I heard Mrs. Ford say, "Merry Christmas, Mr. Pottle." And, just like Jack Benny, I heard Sam dissolve into helpless giggles.

Chapter 16
Records

I'm old enough to remember radio drama. (Sigh.) When I was in boarding school and we were in bed after lights out, Sister Regina Agnes, who was in charge of the dormitory, would turn on her radio and we would fall asleep listening to *The Lone Ranger* and *The F.B.I. in Peace and War*. I remember it being a wonderful exercise in imagination.

Later on, when I became a copywriter, I realized how much fun radio was to write. I was free of the strangulation of film production budgets. All I needed was an actor or two and a sound effects library and I could create ship wrecks, rocket launches, cattle stampedes, airplane races, and anything else I dreamed up.

But, in the mid-70s, I got to dust off my radio chops again when I was asked to write some *Sesame Street* record albums. I did a "monsters" album and a couple of Christmas albums, one based on a Christmas television special I wrote with Jon Stone. But the two that were the most fun were *The Count COUNTS* and *Bert & Ernie SING-ALONG*.

For *The Count COUNTS*, we created a hard driving, 1960s, AM radio disc jockey show with the Count as the very "hip" D.J. Sam Pottle and David Axlerod created some wonderful, fast paced musical buttons in that 60s D.J. genre of over-the-top reverberation:

All the swingingest sounds around, it's the Count's Countdoooooown.

Radio One, Two Threeeeeeeeeee!

Who's the Count we're bats about? It's the Count Von Coooount!

You get the idea.

Jim Henson's hyper-hysterical Guy Smiley, Star of Day Time TV, did the opening introduction:

AND NOW! DIRECT FROM THE SESAME STREET STUDIOS LOCATED HIGH ABOVE HOOPER'S CANDY STORE! RADIO 1-2-3 PROUDLY PRESENTS COUNT VON COUNT AND THE COUNT'S COUNTDOWN!!!!

Then came the Pottle/Axlerod theme:

Who's got the numbers all the time and loves to count them and to play them for you? No one but the Count! He's got the crown!

He also has the numbers and the cat is gonna lay them on you one by one at the Count's Countdooooooooown!

Que Pasa?! And Vot's happening?!, the Count opened. He then went on to start counting listeners.

Starting at the bottom, the Count played this week's top twelve hits, working his way up to number one with appropriate fanfare.

During the show, we inserted as many radio elements as we could – *Sesame Street* style:

We had an ad:

GUY SMILEY: *Friends, has your counting been a little dull lately Not much fun, Hmm? Well, maybe it's because you can only count to ten. So, let me tell you about the wonderful number, 15!*

Guy then went on to extol the benefits of being able to count up to 15. And, at the end: *Ask your local adult for a demonstration!*

We did a weather report: *Today's high was 72 at 11 o'clock! The low was 46 at eight o'clock! The barometric pressure is 28 and falling! There is a 60 percent chance of rain and wind from the east at 12 miles per hour! And there is a light overcast at 15,000, 15,000 vonderful feet!*

The Count did dedications to David and Maria, and Gordon and Susan. He counted the holes in the microphone. He played "Moldy Oldies" and blasts from the past.

Numbers in the news: Three little pigs whose visiting cousin made four little pigs! Ten is the number of toes most people have! (We also did sports news, which consisted of nothing but scores.)

Since I was the sole writer on the album, I decided to indulge in a little good natured nepotism and include two of my favorite *Sesame Street* songs. They are two of my favorite *Sesame Street* songs because I wrote the lyrics for them.

The inspiration came when *Sesame Street* decided to do a network musical variety show in which I was not invited to participate. In retaliation, I decided that my next regular *Sesame Street* script would be a musical variety show set on *Sesame Street*, called, *Two Plus Two*. The opening number was called, *I Just Adore Four!* The production starred Big Bird backed up by a chorus of male Muppets called, the Tarnish Brothers, although, I can't for the life of me remember why. But, The number had a big, Broadway musical feel to it.

I Just Adore Four
I just adore four.
The number for me.
You can't deplore four,
It's less than five, more than three!

You can have four doors,
Or four dinosaurs,
Four janitors,
Or even four grocery stores!

I Just adore four.
The number sublime.
I love to draw four,
It's just an angle and a line!

I can't get sore for
It's plain, you see,
I just adore four,
The number for me!

(Spoken)

Ah, yes. I used to fret a lot and fidget.
Until I met that dazzling digit.
And now you see a brand new me for
I found a number I can be for and count 1, 2, 3, 4.

Now the Tarnish Brothers join it.

I just adore four.
The number for me.
You can't deplore four,
It's less than five, more than three!

You can have four floors,
or four army corps,
Four dresser drawers,
Or even four crashing bores!

I Just adore four.
The number sublime.
I love to draw four
It's just an angle and a line!

I can't get sore for, it's plain to see
I just adore four, the number 1, 2, 3,
Four me!

And, as long as I was being self indulgent, I gave the Count the line: *Vel! They certainly don't write them like that anymore!*

The title for the second song just came to me while I was deep in concentration about subtraction. Flash! *The Subtraction Blues.* Take it away. Take it away!

The number was performed on the show and on the record, by Northern Calloway, the talented Broadway performer who played "David" on *Sesame Street*, in his best Kansas City blues style.

The Subtraction Blues
I've got the subtraction blues,
Sitting and crying all day.
I've got the subtraction blues,
Sitting and crying all day.
Got the subtraction blues.
Take it away. Take it away.

I had four pieces of pizza.
I was saving them all for me.
I swapped one for some chocolate milk,
And four take away one is three!

Got the subtraction blues.
Sitting and crying all day.
Got the subtraction blues.
Take it away. Take it away.

I had three pieces of pizza,
Just waiting for me to chew.
I gave one to a friend of mine.
And three take away one is two!

Th subtraction blues.
Sitting and crying all day.
I've got the subtraction blues.
Take it away. Take it away.

I had two pieces of pizza.
I was saving to eat in the sun.
One slipped into the gold fish bowl.
And two take away one is one!

Got the subtraction blues.
Take it away. Take it away.

I had just one piece of pizza.
Then my dog grabbed it on the run.
I had just one piece of pizza.
But one take away one is none!

I've got the subtraction blues.
Sitting and crying all day.
I've got the subtraction blues.
Take it away. Take it away.

At the end of the record, the Count had played his way up to number one, which, of course was the Song of the Count. *Counting is Vonderful! Counting is Marwelous!*

I found the inspiration for the *Bert & Ernie SING-ALONG* album in the classic 1935 Marx Brothers hit film, *A Night at the Opera*. The movie contains one of the most famous comedy scenes of all time. It takes place in a small, trunk-filled steamship cabin. At the beginning, Groucho, Chico, Harpo and the ship's doctor are in the room. For some reason, Harpo is asleep and can't be awakened.

Over the next two and a half minutes, two maids, the ship's engineer, a manicurist, the engineer's assistant, a woman looking for her Aunt Minnie, another maid and finally four stewards with large trays of room service all cram into the tiny stateroom, while Groucho does a continuous stream of one liners. At the end, there are some 15 people crawling all over each other trying to clean the room, fix the heat, give a manicure, make a phone call and serve dinner.

For a finish, Margaret Dumont, who played the clueless matriarch and was the brunt of Groucho's double entendres, comes down the hallway. When she opens the cabin door, the rest of the cast explodes through the door like they've been shot out of a cannon. It was the kind of lunatic anarchy that was perfect for the Muppets.

The *Bert & Ernie SING-ALONG* album starts simply enough with Bert in the bathtub singing to himself. But then Ernie comes in and decides that the acoustics are so good that the bathroom is the perfect place for a sing-along.

So, he brings in his piano. He and Bert do a duet called, *I Refuse to Sing Along*.

As the record progresses, more and more of the *Sesame Street* cast hear the singing and show up to join in. First comes David. Then Gordon comes in *with* his bass fiddle. Then comes Bob and Susan and Maria, causing Bert to plead for a towel or at least more bubble bath. Big Bird comes in with his bells. And the Count starts to count the bathroom tiles until the rest put him in the shower.

We hear a motorcycle roar down the hall and crash through the door with the *Sesame Street* monsters, Herry, Grover and Cookie aboard.

How did you get a motorcycle in the bathroom!?

Simple. I made a left in the bedroom.

Then Oscar comes in to complain about the noise.

The album ends with the University of Michigan Marching Band marching in playing *Stars and Stripes Forever*.

Jon Stone liked the finish record so much that we recreated as much as we could for an episode of *Sesame Street*.

Some 30 years after the album was produced (and 70 years after *A Night at the Opera* appeared), Lawrence Downes, of the *New York Times*, wrote in his column that he had found a copy of *SING-ALONG* at a garage sale, bought it for his daughter, Sophie. He was kind enough to mention just how much they had enjoyed it.

So Groucho, Harpo, Chico, Zeppo and Gummo, wherever you are, thank you.

Chapter 17
Joe Raposo

Joe Raposo was the musical force behind the creation of *Sesame Street*. A classically trained musician, Joe could compose, orchestrate, and conduct with equal virtuosity.

As the show's original Music Director, he wrote the music for the *Sesame Street* theme and composed or co-wrote the early *Sesame Street* hits including *It's Not Easy Being Green, and, Sing! (Canta!)*. Joe wrote, *Green*, in one night with no more direction than a note in a *Sesame Street* script: *Kermit sings a song*. He also composed the occasional music and songs that underscored the show's Muppet and animation pieces (including my personal favorite, *I'm An Aardvark and I'm Proud!*).

Occasionally, Joe and I would go out for a beer after work. Most of his background and impressive other credits are scattered all over Google and Wikipedia. But here are a couple of my favorite Joe Raposo stories that you won't find on the Internet:

When Joe first came to New York after graduating from Harvard, where he worked on *Hasty Pudding* productions, he supported himself by picking up occasional cocktail piano and off Broadway gigs. Eventually, he joined the musicians' union, Local 802. And suddenly, his work load surged.

Joe was getting booked in bands that were playing elaborate celebrations in Brooklyn and on Long Island – weddings, first communions, confirmations, graduations and anniversary parties. Joe said he always got paid well, in cash, got fed as well as the guests, and more often than not, got a bottle of wine or liquor on the way out. Joe couldn't figure out his good luck. He was a talented piano player, but New York was full of talented piano players.

Finally, it dawned on him. All of the affairs he worked were thrown by Italian-American families connected to, "friends downtown," as the expression goes. Because of his last name, the union guys figured he was Italian. So, until he got a steady gig, Joe feared his only source of income would dry up immediately if it was discovered he wasn't Italian at all, but a full-blooded Portugese from Fall River, Massachusetts.

Right after *Sesame Street* became a tremendous hit, Joe was on business in Los Angeles with Jeff Moss, the show's first Head Writer. At a party, Joe struck up a conversation with a man who claimed to be a *Sesame Street* writer. Joe had never seen him before in his life.

Without revealing his connection to the show Joe casually mentioned that he thought *Sesame Street* was written and produced in New York. The "writer" assured him that was true. But the show liked his material so much that they let him write from Los Angeles. And his scripts were delivered to *Sesame Street* via the daily William Morris mail pouch that was hand carried from Los Angeles to New York by messenger.

Feigning fascination, Joe then called Jeff Morse over to the conversation without revealing Jeff's position as *Sesame Street*'s Head Writer. Joe and Jeff then let this unsuspecting fool rhapsodize all night about his contribution to *Sesame Street*, which in his estimation was enormous, and never let on about their connection to the show.

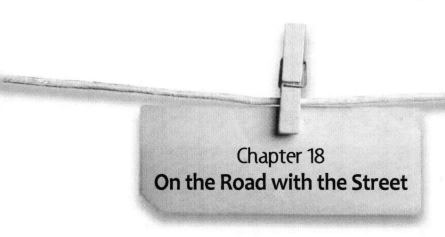

Chapter 18
On the Road with the Street

I n the mid-1970s, *Sesame Street* decided to take the show on the road. Video taping equipment was becoming relatively portable, although, not by present standards – television was still recorded on two-inch wide tape. But it was common enough that *Sesame Street* could afford it. We started by doing some local "remotes" in and around New York City.

One show was shot in the rolling hills northwest of New York City. The show's premise was that Bob, Susan, Gordon, Mr. Hooper, Big Bird, Oscar and several kids take a camping trip to the woods with predictably disastrous results.

But during that shoot, I got to create a wonderful spoof on old time adventure films. It was a creative element on *Sesame Street* to do our own spoofs on adult genres like adventure films or quiz shows.

I must have been in an impish mood when I wrote it because I saw an opportunity to take Bob, a pretty clean cut, straight-laced character, and use him against type in some outrageous visual comedy.

Since Big Bird was on the shoot, I knew Kermit Love would be along to protect him in the wilds. Kermit, who also had a theatrical background, made occasional appearances on *Sesame Street* as Willie the Hot Dog Man. Visually, Kermit is positively Santa Claus-esque with long silver hair and matching full beard.

So, this would be one of those bits where the *Street* characters would be playing other, cartoon-like characters. Finally, the entire piece could be shot on the locations of the other segments. So, it was practically a Freebie.

With adventure music underneath, the piece starts with a series of quick shots of Bob: 1. In a safari jacket and pith helmet struggling through some brush. 2. In torn clothes with a raggedly beard struggling up a beach. 3. In longer beard and more ragged clothing climbing a mountain.

As the music fades, we cut to a forest clearing, where Kermit the Person is playing Kermit the Hermit. In a still longer beard and tatters, Bob crawls in on his hands and knees.

"Are you Kermit the Hermit, Wise Man of the Forest?"

"Yes, my son."

"I've crossed the wildest jungle, swum the deepest ocean, and climbed the highest mountain to get here. Tell me, oh Wise Man, What is the secret of life?", asks Bob.

"The secret of life," Kermit replies, "is A-B-C-D-E-F-G-H-I-J-K-L-M-N-O-P-Q-R-S-T-U-V-W-X-Y-Z.", as the letters appear on the screen.

"A-B-C-D-E-F-G-H-I-J-K-L-M-N-O-P-Q-R-S-T-U-V-W-X-Y-Z!", Bob exclaimed, with the letters appearing again. "I didn't cross the wildest jungle, swim the deepest ocean, and climb the highest mountain to hear A-B-C-D-E-F-G-H-I-J-K-L-M-N-O-P-Q-R-S-T-U-V-W-X-Y-Z. That's the alphabet!"

"A-B-C-D-E-F-G-H-I-J-K-L-M-N-O-P-Q-R-S-T-U-V-W-X-Y-Z, is the alphabet? Are you sure?"

"Sure, I'm sure."

As Kermit exits, he hands Bob his staff and says, "Well, I guess that makes you the next Wise Man of the Forest."

Another *Sesame Street* "remote" was shot on City Island, a small nautical community that actually is a small island and a part of New York City. City Island is best known for its sail makers. City Island sails can be seen on sailboats around the world. But I remember City Island for another reason.

We had incorporated a multi-generational Puerto Rican family into our City Island story line. The grandfather of the family had been a farmer in Puerto Rico before coming to New York. And he never really lost his passion for farming in all his years in the city. So, the family had enclosed the generous back yard with a greenhouse.

And as the women in the family traveled back and forth to the island, they brought back small clippings of Puerto Rico's tropical flora in their pocketbooks. The tips were wrapped in wet cotton with tin foil on the outside. This kept them alive just long enough to make the trip from San Juan to City Island, where the grandfather rooted them.

Over the years, the grandfather had multiplied the plants until the entire back yard was a little piece of glassed in tropic paradise. I remember having coffee on the deck and looking over and through coffee plants, banana trees, bougainvillea, and coconut palms – another little hidden New York gem.

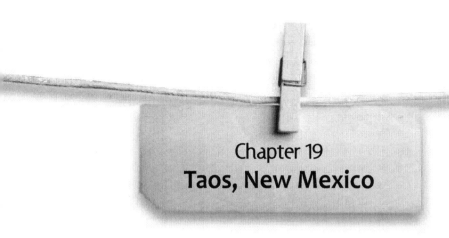

Chapter 19
Taos, New Mexico

After the success of the local remotes, in 1976, *Sesame Street* planned and budgeted two weeks of remote shows, shot in a completely different part of the country. I was appointed the writer for the project.

After much research, it was decided that Taos, New Mexico would be the ideal destination. Its western, mountain location was as far as you could get from *Sesame Street*'s urban setting. It was culturally diverse, with a combination of white and Hispanic populations and a nearby Indian pueblo. And, the scenery was just plain gorgeous.

We created a story line around Luis, *Sesame Street*'s resident Mexican-American, going to Taos to visit his uncle, who was building a new adobe house. A suitably beat up pick-up truck was procured for the trip. Bob, Maria, Gordon, Buffy St. Marie and Big Bird decided to go along for the ride. A large Hispanic family was recruited in Taos to play Luis' relatives, along with a few local actors to handle the occasional speaking roles.

We shot for about ten days in and around Taos in some of the most beautiful scenery in the world. What I remember most was how beautiful Big Bird looked in all his yellow grandeur against that blue western sky.

One of the benefits of location travel is that you get to spend an extended period of time in a place you would probably never go, otherwise. And, since the location is an integral part of the production, you really get a sense of the place. New Mexico is cattle country. And, even though it's still the United States, to an eastern city boy like me, it might as well be another planet.

I realized how foreign it was one morning in the hotel coffee shop. Three ranchers were having breakfast and talking very, very seriously about water. Water, to me, has always come out of the wall when I turn a tap. So, after a while, I became so intrigued, I said to them, "You guys talk about water the way we talk about closets in New York."

That prompted an explanation from one of the ranchers of how scarce water was in that part of the country. Taos's water comes from melting snow at the upper altitudes of the *Sangre de Cristo* mountain chain. The water travels down through an intricate system of ditches. The main ditch, the Arroyo Madre, is said to have been started by the Indians a thousand years ago. How much water is available, dictates how long ranchers are allowed to draw water from the arroyos onto their land.

When he was finished, the rancher asked me about my reference to closets. I told him that space in New York City is as scarce as water is in Taos. Then I asked him where he put his stuff. The, stuff, I explained, that he didn't need right now, but he might need later or just didn't want to throw out.

"That's easy.", he replied. "We just put it in the old barn."

That's when I knew it would be futile to continue that conversation.

Early one morning, Jon Stone and I went out to the Taos Pueblo to scout locations for the segments we were going to shoot there. Physically, the Pueblo hasn't changed in 1,000 years. It rises from a valley floor up into the cliffs on both sides of a fast running mountain stream, which is the community's only water source. Individual dwellings are carved out of the cliffs and hand made ladders are the only access from one level to another. On the "ground" floor, flat roofed, one and two story adobe buildings are separated by winding streets and small plazas, making it feel like a biblical Arab village.

The Pueblo is run much like a co-op or a condominium. Each dwelling is owned individually by local Indians and used primarily as a weekend retreat. These people can return completely to their ethnic roots with one short drive. Tewa Indian customs were rigorously observed. The most obvious was the Blanket Rule for Tewa men: If a man was outside anywhere in the Pueblo, he was required to wear an Indian blanket. It could be over his shoulders or around his waist, but he had to wear a blanket. A Tewa man without a blanket meant he was on the war path.

Since the Pueblo is, in effect, private property, tourists are restricted to certain areas and certain hours. Entry at any other time is possible only with a permit from the Pueblo's Governor.

Jon and I had the Governor's permission to visit the Pueblo that morning. The weather was just miserable. It was cold, overcast and windy. Occasion rain squalls blew down from the mountains. Because of the weather, the narrow streets were empty, adding to the sense of eeriness.

"This reminds me of a bad dream I kept having back in New York.", Jon said to me. "I'm out here with a full cast and crew and I haven't got the foggiest idea of what the hell I'm doing."

"Jon," I told him. "Please don't ever say that again. The only thing that keeps the rest of us going is we all figure at least you know what the hell you're doing."

By this time we had worked our way deep into the Pueblo. We had come to a small picturesque square that Jon thought had possibilities as a location. We began discussing the square's cinematic possibilities and the logistics of bringing in cameras, lights, crew, and shooting in the space.

Suddenly, an Indian woman appeared over us on the roof of an adobe building. She was tall and long legged in boots, jeans and a vibrant red Indian shirt with a sash. Her waist length black hair was blowing in the wind. She was gorgeous against the stormy sky.

In language that would make a rapper blush, she told us in no uncertain terms that this was private property not some kind of zoo and we, outsiders, were by no means welcome.

Her verbal attack was so virulent that Jon and I beat a hasty retreat, tails between legs, as expletives echoed through the narrow streets. We knew it was futile to try to explain our presence. As we walked to the car in the rain, an unspoken sentiment hung heavily in the cold damp air that this whole pueblo shoot had a very bad feel about it.

The next day, Jon and I had a script meeting about the Pueblo shoot. The only productive thing to come out of it was a mutual decision to scrap most of the Pueblo pieces I had written back in New York. I went back to my room to write some new material.

After a bit of hand wringing and head banging I came up with the germ of an idea. As usual, simple works best. But simple is so damned elusive.

The day of the Pueblo shoot arrived warm and sunny. Neither of us would admit it, but after our encounter with the Indian woman the day before, we were both surreptitiously checking to make sure the Pueblo men were still wearing blankets.

But in the balmy weather, our spirits and expectations began to rise. And on this visit to the Pueblo, with a full video crew and compliment of equipment, it was pretty obvious that we had the Governor's permission to be there. In fact, we had the Governor there, too. And the Pueblo residents were nothing but cordial and helpful to us.

In deference to the Governor and other elders of the Pueblo, we had set up a special viewing area for them with a television monitor on the back of a station wagon. There were four or five of them sitting there, staring expressionlessly at the screen. Not a word passed between them. A small crowd of other residents formed respectfully behind them, as our script began to unfold.

The *Sesame Street* characters involved in this segment were Maria, our Puerto Rican character, and Buffy Saint Marie, who was then also a cast member and is a full-blooded Cree Indian.

In my new script, Buffy is going to visit some friends in the Pueblo and asks if Maria and Big Bird would like to go along. The three jump in the pick up truck and head for the Pueblo.

But at the entrance to the Pueblo, Big Bird becomes apprehensive. He has never been in a pueblo before. In fact, he's not even sure what a pueblo is and what he's supposed to do when he gets there.

Buffy and Maria gently explain to him that a pueblo is just a place where Indians live. It's just a home, and you behave the way you behave in anybody's home. The way you'd like people to act in your home. And, if you have any questions, just be polite and ask.

This placates Big Bird a bit. But then he remembers he's never met an Indian. But he's seen pictures and they look pretty scary with all their feathers. Those feathers have to come from some place or somebody.

Buffy explains, much to Big Bird's incredulity, that *she's an Indian*. And, that Indians only wear feathers for ceremonies and special occasions. The rest of the time, they just look like everyone else, leaving Big Bird to ponder that if he took off his feathers, he'd look just like everyone else. With a greatly relieved Big Bird, the trio entered the Pueblo.

The rest of the day went well. Buffy did some wonderful music numbers surrounded by Indian kids. Big Bird looked beautiful and was the instant hit he always is. And, since he naturally sheds a bit, by the end of the day many of the Pueblo residents had decorated their hat bands with brilliant yellow feathers.

Our final set up was the little square where Jon and I had encountered the Indian woman several days earlier. The scene went very well and Jon called it a wrap for the day.

As the crew started to pack up, the effect our opening piece had on the Pueblo residents became evident, when the same Indian woman who had cursed out Jon and me a few days earlier approached us. "Would you like to see my pueblo?", she asked.

So, Jon and I climbed up two flights of rickety outside ladders to tour her home. (Jon *hated* heights.) During that climb, I came up with another piece of visitation advice for Big Bird. Wherever you are in the world, it's always a compliment when somebody invites you into their home.

The day after the Pueblo shoot, Buffy had to leave for another engagement. But Jon still needed some traveling footage of the pick-up truck going to the Pueblo. A quick survey of the cast and crew revealed that I was the only available person who could drive the standard shift pick-up.

Since most of the footage was going to be wide, long shots, it really didn't matter who was driving. The truck was too far away to determine who was behind the wheel. For closer shots, I wore Buffy's hat and turned away from the camera and slouched as low as I could in the seat and still drive. I can still hear Jon's voice from the walkie-talkie on the seat beside me, *I don't want to see one hair of that beard!!!*

It was like a day off for me. All I had to do was drive Big Bird through the mountains in the pick-up truck. We stopped for lunch in the middle of the afternoon at a local Mexican restaurant. Since we were almost finished shooting the shows, we all got a little lax. The one hour lunch turned into two hours and then two and a half hours.

Suddenly, Jon realized how late it was getting. He had one more shot he needed to get that day. It was the pick-up driving into the sunset at a location about 20 miles away.

There's a director's trick for gauging a sunset with a hand: If you can put your fist between the sun and the horizon, it's roughly an hour until sunset. After that, it's fifteen minutes a finger. Jon could barely get three fingers between the sun and the horizon.

"Saddle up!!!", Jon commanded. We paid our checks and raced to the parking lot. I jumped behind the wheel of the pickup. Jimmy Baylor, the Assistant Director jumped into the passenger side. Our convoy, let by the camera truck roared out of the parking lot onto the highway. The pick-up looked like it had been through a couple of wars. But it was a lot faster that it looked. It had a well-tuned, big bore V-8 engine and a four-on-the-floor transmission.

Later, I found out that the last job the camera truck driver had done was shooting race car footage in front of racing legend, Mario Andretti. This guy could drive! And, at Jon's urging, he was leading us through those mountain roads at speeds over 80 miles per hour. And, I was hanging in right behind him with the pick-up.

I vaguely heard something banging around in the truck's bed, but keeping up with the camera truck required all my attention. I knew there were a few props back there, Oscar's trash can among them.

We reached the location with no time to spare. I screeched up next to the camera truck in a cloud of dust. That's when I discovered the production's still photographer had jumped into our truck bed as I pulled out of the restaurant's parking lot. It was he who had been banging around in the back of the truck along with Oscar's trash can and various and sundry other things. I can only imagine what it was like bouncing around in that truck bed while I careened through the mountains at 80 miles per hour.

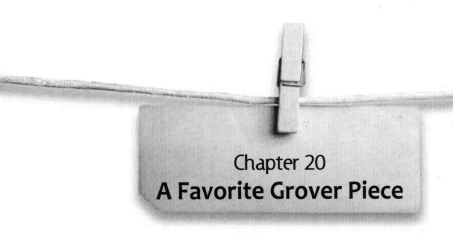

Chapter 20
A Favorite Grover Piece

Educational Goals: Full/Empty – Man Made Environment - Telephone

OPEN TO A MUPPET STREET SET.   ON THE STREET IS A TELEPHONE
BOOTH.

ENTER GROVER

                        GROVER

Oh, dear! I must make a telephone call. It is very important. I must find an
empty telephone booth. Hello! There is a telephone booth, and I think, yes,
there is no one in it. It is *empty*. Look at that! An *empty* telephone booth.

                    OFF CAMERA VOICES

What'd he say? An *empty* telephone booth? Hey! There's an *empty* telephone
booth!

A GAGGLE OF ABOUT 17,000 MONSTERS GALLOP INTO CAMERA AND JAM
INTO THE TELEPHONE PHONE BOOTH WITH GROVER. NOTE: THIS COULD BE
DONE WITH SPEEDED UP TAPE.

                        GROVER

Hey, fellows! What is going on here? What are you doing in my telephone booth?

                        MONSTERS

We're making a call.

                        GROVER

But nobody can make a telephone call, because the booth is *full*!

MONSTER

I thought something was wrong.

GROVER

Okay, everybody out! Out! Out! Out!

GAGGLE OF MONSTERS EXITS PHONE BOOTH IN SPEEDED UP MOTION. GROVER FLOPS OUT.

GROVER

Aaaaaaaaaaaaaaa! That is better. Now, I can make my telephone call, because the booth is *empty*.

OFF CAMERA VOICES

Hey! Did I hear there's an *empty* telephone booth! Etc.

GAGGLE OF 17,000 MONSTERS (IN FAST MOTION) ENTER CAMERA AND SQUASH GROVER INTO THE TELEPHONE BOOTH..

GROVER

Oooooooch! Now this telephone booth isn't *empty* any more! It is *full* of Monsters.

MONSTERS

Hey! That's my foot! Can't you move over a little! Etc.

GROVER

I told you, nobody can make a telephone call when the telephone booth is *full*! Everybody out!!!

MONSTERS EXIT GRUMBLING.

GROVER

Ah, now the telephone booth is . . .

SFX: TELEPHONE

GROVER ANSWERS

GROVER

Hello? . . . Who? . . . Don't think so. But, I'll ask. (CALLS SOFTLY) Anybody here named Monderporg?

MONSTERS RUSH IN AND FILL THE BOOTH, CRUSHING GROVER.

MONSTERS

Monderporg My name's Monderporg! It's probably Uncle Rufus Monderporg from Cleveland! Monderporg! I'm Clarence Monderporg! Etc.

MUSIC BUTTON

FADE OUT

Birthday card drawn by Big Bird puppeteer, Caroll Spinney, in the style of Chester Gould, the cartoonist who created Dick Tracy. In one page, Caroll kids me about my smoking (I've since quit), my motorcycles, my jaunts to the Carribean, and my insistence on using my middle initial, "A" in my TV credits.

Bob descending into Oscar's trash can.

Itchy the Prospector.

The author with his wife, Gail Frank Bailey.

Mad Man – 1960s

Muppet Man – 1970s

Richard Hunt and Frank Oz *perform Cookie Monster as he eats Hooper's Store.*

Chapter 21
Starting The Muppet Show

In March of 1977, when Al Gottesman finally returned from vacation, I solidified my deal to write *The Muppet Show*. I was to get so much per script plus appropriate Writers Guild residuals, so much *per diem* expenses; a certain number of trips home from England and first class travel.

The deal was made quickly and cordially to the satisfaction of the both of us. In fact, I have to say that doing business with the Muppet organization was always a pleasure. Al Gottesman is such a decent, straightforward guy that I never needed "people" to talk to Jim's "people." I could talk to Al myself.

Several weeks later, Jim and I flew to Los Angeles for a series of creative meetings. We stayed at the Beverly Wilshire Hotel, which was one of Jim's favorites, but not because of the rooms or cuisine, which were outstanding.

Jim traveled constantly. He had projects in New York, London, Toronto, and of course in Los Angeles. So, clean laundry was always a problem. The reason Jim was so fond of the Beverly Wilshire, he told me, was that you could get laundry and dry cleaning done in two hours.

Sure enough, when we arrived at the hotel, Jim pointed to two very large suitcases in the trunk, all of his luggage. He told the bellboy, "Take these directly to the laundry, please."

The creative meetings, along with Jim, Jerry Juhl and myself included Bernie Brillstein, Jim's manager, Larry Grossman, the music director and Don Hinkley, the third member of the writing staff. If you wonder what goes on in a "creative" meeting, the subject matter ranged from new Muppet characters to potential guest stars and possible musical numbers.

Of course, an awful lot of navel contemplation goes on at these things, too. But I remember during one of those sessions around the hotel pool, we created *Pigs-in-Space* and named the Spaceship: the *Swinetrek*. We also created First Mate Piggy's two ship mates: Commander Link Hogthrob; and Science Officer, Doctor Julius Strangepork.

After attending Kermit the Frog's 21st birthday party at Chasen's restaurant, I returned to New York where I spent the next few weeks preparing for an extended stay in London.

Chapter 22
The Queen Elizabeth II

May 8, 1977, the date of our sailing from New York was fast approaching. Jerry Juhl and his wife, Susan flew in from Cambria, California, which was then their permanent residence. Don Hinkley, his wife Karen and their two young sons, left their home in Santa Monica and wound up crowded into a tiny hotel suite along with piles of suitcases full of enough clothing to last the entire family for a year.

I called Don at the hotel to see how they were doing. Don told me that his son, Tommy, wasn't feeling well at all.

It turned out May 8th was Mother's Day. So, I went to New Jersey to spend it with my recently widowed mother. After dinner, my wife and I went to the pier.

Unfortunately, even in 1977, the lovely tradition of *Bon Voyage* parties had ended, a practice which is still sadly in place today. Because of the fear of terrorism, security was tight and only passengers were allowed to actually board ship. The only difference between then and now was the terrorists. In those days the fear was the Irish Republican Army instead of al Quaeda.

So, the Muppet contingent boarded the Queen Elizabeth II. Besides the Juhls and the Hinkleys were Jim and Jane Henson; Jim's manager, Bernie Brillstein and his wife, Debbie; puppeteers Jerry Nelson, Richard Hunt and Frank Oz, and me.

I checked into my cabin and then went on deck to watch the ship's departure. There, I ran into Don Hinkley. As the tugs pushed us away from the pier and out onto the Hudson River, I asked Don, "How's your son, Tommy, feeling?"

"Oh, he's coming along.", Don replied. Then, with an evil twinkle in his eye, he continued, "It's just a touch of cholera."

The QE-2 was a real throw back to the days when ocean liners were the only transportation across the Atlantic and the formalities that were observed then. Since we were traveling first class, it was black tie for dinner every evening. We had two tables in the dining room with our own waiters for each. Someone had even consulted Emily Post to make sure that every night we each had a different seating and, thus, different dining companions.

It was at the end of dinner one night when Jim and I independently came to a realization. The QE-2, being a British ship, has one of the most elaborate dessert menus on the planet. The English are real sugar junkies. They've actually gone to war over it once or twice. While trying to decide on dessert, a number of guys in our party started complaining about their diets and their weight while they lamented having to pass up all these amazing desserts.

Jim and I were the exact same body type. I'm 6'2" and at the time, I weighed 135 pounds. Jim was my height and not much heavier. I was regularly mistaken for him from behind. We also shared a metabolism which allowed us to eat whatever we wanted and not gain an ounce.

While the chubbies were groaning and drooling over the dessert menu, an evil grin crossed Jim's face, and he impishly asked me if I thought the raspberry torte had enough calories in it. I quickly realized that Jim's "Ernie" personality was surfacing and replied I thought so, but then went on to suggest the almondine strudel might be more fattening.

In an instant, Jim and I realized this was the Skinny Kids revenge against all the muscle guys who were the athletes in high school and took all the girls. Now all the jocks were at the age where weight was becoming a problem. Revenge really was going to be sweet.

So, Jim and I proceeded to devilishly discuss the merits and caloric value of every item in the dessert menu, as the ex-athletes and other dieters suffered. Finally, we both decided on separate sugar laden, whipped cream and candied fruit extravaganza.

After we ordered, and the subject of conversation had just changed to the relief of the others, Jim said loudly to me, "And, we can have some deep dish apple pie with double Devon cream sent down to our cabins later." Richard Hunt quipped, "You know, you need a prescription to get that in the States."

On another evening, our two waiters invited us to go bar hopping with them in the crew's quarters. I declined and have regretted it ever since.

Richard Hunt accepted the invitation and reported back of a parallel universe of neon and linoleum instead of paneling and carpet. There were six crew bars (called "pigs") on the QE-2. By tradition, crew members do not wash glasses for each other. So, bar hoppers carry their own glasses as they travel from one pig to another.

Sailing the Atlantic on the Elizabeth was a wonderful experience and something I never would have done by myself. It was one of those lovely things that seemed to happen whenever I was associated with the Muppets.

But the writing staff was also expected to turn in a script when we reached South Hampton at the end of the week. So, although our evenings were spent in Cary Grant splendor, our days and nights were spent in cramped cabins trying to write comedy on a pitching ocean liner.

Late on one of those nights I was struggling mightily with a sketch that just wasn't coming together. Frustration is an occupational hazard of comedy writing. But this particular night, the late hour and the boat's pitching were really getting to me.

In desperation, I pushed the steward button on my night table. (First Class QE-2 cabins had 24 hour steward and maid service.) Moments later, the steward arrived at my door. As far as I can remember, I snarled something absolutely incomprehensible at him.

"Not to worry, Mr. Bailey.", he replied soothingly. "How about a bacon, lettuce and tomato sandwich, a few bottles of cold Heineken and a hot pot of coffee?"

I immediately realized that was exactly what I wanted.

My snack arrived almost immediately. The sandwich was perfect. The beer was presented in a champagne bucket full of ice and the coffee was fresh brewed. *This* was real service. Forget about mints on the pillow and extra shampoo. Real service is anticipating what the patron wants before he knows it himself. Alas, this kind of service is all too rare these days.

Of course, the Queen Elizabeth was ideal for the kind of benign mischief that hovered around the Muppets wherever they went.

One night, puppeteer Frank Oz invited me to have a drink with him after dinner. Frank had scoped out the bar at the highest point of the ship that had a dance floor. The day had been a bit rough. And since a ship pivots at the water line, the higher up you go, the more pronounced the ship's rocking becomes.

Frank and I got ourselves securely seated on a couple of bar stools, which were bolted to the deck, and spent a pleasant evening watching the other patrons, after a few drinks, trying to dance as the ship continued to pitch and roll precariously. To make the evening even more entertaining, we surreptitiously requested the orchestra to play tangos, rumbas, cha chas, with the occasional hula or Mexican Hat dance thrown in for good measure.

Another evening, during a cocktail party in the cabin of Richard Hunt, he announced that he had made a startling discovery. The main hallway on our cabin deck ran the length of the ship from bow to stern. It was periodically intersected by smaller halls that ran across the ship from port to starboard.

I can tell you from experience, when you're walking these halls, out of sight of the horizon, it's easy to become confused about which direction the ship is actually traveling as it plows through the Atlantic at approximately 25 mph.

Richard ushered us to a corner of one of the cross halls where we would be unseen from the main corridor but still be able to see it. He went to the opposite corner to wait for an appropriate prey. Along came three elegantly dressed couples, togged out in tuxedos, evening gowns and high heels, walking unsurely up the main hallway.

When they were about 30 feet from our cross hall, Richard nonchalantly walked across their line of vision, *backward*. This caused them to lose the last tenuous hold on which direction was forward, back, or side to side. The six of them collapsed against each other like rag dolls. It was as though someone had removed their skeletons. So, this became our nightly pre-dinner entertainment for the remainder of the voyage.

The QE-2's first stop out of New York was Cherbourg, France. After docking for a few hours, she set out across the Channel for South Hampton. For safety reasons, all north/south traffic on the English Channel is usually stopped when the Elizabeth crosses.

It was after sunset and we were having dinner as we made the crossing. Suddenly, out of the dark appeared another ocean liner headed in the opposite direction. It seemed like every window and porthole was lit, and her rigging was outlined in lights as well. She came and went quickly from view. It was one of the most spectacular sights I have ever seen – literally, ships that pass in the night.

We arrived in South Hampton the morning of Saturday, May 14, 1977. And South Hampton was in the middle of a dock strike.

In the 1940s and 50s, before trans-Atlantic air service became common, American celebrities sailed to Europe on the great liners. Their arrival at South Hampton was always a big deal and a staple of Pathe News, which ran in movie theaters. Not infrequently, the port would suffer longshoremen strikes, providing news film of celebrities pushing their own mounds of luggage off the dock by themselves. I have a vivid, romantic memory of Marilyn Monroe, in a sweater, hobble skirt and mules, pushing a dolly piled high with her matching luggage as the striking British dock workers looked on stoically.

Well, in 1977, England was in strike mode again. We arrived in the middle of the classic South Hampton longshoremen strike. The pier looked the same as when Marilyn swivelled down it 25 years before. I'd swear the same dock wallopers with the same tweed hats and dangling cigarette butts hadn't moved in a quarter of a century, either.

The union rule was that only passengers were allowed to carry anything off the dock. Most grumbled as they lugged their baggage down the pier. But we, Muppets, in addition to our personal luggage, also had five tons of Muppet materials, puppets, props, wardrobe, etc., in the hold of the ship.

Now only we could unload it from the dock. The same hand trucks and dollies that were available to Marilyn in 1953 were now made available to us. All of our guys grabbed dollies and hand trucks to move this five ton pile of boxes off the dock. Jim and I took a two-man dolly.

To handle our five tons of Muppet freight, A.T.V. Studios had sent a lorry with a crew. What made it so surreal was that the studio had also sent a fleet of those wonderful Daimler Princess limousines to take us to London. The cars were piloted by very professional chauffeurs dressed in grey, brass buttoned uniforms with white gloves. But all these guys were restricted to the *outside* of Customs and Immigration.

So out on the dock, Jim and I would heft a load of boxes onto the dolly and then push it slowly through Immigration and Customs. Like most reprobates, I've had a few jobs that involved moving freight, so I fell into my freight-moving pattern. But as soon as we got the load through the door, a brigade of these very British, very solicitous chauffeurs would rush to us saying, "Oh, Guv'nor, allow me to take that."

They would take immediate control of our carts, push them over to the van, briskly unload them and return them to us with a tip of the hat. It was a bizarre introduction to England to start off transforming from a stevedore with a hand truck into a chauffeured "Guv'nor" and back again within a few hundred feet.

Chapter 23
London 1977

We arrived in London at midday and checked into the Sloane Square Hotel. 1977, it turned out, was the Silver Anniversary of the coronation of Her Majesty, Elizabeth II. All of England was in the midst of a year long celebration, which meant that hotel rooms were at a premium.

We were told that our rooms at the Sloane were reserved for 12 days and that was it. We could not extend our reservations. We had exactly 12 days to find an apartment and move into it. (During our stay we heard what sounded like muffled gun shots and were told that some Arab guests had taken umbrage to the 12-day reservation rule.)

Most of our crew had worked in London the season before and had made living arrangements for this season at the end of last season. But the Hinkleys and I were first timers. So, when we weren't writing the TV show 10 hours a day, we were frantically chasing around London with real estate agents looking for places to live. I was just looking for a flat. But the Hinkleys, with two kids, needed a house!

Of course, the premium on hotel rooms also extended to flats. It seemed like everyone in London with a flat was renting it out for outrageous amounts of money. And by mid-May, most of them were gone. To make it more difficult, I knew nothing of the geography of London. I had only been there once before on vacation in 1969. I had no idea of good and bad neighborhoods or where anything was located.

London is also a very confusing city. Even life-long Londoners keep an A to Z(ed), the city's street atlas, on their dashboards. London streets change names every few blocks. In certain areas street names are repeated. You can have a Lenox Street, Lenox Road, Lenox Gardens, Lenox Muse and Lenox Close (whatever a *close* is), all in one small area. Added to that, there isn't a straight street in the whole town except Brompton Road, which is the old Roman Road north to Sheffield.

Don Hinkley, said it was the most confusing city he had ever inhabited. He claimed it was the only city in the world where you couldn't walk around the block. "I tried it last week.", he told me. "And, I wound up in Scotland."

So for several days, I flew around town with a series of estate agents looking at flats. One was a South African woman, with whom I got into a conversation about how reserved the Brits are. "Yes.", she told me. "But as soon as there is a little bit of sunshine, they'll strip down to their knickers and lie in it."

Sure enough, one day in Green Park, the overcast parted and brilliant sunlight appeared. Instantly men and women stripped down to their underwear and lay down to bask in it until the overcast returned about ten minutes later.

My expense allowance was $500 a week. When I first heard that in New York it sounded like a fortune. This was 1977. I thought, "Gee, I know it rains a lot in London, but I always wanted a penthouse." And, "Maybe there would be enough left over to rent a Jaguar." For a while I even entertained the idea of hiring a real English butler.

But as my 12-day hotel reservation dwindled and I was forced to shoehorn my flat searches around long work days, reality set in. I was being shown dark, dank, cellar studios where you wouldn't commit suicide - you'd be too embarrassed to have the body discovered there. These places were renting for $800 a month and up. If the original tenants were paying more that $100 a month, they were being robbed blind. I finally settled on a flat in a 1950s hi-rise building opposite Regents Park. The rent was $1,300 a month.

It had light and a view of the Park, which was quite lovely. But it was still the strangest place I've ever lived. The building was a giant semi-circle to insure every flat had a view of the Park, rather like a seaside resort hotel. Glassed in walkways radiated like spokes from the street to each of the building's five entrances. So, coming home always felt a little bit like flying to Cleveland.

The flat had started out as a one bedroom, with a living room and kitchen. However, they had turned the kitchen into a second bedroom, which featured a kitchen sink as part of its decor. A galley kitchen had been hacked out of the entry hall.

Its most distinctive feature was its attempt to create a sunken living room. Someone had installed a ten-inch high box in the middle of the living room doorway. So, to enter the living room, you had to step up and then step down.

A photographer friend of mine camped out with me for a few months and he must have fallen over it at least once a day, usually while carrying cases of very expensive photographic equipment.

Moving to London was real culture shock. To begin with, I had spent the past four years hibernating in my New York apartment, churning out *Sesame Street* scripts. Since my wife was constantly on the road shooting documentaries, I pretty much lived on Chinese, deli and pizza, all delivered. So, even getting outside into New York City was a rare occasion. Now I was not only in a different city but a different country as well.

The first thing I discovered was how wrong Winston Churchill was when he described the U.S. and England as, "Two great countries separated by a common language."

There's nothing common about our languages! It was a full two weeks before I understood everything that was said to me. And, when my wife came through town, I actually had to translate for her.

For a while, I suffered from a paranoid delusion that the English put on that accent just to put on us Yanks. I had this fantasy that when we Yanks weren't around, the Brits talk just like people in Chicago or Canarsie. But, thanks to my time in London, I can now understand anyone from anywhere in the English-speaking world . . . except the Scots.

Then, of course, there was the London weather. They say in London you can experience all four seasons of the year in one day. What they don't tell you is that 23½ hours of that day are winter. Evenings in June, I would come home to my $1,300.00 a month flat and turn on the gas stove to warm the place up, just the way I did when I was broke and living in a $75.00 a month studio on Beacon Hill.

Richard Hunt used to make the point of how rare sunlight is in England by asking a group of five or six Brits which way was North. Inevitably, they all would point in different directions.

The BBC-TV daily weather reports were all depressingly the same: *overcast with occasional bright spots* – the bright spots being those brief moments when the clouds parted, the sunlight appeared, and the above-mentioned Londoners stripped down to their skivies in a vain attempt to get tan.

Additionally, the weather reports gave the temperatures in Celsius, a perfectly logical measurement system which, like the metric system, made no sense at all to me. In order to translate Celsius into good ol' American Fahrenheit, I had to get out the calculator, feed the Celsius temperature into it, multiply by nine, divide by three, and add 32.

Once I figured out what the real temperature would be, I still wasn't out of the woods. The usual BBC weather graphic was an outline of England with the day's high temperatures on the appropriate places on the map. However, the map lacked any other geographical information, *including cities*. So, since I had no idea where London was located in the country of England, I still had no idea what the temperature would be that day. Eventually, I just gave up and assumed it would be overcast with occasional bright spots.

I also wasn't prepared for London humidity. Since it was May when we left, I only packed two sweaters. But, I needed a sweater every day in London. At the end of the first week, I rinsed the first sweater out and laid it on a towel to dry. The second week I wore the second sweater every day. At the end of the second week, I rinsed out the second sweater. That's when I discovered I now had two wet sweaters. On the third week, I broke down and bought a half dozen sweaters, an electric heater the size of a two-car garage, and a sheepskin jacket that we still refer to as my English summer coat.

The English, of course, are impervious to weather – stiff upper lip and all that. Many homes do not have central heating. The Brits prefer to lug an electric heater from room to room all winter long.

Even heat doesn't bother them. I've met Brits on vacation in the Caribbean who didn't think they got their money's worth unless they went home with a second degree sun burn.

Jerry Juhl told me that in 1976 London suffered from a very rare heat wave. Jerry was having lunch with some people in a restaurant, and since air-conditioning was practically unknown in England, the temperature in the restaurant was in the high 90s (Fahrenheit). Jerry asked the maitre'd if they could take off their suit jackets. "That just isn't done here.", was the reply.

A few minute later, there was a cacophonous crash as a waiter, carrying a large tray of food, passed out from heat prostration. Jerry then asked again if they could remove their jackets. An exasperated maitre'd reluctantly agreed.

In England, 1977 was also the Year Of The Strike. And the unions seemed to be trying to outdo each other. Mornings in London, I would turn on the radio, much the way you would in the States to get baseball scores. But in London, I did it to see who was on strike today. Some days there would be no milk, some days no newspapers. Auto workers were striking because they didn't have clean coveralls.

The electrical workers made their unhappiness known by indiscriminately cutting the power to large sections of the country. They only did this at night because cutting power in the day time could shut down factories and put fellow union members out of work. So, it was not unusual, while driving home after work, to suddenly have the street lamps, traffic signals and all the surrounding buildings go dark.

To show you how popular *The Muppet Show* was in England, the electrical union put out a news release stating that they would not cut the power anywhere while *The Muppet Show* was being broadcast. They genuinely feared the public's reaction. The show ran on Tuesday nights in England. And when the credits started to roll, I would look out my windows and watch 60 or 70 blocks of London instantly go black.

To make matters more interesting, at the same time the electrical union was haphazardly cutting the power around the country, and people were lighting candles against the dark, the national Fire Department also went on strike. So, the National Guard took over.

Since virtually all of England belonged to one union or another, no one would cross a picket line to get to the fire engines. The only fire fighting equipment available to the Guard, without upsetting the unions, was a fleet of military trucks that had been built in the 1950s to respond to a nuclear attack. They had been mothballed ever since. They were dubbed, "Green Monsters," and evidently were very difficult to handle since they regularly rolled over on their way to fires, causing more mayhem. The Brits took it all in stride. Nothing seems to cheer up the English like adversity.

Looking back, despite, or maybe because of all the madness, I enjoyed my time in London. No doubt about it, the English are a great people. But Londoners are as crazy as New Yorkers. They just have better diction.

Chapter 24
Moon over the A12

The Muppet Show was taped at Lord Lew Grade's A.T.V. Studios in the town of Elstree, about a 45 minute drive north of London. We got there each day by car service, not the Daimler limos we rode up from South Hampton in, just regular English sedans. The cars would pick several of us up in front of our residences. Routes had been worked out since the Muppet crew was spread out all over London. My car picked up Jerry Juhl, the Head Writer, first, then me, and then puppeteer Jerry Nelson.

The car service came about through rather strange circumstances. When the show first went into production the year before, one minibus was used to pick up the entire Muppet cast and crew. That meant that the people who lived in south London, around Battersea, had to get on the bus at about 8:00 a.m., and spend close to two hours on the bus as it meandered through the city picking up the others on its way north. And, they faced the same two-hour commute to get home at night.

One day, as the bus approached Elstree, Richard Hunt, spotted Lew Grade's Rolls Royce limousine up ahead in the heavy traffic on Highway A12. Richard asked the driver to maneuver into the lane next to the Rolls, and pass it.

The bus passed the limousine with a blare of its horns and a hearty, "Hey, Lew!!!", shouted in unison by the passengers. The view from the back seat of the Rolls must have been fantastic, because every window on the left side of the bus flew open and a bare bottom instantly appeared in every one of them. Lew Grade was being magnificently mooned at 9:30 in the morning on the A12.

When the bus arrived at the studio, word came down that Lew Grade wanted to talk to Richard Hunt. There was no question that the irrepressible Richard was the instigator of the revolution.

"That's great!", Richard responded. "It just so happens I want to talk to Lew."

Evidently, now that Richard had Lew Grade's attention, he complained about the minibus and Sir Lew ordered the car service. You can't ever say that Lord Lew Grade wasn't a good sport. In fact, it was well known that the Dr. Bunsen Honeydew puppet of *Muppet* Labs is a caricature of Lew Grade.

Chapter 25
Jerry Juhl

can't write much further about *The Muppet Show* without mentioning Jerry Juhl, the show's head writer and my immediate boss. Jerry started as a puppeteer with Jim in the very early days of the Muppets in Washington, D.C. But, due to what Jerry described as "terminal stage fright", he soon segued into being Jim's writing alter ego, functioning basically as Jim's second creative brain. Jerry wrote the early Muppet television specials, Muppet material for guest spots on other shows, *Sesame Street* Muppet pieces, and several of the Muppet films.

Jerry remembered the early days of the Muppets, when he had trouble finding a cheap apartment in Washington, D.C. because Jim insisted Jerry go house hunting in Jim's second-hand Rolls Royce.

He also remembered how Jim, in the early, pre-security 60s, rarely bothered with airline reservations. Instead, he would go to the airport, find a flight he liked, and then offer a service man on that flight the price of the ticket and $50.00 to give Jim his seat and take the next flight.

One of Jerry's favorite *Muppet Show* stories was his experience writing for N.A.S.A. The space agency has a tradition of waking up astronauts in space every morning with a radio transmission of special music, e.g., *Up, Up and Away!*, or personal announcements about things like astronauts' birthdays or wedding anniversaries.

Because *The Muppet Show* was so popular in 1981, N.A.S.A. asked the Muppets if they would produce a couple of special Pigs In Space radio segments to use as wake up calls during the November mission of the Space Shuttle Columbia. Of course, the Muppets agreed and Jerry was asked to write the skits.

The first thing Jerry asked for was an interview/bull session with some of the inside N.A.S.A. people who knew the Columbia crew well. The bits had to be laced with inside dope like who forgot to put the wheels down on the simulator or who sat on a peanut butter sandwich. All of this had to be in secret to protect the surprise. So, Jerry started making plans to go to Houston and have an off-campus meeting with some N.A.S.A. personnel.

"Not to worry.", N.A.S.A. tells Jerry. A few of the astronauts will fly up from Houston and visit Jerry in his home in Cambria on the northern California coast. And they did – each in his own F-16 fighter jet!

This actually made some sense. All of these astronauts were fighter pilots. And, as such, they had to log so many hours a month flying fighters. So, they may as well fly from Houston to Cambria.

Jerry was still impressed, until the interview was over. Jerry had just gotten a new computer. While demonstrating it to the astronauts, he opened up his new flight simulator.

Incredulously, Jerry told me, *Not one of them could land the flight simulator without crashing!*

So, after an afternoon of crashing Piper Cherokees, the astronauts climbed back into their F-16s and flew back to Houston. *The Pigs In Space* pieces were a great success. But Jerry always seemed a little nervous during shuttle landings.

I can tell you from personal experience that being a head writer is a very tough job. Don Hinkley was offered the position on several shows and he always refused. He told me that no matter how much they paid you, it wasn't worth it.

The head writer is responsible for every word in the script. And, if the rest of the writing staff dies of simultaneous heart attacks, he has to write the whole script himself. The head writer sets the tone, balance, and direction of the show. He's the sounding board for ideas. He assigns segments to writers. It's also his job to ask for re-writes or outright reject material, not an easy job when you're dealing with writers' egos. Jerry handled it all with great grace and humor.

It was Jerry who first taught me the cardinal rule of writing for the Muppets: After you finish writing a piece, read it over. *If it can be performed with human beings, it's not Muppet material.*

There was another Muppet writing rule that constantly gave me problems: *A joke that's too bad to be used once may be bad enough to use three times.* This was most evident in the *At The Dance* and *Veterinarian's Hospital* segments of the show. Even though these segments were very funny when produced, I didn't feel I was earning my salary by just turning in corny old jokes. So, I'd write new ones, which wasn't really following the structure of the show.

So, Jerry had a double quandary with me: Most of the time when I had to re-write my material, it was to make it sharper and funnier. But, very rarely, I had to do re-writes because, as Jerry explained, my material was too funny.

Jerry had another quality which made him a great head writer -- the courage to defend his staff's material, a quality all too rare in television.

As I said, before I wrote my audition material for *The Muppet Show*, I recorded several episodes so I could analyze it. I determined that the premise of the Swedish Chef was that whatever he was cooking, the food always fought back -- and won.

So I came up with the idea of the Chef making lobster thermidor. Of course, there was a Muppet lobster who refused to get into the pot. After an epic battle, the Chef finally managed to subdue the lobster and get him into the pot.

As soon as that happened, we heard, off-camera, the blare of a mariachi trumpet and the thunder of horses' hooves. Suddenly, three Muppet lobsters, dressed as Mexican bandits with sombreros and bandoliers, burst into the Chef's kitchen with guns blazing, rescued the lobster in the pot, and rode off.

Jerry liked the piece and put it into a script. But Jim rejected it. (Since Jim had seen the piece in my audition material, I guess he hired me in spite of it.) Normally, that would be the end of the piece. But Jerry still liked it and inserted it in the following week's script. Again, Jim bounced it. This continued for several weeks and became a good natured inside joke between Jim and the writing staff.

Finally, Jim's beautiful teenaged daughter, Cheryl, who was visiting her father in London, sat in on a script run through. Cheryl liked the piece and told Jim that she thought she could design and make some great lobster puppets for the piece. Jim relented and Cheryl built the puppets. One of them even wore the handlebar moustache I was sporting at the time.

When the piece went in front of the cameras, it played like Gangbusters! The lobster puppeteers, immediately became Muppet versions of the Mexican bandits in The Treasure of the Sierra Madres, ad libbing (as I knew they would): *We don't need no stinkin' badges! We're Federales. Jou know, mounted police.*

Jim loved it. And, I'm proud to say that the Lobster/Swedish Chef piece is now a part of the permanent Muppet display in the Smithsonian Museum.

(Just to give you a little writer's insight, I had an alternate version of the lobster sketch that I think would have worked equally well. In it the Chef is making lamb stew and forces a cute little fuzzy-wuzzy lamb into the pot. Then three lambs dressed as gangsters with fedora hats and Brooklyn accents burst in and execute the rescue.)

In fact, Jim liked the lobster sketch so much, he said to Jerry, "Let's take another look at your chicken-gunfight-in-the-western-saloon bit". The chicken-gunfight-in-the-western-saloon bit was something I dreamed up after a conversation with Jerry and Don about how many countries were broadcasting The Muppet Show. We were syndicated in 104 countries, with the local language dubbed over in most cases. So, I'd occasionally write a punch line and say to myself, "I wonder what that sounds like dubbed in German or Tibetan."

I began to look for ideas that didn't require dialogue. That way, the laughs would all be visual, and visual comedy transcends language. After some thought, I came up with the idea of doing cliche' movie scenes that the whole world has seen a million times. But, I wanted to do them with animal puppets, making their particular sounds, instead of dialogue, so the scenes wouldn't have to be dubbed. I know, that sounds strange. But, here's how it worked:

I decided to do an old fashioned western saloon gunfight. But, all the participants would be Muppet chickens and all the dialogue would be clucking in the appropriate attitude.

The sketch opened in a Muppet western saloon set. The bar is packed with chickens. A rinky-dink piano is playing. Several chicken couples are dancing. Gonzo is behind the bar.

There's a sting of music. The swinging doors fly open and in walks the toughest looking black rooster wearing a black hat and two six guns. He strides over to the bar to a chicken looking fetching in a mantilla. He clucks coarsely and suggestively in her ear.

She screams and slaps his face. Enter the good guy rooster with his white hat. He comes to the lady chicken's defense. He and the gunman start to circle each other, clucking ominously.

This was some of the best puppeteering I've even seen. Jerry Nelson as the Good Guy and Frank Oz as Black Bart milked every bit of melodrama they could from the scene. Pure and simple, it was just great comedic acting.

Finally, Black Bart pulls a six gun and fires. But the Good Guy holds up a frying pan and the shot ricochets off it. The bullet continues to ricochet around the barroom, breaking china and bottles on its way. Eventually, it hits the chain on the chandelier, causing the chandelier to fall on Black Bart, knocking him out. The final shot is Good Guy and Mantilla Chicken riding off into the sunset – on a cow, Jim's contribution.

After his wonderful wife, Susan, Jerry loved travel, penguins, exotic cars (he once owned a V-8 Morgan with an oak wood frame) and puns – the more groan inspiring, the better. One of his favorites involved a tourist in Mercy, England being recommended the local specialty, koala bear tea. When he complains about the lumps in it, he is told: *The koala tea of Mercy is not strained!"*

My favorite Jerry Juhl pun story also involves Jon Stone. Sometime in the 1980s, Jon and I were working a script together. This was just about the time fax machines became standard equipment. Jon and I were both working at our New York homes, and faxing the material between us.

One afternoon, Jon and I got a little goofy and started faxing puns back and forth in a kind of, "Can you top this?", contest. (Hey, we're comedy writers. We're allowed. Besides, Jon was the Executive Producer.) Jon was also a great connoisseur of the *punus terriblus*. So, in desperation, I faxed Jerry at his home in California:

Help!!! I'm in a punning contest with Jon Stone! Send me your worst!

Almost immediately, my fax machine spewed out Jerry's reply:

Sorry. We're all out of sausage!

Coincidentally, when Jerry and Susan Juhl came to New York with the Muppets in the early 1960s, they moved into the same apartment building where I now live. They did so because Don Sahlin, one of the earliest and most talented Muppet designers and builders already lived here. Not coincidentally, the first New York Muppet studio was located only three blocks away. By the time I moved in, the Juhls had already moved to California. But Don still lived here.

Jerry and Don were great friends. Don lived two storeys above the Juhls in the same apartment line. Occasionally, Don would create some strange or scary creature in the Muppet studio and bring it home. At night, he would lower it out the window and sit it on the Juhls' air conditioner to greet Jerry and Susan when they got up the next morning. There was a lot of speculation about what the people who inhabited the apartment in between them thought as those strange creations descended past their living room window.

Don Sahlin also had a strange appreciation of Jean-Philippe Rameau, an obscure 18th Century Baroque composer. He dreamed of composing an opera around Rameau's music. In order to promote Rameau's popularity, which was pretty much non-existent, Don and Jerry inscribed, *Viva Rameau!*, in various locations around the world in the same spirit as the people who have been inscribing, *Bird Lives!*, since the great saxophonist, Charlie Parker, died in 1955, and *Kilroy was here* since World War II. Jerry told me that he had inscribed it in Antarctica and on the Berlin Wall.

Both Jerry and Don are gone now. Per Susan's request, some of Jerry's ashes are interred in my living room over my fireplace. So, I hope some of Jerry's spirit graces my home. The rest of Jerry's ashes are located in the various other places around the world that he loved.

Don Sahlin has become a permanent part of Muppet lore. In Muppet theology, when a Muppet member crosses to the other side, he or she is met by Don Sahlin, who presents them with a rubber chicken.

Here's a small sample of Jerry Juhl's humor. It's a disclaimer Jerry wrote for a Muppet holiday card.

THE FOLLOWING INFORMATION MUST
BE READ BEFORE THIS CARD IS OPENED!

The Muppets©"**TM**" are trademarked and copyrighted properties belonging to The Muppet Studio LLC (TMSLLC). The project herein described is independent of TMSLLC, The Sesame Workshop, and/or The Jim Henson Companies ("Organizations"). The pig-like, bear-like and other anthropomorphic images on the inside of this card exist as an attention-getting device only and in no way implies an endorsement by the Organizations.

Furthermore, the Organizations are free of responsibility for any injury resulting from the misuse of this card, including, but not limited to paper cuts. Setting fire to this card may result in serious injury to the fingers. The card is meant for external use only, and should not be masticated and ingested, brewed into a tea for drinking, or distilled or fermented into an alcoholic beverage. Do not inject intravenously. May cause nausea, headaches, liver damage, skin rashes, pancreatic failure, anal bleeding, dandruff, dry mouth, seizures, and premature explosion. Dispose of this card in a responsible manner. Just read the damn thing first and don't make trouble for us with the corporate lawyers, okay? Bless you.

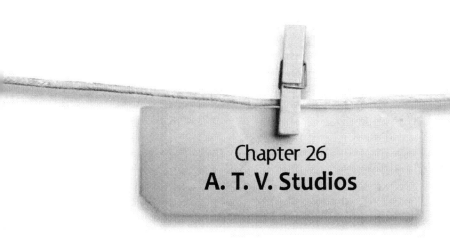

Chapter 26
A. T. V. Studios

Ironically, working at A.T.V. Studios in England was the closest I ever came to working in a real, Hollywood style studio. Television production in New York is mostly a piecemeal affair. Studios are rented for the duration of a production and then rented to someone else. Scenery is built in shops miles from the studio. Props, costumes and much of the equipment all come from different places.

A real old-time Hollywood studio was a movie factory that ran 12 months of the year. Carpentry shops, electricians, wardrobe departments, prop storage, beauticians, designers, writers, actors, directors, producers, as well as the sound stages were all located on studio property. The people all worked regularly for the same company.

A.T.V., located in Boreham Wood, was a real old-fashioned studio with four sound stages. A sound stage, by the way, is a large building dedicated to film or studio production. To do so, it must meet several criteria. Firstly, the roof must be completely supported by the walls. Interior support beams could interrupt or negate a tracking shot. They're basically the same design as an airplane hanger, which has similar requirements.

Secondly, they have to be tall enough to accommodate the massive overhead lighting, which requires a certain distance from the subject to even out. And thirdly, it has to be sound proof so that external noise does not end up on the sound track.

Finally, for television, each sound stage or studio must have its own control room, where the director, his assistant, the sound man and technical people sit and actually put the show together.

Since the 1950s, television has worked on a three-camera system. Each camera has a monitor in the control room. A fourth monitor continuously shows what is actually being broadcast or recorded.

The way it works is while camera number one is shooting the action, camera number two is positioned for the next shot. And camera number three is moving into position for the shot after that. As soon as the feed cuts from camera one to camera two, camera one moves into position for the next shot after camera three's. The cameras keep rotating like this as the scene unfolds.

How each shot is composed and when to cut from camera to camera is decided by the director in his pre-production preparation. The sequence is then practiced during the camera rehearsal. The director is also responsible for the theatrical performance by the cast. As you might imagine, the more complicated the scene, the more rehearsal and studio time is required.

A.T.V. also had a wardrobe department, a prop (short for properties) department, an in-house orchestra, a carpentry shop for building scenery, dressing rooms, offices for production staffs, a commissary and even a pub. The buildings that housed all of them were deliberately different periods and styles so they could be used for various exteriors. The building we worked in became a hotel, an office building or a hospital emergency entrance, depending on how it was dressed.

Out in the back lot, there was an entire Elizabethan village for Shakespearian productions. I used to wander through its Globe Theater looking for inspiration.

Don Hinkley and I shared a cheerless office furnished with a couple of battered desks and typewriters from the 1950s. Jerry Juhl had an equally attractive office next door connected to ours with an adjoining door. Nobody wastes money on writers.

We also had a rather unique phone system. Four lines came into our office. The phones were heavy, black Bakelite instruments that dated back to the 1940s. Since multi-line phones didn't exist in 1948, we had a phone for each line. None of them had a long enough cord to reach a desk. So the four of them sat on the floor, lined up against the wall.

Answering a phone call was a comedy routine. Since the phones had no lights, whenever the phone rang, Don or I went over to them, bent over and kept answering one after another until we got to the right one. Regardless of whether we started at the left or the right of the line, Murphy's Law kicked in. Inevitably, the call was always on the fourth phone to be answered, assuming the caller hadn't hung up.

The office of David Lazer, *The Muppet Show*'s Executive Producer, was located right next door to Don's and my office. The walls were so thin, we could hear every word Dave said on the phone. We could even tell if he was speaking to an American or a Brit, depending on how he spelled his last name: L-A-ZEE-E-R for the Yanks and L-A-ZED-E-R for the Brits.

But the real problem was that much of the business Dave did over the phone was delicate and confidential. We reminded Dave constantly. But he would forget when his mind was on business.

So, Don and I put up a sign on our common wall:

HEAR!

BIG TIME SHOW BUSINESS DEALS

ON TRANSCONTINENTAL TELEPHONE CALLS!

YOUR SALARY AND RAISES DISCUSSED!

WHAT THE BOSS REALLY THINKS OF YOU AND YOUR WORK!

WHO IS CANODDLING WITH WHOM!

PLACE 50 PENCE IN THE DISH

AND PLACE GLASS HERE

At the bottom of the ad was an appropriately sized circle.

On a small table, right under the sign, Don and I installed a small table with a glass and a saucer with some change in it. We made sure Dave saw the sign. So, whenever the volume of Dave's phone calls went up, we would drop some change in the dish and he would get the hint.

And now, an anecdote that will simultaneously amuse every soccer/football fan out there and prove once again that there is nothing funnier than the truth.

One of the more civilized aspects of working at A.T.V. Studios was that A.T.V. had its own pub on premises. So, every night when we quit work at eight p.m., most of the Muppet gang retired to the studio pub for a pint while we waited for the car service to take us home.

But, we Americans had no idea that the whole world, except us was gearing up for an event second only in import to the signing of the Magna Carta, or, perhaps, the Resurrection -- the 1978 World Cup.

But in 1977, we Americans knew virtually nothing about soccer, a game so popular in the rest of the world that wars have broken out over it. There were no cable sports channels. American kids hardly played it. Europeans in the US had to wait days for foreign newspapers to get their soccer scores. I was 27 before I ever saw a soccer ball.

As it got later in the season, it seemed like every week there was *THE MOST IMPORTANT FOOTBALL GAME IN THE WORLD* on the pub's TV, only to be followed a few days later by an *EVEN MORE MOST IMPORTANT FOOTBALL GAME IN THE WORLD.*

During every game, the Brits in the pub went absolutely nuts, cheering and whistling or groaning and booing at the top of their lungs. Meanwhile, we Yanks stood in muted confusion while the cacophony raged around us.

Finally came one of the last and most very, very important games of the season. The pub was jammed with clamorous English soccer fans. I had gotten there early enough to get a space at the bar. But the rest of our gang came later and were forced to stand in the back.

After a particularly noisy explosion from the Brits, a cartoon Muppet voice with a very heavy American accent, boomed from the back of the bar: *Why don't ya pick it up and run with it, ya dumb S.O.B.!!!*

Immediately, the Brits collapsed with laughter, because they realized that every American's reaction to soccer had just been verbalized. I've told that story to every soccer fan I've met. And, it never fails to get a big laugh, because the funniest thing is always the truth.

Chapter 27
Writing The Muppet Show

Firstly, the basics: We worked a five-day week, which sometimes stretched into six if production got behind. Our work week ran from Sunday to Thursday. That's because it was designed for the convenience of the guest stars. Since most of our guest stars came from Los Angeles and New York, this schedule allowed them to fly to London on Saturday, work Sunday through Tuesday and return home on Wednesday.

This schedule had unforeseen consequences in that our guest stars suffered from chronic jet lag. There must be hours and hours of out-takes of very famous people stopping in mid-scene, looking directly into the camera and saying, "I have no idea of what the hell comes next."

Our work day ran from 10:00 a.m. until 8:00 p.m. Those were the hours agreed upon by the studio unions -- cameramen, carpenters, grips (stage hands), electricians, etc. As long as they were shooting in the studio, we writers had to be available for any necessary changes. A writer's job isn't really finished until his piece is "in the can," or finished in the studio.

Sunday morning started with a full staff meeting, where the staff was introduced to the guest star and the script was read through with all departments making notes and suggestions. After the meeting, we writers went to our offices to make changes if necessary. If there were no changes (a very rare occurrence), we would start on the script to be produced three weeks hence. The rest of the staff also goes back to work. The cast does some rehearsing with the guest star, who is also available for wardrobe fittings.

Monday was music record day for both the guest star and the Muppet cast. All the singing on *The Muppet Show* was pre-recorded for a very good reason. It's difficult enough to sing, on key, in a character voice one time. But in television, with its many retakes, the puppeteers could be singing in those voices all day long. And if a puppeteer lost his or her voice, it could cause enormous production difficulties working around the missing characters.

Tuesdays in the studio were dedicated completely to shooting all the guest star segments so they could go home on Wednesday. In theory, the rest of the week's show was shot on Wednesday and Thursday. Three days, or thirty hours may seem like a lot of studio time to produce a half hour television show. But it really isn't. Scenery has to be moved in and out, lighting has to be changed and technical problems arise with monotonous regularity. Additionally, by their nature, puppets also slow down production.

To give the scenic and wardrobe people and the puppet makers enough time to properly perform their responsibilities, scripts had to be finished and approved three weeks before production. And, we turned out a script a week.

Every show had to have a guest star. That's because after Lord Lew Grade decided to produce *The Muppet Show* and get it on British television, CBS agreed to run it on the five stations they owned and operated in the United States. After that it was syndicated across the country.

But CBS agreed to run it only if each show had a celebrity guest star, *and* that guest star had to be billboarded in the opening of the show to hold the viewers. That's why the show always opened with Scooter announcing how long before show time to the guest star in the star's dressing room. Jim determined that Scooter's dialogue would coincide exactly with the length of the skit. If the skit timed out at 19 seconds, Scooter would announce to the guest star, "19 seconds 'til curtain!"

Initially, it was difficult to attract guest stars, mostly because of the American belief that puppets on television were only for kids. (They thought the same thing about animation until *The Simpsons* and *South Park*.) However, after the show became a hit in 1976, stars were lining up to appear on it.

It was the culture of *The Muppet Show* to make sure every guest star was made to feel welcome and comfortable. So, a week or so before we started a script, Jerry Juhl would talk to the star's manager or the star himself, or herself, to get a feeling of what they would be comfortable doing on the show. Usually singers wanted to sing, and dancers wanted to dance.

But, occasionally, stars saw the show as an opportunity to play against type. I remember Beverly Sills, the great opera singer, told Jerry Juhl she always wanted to tap dance and sing Country and Western music. Since the Muppets operated in a parallel universe, we could usually accommodate the guests. (We did for Ms. Sills.)

Once a week, the writers also met with Jim to get his input for the next script. Sometimes Jim had an idea for a back stage story line. Sometimes he had ideas that involved the guest stars, or a *Pigs In Space*, or a music number. Jim thought about the show constantly. So, it was very important for Jim and the writers to stay in creative touch. *The Muppet Show* really was the product of Jim Henson's imagination.

So, when the writers started to construct the show, we knew what the guest star wanted to do. We also knew the guest star had to be in the dressing room opening, star in two skits or musical numbers, and do a "talk" spot with Kermit. These pieces, along with Jim's input, were sacrosanct. But, we could also use the guest star in other pieces if it was appropriate. Also, every script had to have a four-scene backstage story line.

Here is a typical writers' run down for the show that starred Helen Reddy as prepared by Jerry Juhl after the initial writers' meeting.

THE MUPPET SHOW NO. 72 – Helen Reddy

1. OPENING (Scooter/Guest Star in Dressing Room)
2. OPENING TITLES
3. COMMERCIAL NO. 1
4. KERMIT WELCOMES
5. OPENING MUSICAL NO.
6. STATLER & WALDORF NO. 1
7. BACKSTAGE NO. 1 – Beauregard, the stage hand, has waxed the backstage floor – no one can stand up.
8. KERMIT INTROS HELEN REDDY
9. HELEN'S FIRST NO.
10. STATLER & WALDORF NO. 2
11. NIGHT COURT – a new magazine element ... maybe
12. HELEN, FOZZIE & AUSTRIAN BAND
13. BACKSTAGE NO. 2 – Kermit has stopped Beauregard just in time. He was starting to wax center stage.

14. KERMIT INTROS FOZZIE - who is going to do a Folk Dance with two other guys.

15. THE SLIP DANCE – Fozzie and his partners try to do their dance, avoiding the one slippery spot on the stage. Guess who keeps finding it.

16. COMMERCIAL NO. 2

17. UK SPOT

18. HELEN & KERMIT TALK SPOT INTO SONG.

19. STATLER & WALDORF NO. 3

20. BACKSTAGE NO. 3 – To cut the slipperiness, Kermit asked Beauregard to toss a little sand on the floor. Everyone is knee deep in sand. Beauregard is apologetic. A camel arrives (?)

21. AT THE DANCE

22. MUPPET SPORTS REPORT

23. BACKSTAGE NO. 4 – Beauregard has swept the sand out of backstage. And put it on stage.

24. KERMIT INTROS HELEN

25. HELEN'S CLOSING NUMBER – desert setting – Arabs and camels.

26. COMMERCIAL NO. 3

27. GOODNIGHTS

28. CREDITS

29. STATLER & WALDORF CLOSING COMMENT

When the run down was finished, Don, Jerry and I would have a meeting to decide who writes what. Usually, whoever came up with the backstage story line wrote those four scenes. The rest would be divided up more or less equally, based on who had an idea for what.

It's been more than 30 years since I worked on this script but I do know I wrote Numbers 12 and 21. In Number 12, Fozzie decides to make Helen Reddy feel at home by surprising her with an Austrian, um-pah band, dressed in lederhosen. When Helen explains she's Australian, not Austrian, the band plays an um-pah version of *Waltzing Matilda* while hopping around like kangaroos.

In Number 21, At The Dance, I thought it would be fun to have the Muppets form a conga line. Each bad joke segued back into a conga. E.g.: *What did Pocahontas sing to John Smith when they danced? The Indian love son-ga!*; *What does the dancing cowboy sing to his cattle? Little dogie get alon-ga.* As you can see, I did learn to write bad jokes.

With the exception of the Sunday morning read-through, we writers just hung out in our offices and wrote. Although we were located in a different building from the studio, we had television monitors that showed us what was going on in the studio. Of course, a writer would closely watch the monitor if a piece of his material was being taped. It's always interesting to see how something you wrote is finally performed.

Occasionally, something goes wrong. You're watching a piece you wrote and it's not working. Maybe it's too complicated. Or, maybe it just isn't funny. Don Hinkley had a technical term for this. He called it a "jokeoid."

A jokeoid, Don explained, feels like a joke when you think of it. It reads like a joke when you write it. It sounds like a joke when you rehearse it. But, when you tell it, nobody laughs.

When things go wrong in the studio, as they do, and you're watching something you wrote die, you *know* what the next step is. The phone is going to ring and it will be the studio asking for a re-write. Here's something you may have spent a day or more writing and they want a new ending – *immediately*! But, as Don used to say: "That's why we get the big bucks."

While the writing staff is frantically trying to come up with a new ending, all studio production stops and the entire cast and crew stand down and wait. Thousands of dollars are being wasted. To make matters worse, while we're scrambling to re-write, the camera pans around the studio so you can watch the cast and crew trimming their nails and twiddling their thumbs.

Basically, our job was to show up every day and be funny. However, there was a certain amount of practicality involved. Television shows have to have structure, continuity and contrast. So, the lunacy had to be channeled.

Obviously, there's a lot of daydreaming. It's part of the job. Don and I also worked out an intricate body language to signal if we were really working on something or were available for some serious breeze shooting. Sometimes, that even led to a useable idea.

Don and I were as opposite as two people could be. I was hirsute and bearded. Don was clean shaven and bald. I was the nervous, edgy New Yorker. Don was the laid back Californian. There was also a twenty-year difference in our ages. And yet, we never had a bad word. We did have a lot of fun. I've often thought of doing a play about the two of us trapped in that tiny office creating comedy.

Every Thursday, at the end of the work day, we writers had to have a finished script. The last thing we did on Thursday nights was time the script. We did that by running a stop watch and reading through each scene ourselves, out loud, approximating the characters' timing and attitude. If it needed trimming, that's when we trimmed it. In other words, we did our own version of the script with the writers playing all the characters. Jerry usually played Kermit and Don and I did the other characters. We were always careful to lock the doors before we started timing the script.

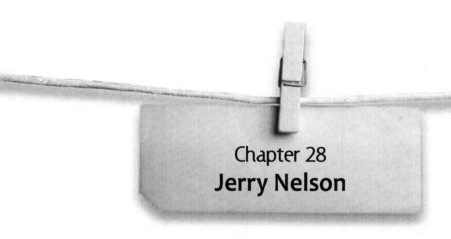

Chapter 28
Jerry Nelson

Jerry and I became friends several years before *The Muppet Show* premiered. Jerry and Richard Hunt were teamed up regularly on *Sesame Street* during my first four seasons on the show. So, we developed a creative relationship between my writing and their performing.

They performed both ends of the Snuffle-upagus with Jerry in front doing the talking. They performed the Two-Headed Monster, Frank-N-Stein. They were Biff (Jerry), the loud mouth hard hat and his partner, Sully (Richard), who couldn't get a word in edgewise. Jerry also performed Herry (pronounced as a cross between "Harry" and hairy) Monster and Count von Count, the numerically crazed Transylvanian nobleman.

During the early 1970s on *Sesame Street*, the Snuffle-upagus was believed by the show's adults to be a figment of Big Bird's imagination. So, the fun, as a writer, was to see how close I could bring this elephant sized mammoth to the adult cast, without their seeing him.

I used him in a show I did about a blackout on *Sesame Street*. After careful negotiation, and minute planning, the adults are about to meet the Snuffle-upagus when the blackout occurred. I also once wrote a party down in Oscar's can, which was basically a radio show. We only saw Oscar's can from the outside. Snuffy's snuffle appears from inside the can and a cast member inside is heard wondering, "Who's that big hairy guy with the trunk?"

"Aw, it's just some friend of Oscar's."

So, according to my *Sesame Street* history, the adults were actually at the same party as the Snuffle-upagus. They were just never introduced.

When *Sesame Street* was in production and the Snuffle-upagus wasn't being used in the studio, the elephant-sized puppet was "flown" from the ceiling. "Flying" is a theatrical term for moving things up and down through a series of pulleys from the top of a studio or theater. Scenic backdrops are "flown." Curtains are "flown." Lighting is "flown."

So, when Snuffy wasn't being used, cables were attached to his head and back and he was hoisted 40 feet in the air, where he was out of the way and safe. When it was time for the puppeteers to suit up, the giant puppet was lowered to the deck.

What made this so much fun was that in those days, we had a lot of kids on the show, playing in the background. There were also a goodly amount of visiting children, friends of the cast and crew. Many of these kids spotted Snuffy hanging overhead. When they did, they went nuts!

Kids would grab the leg of the nearest adult and yell, "Look! Look! It's the Snuffle-upagus!"

And, the adult response was always the same: "Aw, c'mon, kid. You can't fool me. There's no such thing as a Snuffle-upagus."

The Count is really a wonderful character, thanks to Jerry's creativity. I've had him counting bathroom tiles and how many times a piano was carried in and out a door. (Inside dope: The Count's Countmobile license plate is *Transylvania six, five thousand.*)

Jerry also performed Herry Monster, the big furry blue monster with the big purple nose. I based Herry on a friend of mine who was extremely strong and extremely clumsy. Herry didn't know his own strength. Like my friend, Herry just went through life accidentally tearing doors from their hinges. On one occasion, I wrote a song for Herry called, *I Can't Help It*. While performing the song, Herry destroyed the entire Fix-it Shop.

One day, I walked into the *Sesame Street* production offices and was grabbed simultaneously by three or four people.

"You've got to see this!", they exclaimed.

They dragged me over to a monitor that was connected to the studio uptown on 81st Street. It was between takes of a piece where Oscar the Grouch's cousin came to visit. Jerry was performing Oscar's cousin. I hadn't even written the piece, so I couldn't understand what all the excitement was about.

The call for "action" came and the skit started. It was a good bit, but it didn't seem to warrant the gales of laughter from the people around me.

"What's so funny?", I asked.

"Jerry's doing your voice for Oscar's cousin!"

"That doesn't sound anything like me!", which, of course, is what everybody says when they hear their own voice. I like to think I sound like Carry Grant. Please don't break the illusion.

Perhaps my favorite Jerry Nelson *Sesame Street* character from those days was Biff, the opinionated hard hat. Every job site, factory floor and neighborhood tavern has a Biff, a blowhard know-it-all who was seldom, if ever, right. Biff was right up there with Cliff Clavin in *Cheers!* He even antagonized Maria by referring to her as *Little Lady*.

In one *Sesame Street* episode, in an explosion of feminism, I wrote Maria a job on a construction site. While she was working on a steel beam, along came Biff and Sully. Biff decides to teach the *Little Lady* how to rivet. In doing so, he inadvertently riveted his lunch box to the beam.

It's always been fun to be a part of Jerry's characters. They're just so beautifully finished.

But there's another less known but extremely important contribution that Jerry Nelson brings to the Muppets – his musical ability. Jerry can sing on key in all of his voices. Much of the big, Muppet choruses you hear are Jerry's voices over -dubbed several times.

At this writing, December 2010, Jerry recently released *Truro Daydreams*, a CD of his own music, sung with his own voice accompanied by his own guitar. Buy it. In fact, buy three or four.

159

Chapter 29
Writing Assignment:
Gonzo's Song

One morning, Jerry Juhl called me into his office to give me an assignment. The English version of *The Muppet Show* was two minutes longer than the U.S. version because they had fewer commercials. The usual solution was to do a musical number. Music can be timed exactly, and so it's easier to fill a segment that has to be exactly two minutes with a musical production number.

The problem was that a show had to be delivered to the English network, but the musical number wasn't ready. There was a musical number starring Gonzo already produced, but it only ran one minute and forty seconds. Something had to be written to fill twenty seconds so the piece would time out to two minutes.

Normally, Kermit would do an introduction in front of the curtains. But, *Ladies and Gentlemen*, the Great Gonzo will now sing Blah-blah-blah, only takes five seconds. There is still 15 seconds left to fill. Fifteen seconds can be an eternity in television. They do complete commercials in 15 seconds. So, I had to create a 20-second introduction.

Having Kermit talk for 20 seconds seemed contrived to me -- and not very funny. I needed a simple piece of "business" or action for Kermit to fill the time. I came up with this solution:

Firstly, the usual Kermit puppets (there are always several on hand) ended just below the waist, since he's usually shot from the waist up. But I knew there was at least one Kermit with legs for shots where he sits on a chair or a wall.

I had Kermit enter from off camera to start the introduction. But about a quarter of the way in, I indicated that his right foot gets stuck on a piece of chewing gum. This could be realistically accomplished by Jim or a second puppeteer holding Kermit's right leg below camera range.

So, now Kermit's trying to introduce Gonzo *and* get his foot unstuck at the same time. Additionally, during the introduction, he's complaining to someone off stage about the gum and demanding to know who sweeps the stage and why it wasn't swept. It was just a little piece of "business," but Jim played it beautifully. Of course, at the end of the introduction, Kermit's foot pops free and he flies out of the frame. We hear and off camera "crash!" as the curtains open on Gonzo's song.

Chapter 30
Surviving London

I owe my survival during my first few weeks in London to Richard Hunt and Jerry Nelson. At the studio, we were on camera until 8:00 at night, *if* we didn't go into over time. By the time I got back to my flat it was at least 9:00. By then, it was too late to shop. And the English shop owners had strange ideas about closing early on Tuesdays and Saturdays.

In New York, eating late was never a problem. I could leave a studio at anytime of the day or night and find some place to eat. Many bars' kitchens are open until midnight or 2:00 a.m.. There are also all night diners and delis all over New York City.

London, on the other hand, was quite different. First of all, a lot of pub food was frankly awful. And, it's a little known fact that indigestion, along with relationship problems, is an occupational hazard for comedy writers. For that reason, I stay away from strange Mexican, Indian, and Thai restaurants when I'm working. It's hard enough to re-write comedy on the spot when there's a problem and the meter is running. You certainly don't need your bowels on fire to boot.

All of the better London restaurants were very strict about reservations, requiring tables to be "booked" days in advance. Sometimes in New York, if a restaurant is full and you haven't a reservation, they'll let you wait at the bar until a table opens up after the dinner rush.

No such luck in London restaurants. No booking, no table. Their philosophy seemed to be that Londoners were divided into two groups: those who had money and didn't work; and those who worked and had no money. There was no accommodation for people who worked *and* had money.

Since we were never quite sure when we would finish at the studio, it was impossible for us to make dinner reservations. After several weeks, I solved the problem by eating most nights in the London branch of Joe Allen's, the theatre bar on west 46th Street, New York's Restaurant Row.

Joe Allen's had great steaks, cold beer and ice, items in rare supply in most London pubs. Since they served food, they were open until 1:00 a.m., and I could eat at the bar without a reservation. But, until I discovered Joe Allen's, many nights I dined on my "emergency rations," a one pound bar of Cadbury chocolate and a few cans of Heineken beer. I'll admit it's an acquired taste.

Getting around London at night was also a lot tougher that New York. Most taxicabs in New York are owned by fleets. The taxi fleets keep their cabs on the street 24 hours a day. There are privately owned taxis in New York, but their owners also usually hire drivers to work the night shift.

In London, most of the cabs are privately owned and the drivers take them home at the end of their work day. So, it was usual to hail a cab and hear:

"Well, Gov'ner, I'm on me way home to the wife and kiddies down near Battersea. If you're going that way, 'op in. Otherwise . . ."

Sometimes, growling at them in Brooklynese helped.

"I wanna go to Regent Park. *Ya gotta problem wit dat?*"

Kojak was then the hottest show on British television (next to *The Muppet Show*). And, the one thing every Londoner knew about every New Yorker was: 1., We were all heavily armed; and 2., We ate our young. So, sometimes that worked. But usually by evening London cabs disappeared from the streets.

Joe Allen's had the number of a mini-cab service, which was just a group of guys moonlighting with their own private cars. So, when I asked them for a mini-cab to get home, I was never sure what was going to show up. Sometimes it was a 30 year old Peugeot with three fenders. Other times it could be a brand new air-conditioned Volvo.

I once told Jim I had solved the late night, London taxicab problem. I had, I told him, isolate the scent of the female London taxicab and I kept a vial of it with me at all times. When I needed a cab late at night, I simply sprinkled a little around the base of a street lamp. Then I hid in the shadows and waited for a randy buck taxi to show up. After I told him that, Jim said he knew then I was legitimately crazy.

One night, shortly after I arrived in London, and I was about to prepare my usual *Cadbury avec Heineken* repast, my phone rang. It was Jerry Nelson.

"You hungry?"

"I'm starving!"

"How about a steak?"

"You're kidding!"

"Be out front in about 20 minutes."

Twenty minutes later, the oldest, rustiest, dirtiest, dented Ford Cortina I had ever seen rattled up to the front entrance of my apartment building. It was Richard's. (At home in New Jersey, Richard's personal car was a black, eight passenger Checker taxicab.) Richard was at the wheel and Jerry was seated next to him. I jumped into the back seat and Richard roared off into the evening traffic.

Richard had the most extraordinary sense of direction I'd ever seen in a human being. In one year of driving in London, Richard had committed the street atlas of the entire city to memory. In fact, I saw him win "how-to-get-there" arguments with London cabbies who are the best in the world. It takes about 18 months to get a taxi license in London. As I said before, the streets are an indecipherable maze. And the taxi exam has questions like, *What's the fastest way from the Royal College of Needlework to the Hotel Connaught?*

Richard flew through the city so fast that I never got a sense of where we were. We drove for about 15 minutes and pulled up in front of a small hotel called the Portobello.

Richard and Jerry had stayed at the Portobello during the first year of *The Muppet Show* production. The Portobello was London's answer to the

Chelsea Hotel in New York. At the same time the Muppets were staying there, so were the Sex Pistols and J. Paul Getty III, who is said to have skipped out on his bill.

In those days in London, the pubs closed at 11:00 p.m.. However, if you were a hotel guest, you could go to the hotel lounge and pretty much drink all night long. The night manager of the Portobello lounge was an American whom Richard and Jerry had befriended the year before. He let us eat and drink in the lounge after hours while we pretended to be hotel guests. He also had cold beer and made a pretty good chicken fried steak. So, many a night when we worked late, we ended up at the Portobello.

I was always a bit uneasy. Despite assurances from Richard and Jerry, I was always afraid the place would be raided and we'd be all over tomorrow's headlines: MUPPETS CAUGHT IN AFTER HOURS RAID!

"What's the charge?"

"Your Honor, these three criminal aliens were arrested while eating steak and drinking beer at 12:45 a.m.."

"Thirty years hard labor!"

One night we almost did get busted. The hotel's owner came by, something he rarely did at night. "Quick!", Jerry hissed. "Act like a guest."

In a loud voice with my best New York accent, I turned to Richard and said, "Have you seen the johns in this place!?"

The owner did an immediate about face and disappeared. Americans are notorious throughout Europe as being bathroom fanatics. The last thing this guy wanted to do was listen to some loud mouthed American complain about his "can."

Weather reports aside, one of the great things about living in London is the BBC. They do some great programing. But, it's *veddy British* programing.

In 1977, there were only three television channels in London: BBC-1; BBC-2; and a third channel, which was shared by two commercial networks. One network had it during the week. They other had it on the weekends.

So, many nights I'd come home with Chinese take-out, flip on the TV and discover the only thing starting was a program entitles, *The Ponies of the Shetland Islands*. Wow. *But*, fifteen minutes later, I'm thinking, "Wow! That's fascinating!" No doubt about it. The BBC makes great documentaries.

But, their sense of quality extends throughout their programing. John Cleese told us that he had completed 80% of the shooting for his *Fawlty Towers* pilot, and decided he didn't like it. So, he went to the BBC and told them, "This is rubbish. I want to start all over." And, they let him. That's unheard of in American television.

Here's the most esoteric BBC story I know. During a discussion about toilets, a question was poised: If, in the Northern Hemisphere, the water drains clockwise when a toilet is flushed; and it drains counter clockwise in the Southern Hemisphere; what happens when a toilet is flushed on the Equator?

A crew was dispatched to find a toilet located exactly on the Equator. They found one, flushed and reported back that when a toilet is flushed on the Equator, the water actually goes straight down. I don't know about you, but I'll sleep better tonight.

I also enjoyed listening to BBC radio. It is the purest English spoken on the planet. I used to take a short wave on vacation just to listen to BBC English. But the World Service News depressed me on vacation. So, I tuned in right after BBC World Service to the BBC World Farming Report. I would blissfully listen to bulletins and updates on the Rhodesian yam crop and wheat farming in Argentina. I didn't care. I just wanted to hear real English English.

Someone told me that after 6:00 pm, anyone on BBC *Radio* had to be wearing a tuxedo. How appropriate and how British! They always sounded like they were dressed formally.

But then, in England, I heard that in the sixties they abolished that policy. So, now I still like listening to the BBC. But every once in a while, it occurs to me that I could be listening to some yabo in a Hawaiian sport shirt.

If you're as outraged at this barbarity as I am, join me in BBBBBC!, or Bring Back Black Tie to the BBC! Let our voice be heard!

Chapter 31
Lou Rawls

Lou Rawls was one of the greatest jazz singers of the 20th Century. His deep baritone voice was as recognizable around the globe as Frank Sinatra's. And so it came to pass that Lou Rawls was a guest on *The Muppet Show*.

In a writer's meeting about the Lou Rawls episode, Jim asked for a bit where Lou was hanging out by the stage door with some of the guys from the Electric Mayhem band – Zoot, the sax player, Floyd, the bass guitarist, Janice, the lead guitarist, or Animal, the drummer. The assignment fell to me.

I'm not sure how we discovered it, but it seemed that Lou Rawls had a great sense of rhythm but very little sense of comedic timing. So, it took me close to three days to come up with the following bit. I'll outline it for you and then give you the logic behind it.

The sketch opens with Lou hanging by the stage door of the Muppet Theater. Enter Floyd, played by Jerry Nelson and Animal, played by Frank Oz. Animal is wearing a dog collar attached by a chain leash held by Floyd. Floyd explains to Lou that he's out walking the drummer.

When Lou exclaims what a great drummer Animal is, and how he'd like to tell him he can really put some *soul in the bowl,* Floyd tugs on the chain and says, *Animal! Good drummer! Good drummer!*

While Animal chewed on the leash, the conversation continued. Lou says he's going on a road trip and needs a drummer, and how about Animal? Floyd worries that they don't have a long enough chain. So Lou decides to talk directly to Animal. Floyd hands the leash over to Lou with the admonition, *Just don't let him chase any cars.*

As soon as Lou takes the leash from Floyd, we hear, off camera, a car going by.

Car! Car! Car!, cries Animal as he rushes off camera, yanking Lou behind him. We hear another car going by and Animal charges through the scene, pulling a frantic Lou behind him, left to right. Since three is the magic number, we hear another car and Animal drags Lou through the scene once more, from right to left, screaming, *Car! Car! Car!*

The piece "worked" beautifully, as we say in comedy. In fact, I put it on my sample reel. The rationale for it is very simple: Since Lou Rawls had little sense of comedic timing, I literally chained him to Frank Oz, who has an extraordinary sense of comedy. So, Frank's timing controlled the scene.

Chapter 32

Muppet Makers

B esides the cast and production staff, the third component of *The Muppet Show*'s success is the group of people who build and wardrobe the puppet characters. I've always felt the Muppet makers were equally as creative as the writers and puppeteers, and had to be equally in synch with Jim's comedic vision as we were. As a writer, this means after you write something, every possibility of your script is explored to the limit for comedic value by these people.

If you think about it, every character you've ever seen in a Muppet production was made and clothed by hand. These are true artists who create in felt, foam rubber, plastic, feathers and God knows what else.

Many of the original characters were designed by Jim, himself.

But the construction, maintenance and duplication of the puppets were left to the Muppet builders in the various shops located in New York, Los Angeles, London and Toronto, depending on where individual Muppet projects were being produced. Additionally, many of the characters were designed and built by the shops with very little, if any, supervision by Jim Henson.

A case in point is the creation of Miss Piggy. During a shop meeting before the first season of *The Muppet Show*, Jim said, "Make me a gang of pigs." He then got on a plane and flew somewhere.

So, the Muppet shop designed and created a half dozen or so pig Muppets. They surmised that Jim had plans to use them in musical numbers, as he did with penguins. And, that's exactly what he did.

But, between takes of a musical number, a female pig in the chorus started hassling Kermit. To keep spirits up during a production, it's not unusual for the puppeteers to stay in character and ad lib among themselves between takes. Sometimes the ab libs are funnier that the written material.

So this female pig, puppeteered by Frank Oz, started bugging Kermit about when she was going to get her own spot in the show. When Kermit said he had no idea what she was talking about, she replied, "That's not what you said over dinner last night."

As the discussion between Piggy and Kermit heated up, the show's writers were watching this interplay on their monitors. And so, a star was born.

Through the combined imaginations of Frank Oz and the first season *Muppet Show* writers, Piggy's character and importance grew. Calista Hendrickson, a very talented wardrobe designer, took over Piggy's costumes. Calista designed all those wonderful gowns, hats and traveling suits for Piggy while still keeping the original character – basically a Muppet pig.

I once asked Calista what the secret of dressing Miss Piggy was.

"Piggy," Calista explained, "is 15 pounds heavier than she'll admit to herself."

1977 was the beginning of the aerobic craze. So naturally, it occurred to me that Piggy should do an exercise video.

Piggy appeared in a "Pig Power" t-shirt. I had her jogging in place, bending over to touch her toes, doing jumping jacks and squats and complaining bitterly throughout. Of course, Piggy was shot from the waist up through all of it.

For the finish of the piece, I thought it would be funny to have Piggy lay on her back and "bicycle." Since ostensibly, Piggy would be lying on the floor, all we would see are her legs. And so far, Piggy didn't have any legs.

So, it would be up to the shop to create Piggy's legs. I thought this would be a good opportunity for the Muppet builders to design and build a pair of chubby little legs for Piggy. The shot would be a close up of the legs being manipulated by a puppeteer below camera, while Piggy grunted and groaned.

However, I had left one visual element out of the script. When I "saw" Piggy exercising in my mind, I naturally pictured her in work out gear, black fishnet stockings and five inch stiletto heels. I purposely left the stockings and heels out of the script just to see how simpatico the Muppet shop was with the writing staff.

Sure enough, on the day of the shoot, there were Piggy's ham hocks and chubby little calves encased in black fishnet and sporting five-inch stiletto heels.

While I'm on the subject, let me give you a few more examples of the wonderful support I always got from the Muppet shop. Their enthusiasm and creativity always pushed my enthusiasm and creativity.

I had an idea for the Muppet News Man. Just as the food always attacked the Swedish Chef, the news always attacked the Muppet News Man, played, by the way, by Jim Henson. The idea was a running gag with three separate news flashes that we could insert throughout the show.

It was a simple premise. Every news flash announced the opening of another season.

First news flash: "Today is the opening of the Fishing Season." Thousands of gun shots go off. Thousands of Muppet fish fall from the sky onto the News Man.

Second news flash: "Today is the opening of the Hunting Season." Thousands of gun shots go off. A moose falls from the sky and drops on the News Man.

Third news flash: "Today is the opening of the Opera Season." Thousands of gun shots go off. A diva, complete with horned helmet and chrome breast plate, falls on the News Man.

I figured the fish and the diva were a pretty routine request. And, I was right. I did get a call about the moose. There was no problem building a moose. The shop was just curious about whether or not the moose had to be articulated. "Articulated," in Muppet talk means, "Does the puppet have to have a working mouth so a puppeteer can make him talk?"

"No.", I told the shop. "He just has to drop on the News Man."

Well, we got the fish, the moose and the diva. Just in case, the shop articulated the moose. Three shows or so later, he turned up in somebody else's bit as tap dancing Micky Moose. Even better, Jerry Nelson performed him with John Wayne's voice.

You gotta problem with that, Pilgrim?

Chapter 33
Dave Goelz

I didn't meet Dave Goelz until I started on *The Muppet Show* in 1977. So, we've only been friends for 34 years. In those days, Dave appeared to be the most normal of all the puppeteers. But that might be because he was the quietest. "Quiet," of course, being a relative word when discussing Muppeteers. But all appearance of normalcy immediately disappears when Dave inserts his hand into one of his signature characters: Dr. Bunsen Honeydew of Muppet Labs; Zoot, the saxophonist in the Electric Mayhem Band; and my favorite, The Great Gonzo.

I've always thought that deep, down inside, Dr. Bunsen Honeydew has a few sadistic tendencies he won't admit to himself. It can't be coincidental that all of his research ends with the explosion, ingestion, strangulation, depilation, or decapitation of his assistant, Beaker. And, he's so matter of fact about it.

Zoot, the burned out sax player can milk a laugh out of a blank stare. And, we found out last holiday season that Zoot was Jewish, which really made my wife happy.

Head Writer Jerry Juhl said his inspiration for the band was a group of studio musicians that hung out at a recording studio in Los Angeles. This was the 60s, so they looked like spaced out hippies, all hair, beard, torn bellbottoms and tie-dyed T-shirts. And all they talked about were condos in Hawaii.

But, As Jerry listened more, he realized the musicians weren't talking about apartments. They were talking about building hi-rise condo developments and selling them.

Though they looked like simple hippies, studio musicians are the best in the business. They can walk into a recording studio and play an arrangement exactly as it's written with little or no rehearsal. And they can do it repeatedly. So, the good ones work all the time. And besides a session fee, they get a small royalty on every CD that's sold. And all those little royalties add up to big money.

One fairly well known jazz bassist I know told me that even though he's played on albums with Ella Fitzgerald and Frank Sinatra, he'll take all the work he can get. He plays on polka records, country & western, religious, folk, anything to keep those royalties rolling in.

So, Jerry Juhl's take on the *Electric Mayhem* was they were all rich from record royalties and didn't need the gig on *The Muppet Show*. In effect, they were doing Kermit a favor. He needed them more than they needed him. And, they knew it.

But my favorite Dave Goelz character is still the Great Gonzo. Named after the Hunter S. Thompson school of journalism, Gonzo is a pure Muppet. To paraphrase Jerry Juhl, nothing Gonzo does can be done by humans. He's impervious to fear or pain and maybe a little masochistic. And a human being couldn't dream up Gonzo's stunts. (I mean a normal human being.)

Dave just created this maniacal dodo who loves show business more than life itself, and is willing to regularly risk his life to stay in it. He really is *gonzo*. He's pure Muppet off-the-wall lunacy. And, Dave made it so much fun to write for him.

Imagine a character that you could make wrestle a brick blindfolded (and lose!), or tango with a cheese, or jump a motorcycle from the stage to the box where Statler and Waldorf heckle Fozzie. (For their safety, Gonzo had chained them in their seats, earlier.)

Thank you, Dave.

Chapter 34
Sam's Editorials

Hemingway said that writing was the only art that was self taught. He wasn't talking about the mechanics of writing. The novelist was talking about the creative side of writing: where the stories come from; how the characters are formed; how they express themselves; and, in my case, where the jokes originate. Every writer has to find in himself that particular mood or frame of mind that's called inspiration.

There's also a school of literature that says writing is very little inspiration and mostly perspiration. For me that's one of those moot, how-many-angels-can-dance-on-the-head-of-a-pin questions. In my case, inspiration comes from desperation.

As soon as I finish a sketch, the anxiety immediately starts about finding the next one. There are writers who can sit down in the morning, very businesslike, and methodically work their way through a manuscript. They say Neil Simon works that way. So did Don Hinkley.

Not me. I spend hours pacing, doodling, chewing pencils and bounding off the walls, waiting either for God to show up or the blood to come out of my forehead. If Don wasn't such a laid back Californian, I'm sure he would have strangled me by the third week of the season.

The joke in the writer's office was that I could never write anything until at least twelve noon, *New York time*. That meant I would go through my mental and physical gymnastics until 5:00 or 6:00 p.m. London time. Then, if I had come up with anything worthwhile (a *very* big "if"), I would sit down at the typewriter and furiously pound it out until 8:00 p.m., when we quit.

Part of this was also caused by my dislike for and inability at typing. Rather than go through three or four drafts, I run a sketch back and forth through my head like a piece of improvisational theatre. Only when I finally got it right would I put it down on paper.

By the middle of a season, I'd be spending every waking moment looking for laughs. Everything I saw, everything I heard, any idea that came to mind went through a mental filter: *Boring. Boring. Boring. Maybe. Nope, boring.*

Even away from the office, I became very entertaining in a hysterical sort of way. Anything I might say that might be boring or mundane got filtered out. I once had a taxi ride through London where half my brain was looking for a script idea and the other was making polite conversation with the driver. He laughed so hard a couple of times, he nearly wrecked the cab. When we got to my destination, he told me I was the funniest passenger he had ever had, and I hadn't the remotest idea what we had talked about.

One night I was having dinner at the bar in Joe Allen's in my usual state of creative angst. Then I noticed on the wall there was a poster that pictured the most endangered species of animals – the timber wolf, the mountain lion, etc. Among those endangered species was the American Bald Eagle.

In a flash, an idea came to me. *The Muppet Show* had a character, Sam the Eagle. Sam hung around the Muppet Theater and generally disapproved of everything. Politically, Sam was so far to the right, he made Margaret Thatcher look like Mao Tse Tung.

The idea was simple: Sam would come on camera and deliver an editorial about how some, "namby-pamby conservationists" were stopping our progress, by shutting down industry and grinding our highways to a halt for the sake of a few so called endangered species of insignificant animals.

"I have here a list!", Sam declared. (The only time in my writing career I ever quoted Senator Joe McCarthy.) "A list of these so called endangered species!"

Sam then began to read the list about the mountain lion, the timber wolf, etc. Finally, Sam got to the last species on the list: "The American Bald Eagle. *The American Bald Eagle!!!?*"

"Sorry. This list is now *inoperative.*", said Sam as he slunk off camera. (The only time in my writing career I ever got to quote Richard Nixon's Watergate Press Secretary, Ronald Ziegler.)

The show did it up right. They gave Sam a podium with an official looking eagle seal, columns behind him and some pompous entry music. I even got two more bits out of it as Sam's Editorials became a part of *The Muppet Show*.

In the second piece, I had Sam railing against nudity. He had just realized that underneath their clothing, the entire population of the world was walking around naked! *Completely naked! Naked!* And, Sam went on, it wasn't just people! Underneath their fir, even cute little doggies and pussycats, *absolutely naked!* Even worse, Sam continued, underneath their fine feathers, birds, yes, birds were completely . . .

At this point, Sam had a moment of terrible realization. He covered his nether regions with his wings and, greatly embarrassed, slinked off the stage.

Sam's third editorial was about the crime rate, which was rising at an incredible rate. While Sam ranted about it and demanded immediate action, a gang of Muppet thieves stole the columns and everything else off the stage behind him. After Sam exited, the stole the podium, too.

Jerry Juhl was happy with all three of them. So after a brief relaxation period of five or six minutes, I slipped back into my permanent mode of creative panic.

The author and
Mrs. Gerald R. Ford.

Sesame Street writers
Norman Styles, Emily
Pearl Kingsley, the
author and Jon Stone.

Aboard the Queen Elizabeth II.
Standing: The author; Jerry Nelson; Susan Juhl; Jerry Juhl; Frank Oz; Jim Henson. Seated: Karen Hinkley; Don Hinkley; Debbie Brillstein; Bernie Brillstein; Jane Henson; and Richard Hunt.

The Snuffle-upagus and friend.

The Sing-Along episode in Bert and Ernie's bathroom.

Chapter 35
Guest Stars

O ur work week on *The Muppet Show* began on, "the Sunday", as the Brits say. Working on Sunday was pretty depressing, especially in England where the rest of the world was off. It rains a lot in England but the Sunday morning storms always seemed wetter and windier.

Once we got to our office, there was little for Don and I to do but twiddle our thumbs and watch the rain teem down while we waited for the guest star to arrive. Even Don couldn't write comedy under those conditions. And Don had written for Steve Allen, Bob Newhart, Carol Burnett, and Flip Wilson.

To kill time, we'd make up mythical English geographic locations like, *Blight-on-Thames* or *Isle of Lout*.

One Sunday, with the rain pelting the windows of our shabby little office, Don would mention that in all the shopping he had done in England, he had never seen suntan lotion. He had asked in drug stores, supermarkets, department stores, but never found suntan lotion. It was unknown to these people.

Then Don would let me in on his secret. He was going to secretly acquire the Bain de Soleil suntan lotion franchise for England, and monopolize the market before they knew what hit them. Don would rhapsodize about cornering the English suntan lotion market and becoming a zillionaire while the rain pelted against the windows behind him like large caliber machine gun bullets.

On another rainy Sunday morning, Don brought up the fact that although it was cold and rainy in England, in the Sahara Desert the temperatures reached 120-degrees Fahrenheit. Then he segued into an item he had seen in the morning newspaper:

There is actually a trans-Sahara vacation bus tour. The last trip had been booked by a group of German vacationers. During the tour, two passengers died of heat prostration.

"Only the Germans," Don said, "would think of busing across the Sahara Desert as a vacation."

Eventually, we would get word that the guest star had arrived. Don, Jerry Juhl and I would dutifully trudge upstairs to the rehearsal hall for the first script read through.

The Sunday rehearsal hall was even gloomier than our office. It was big and mostly empty with one wall lined with windows and the opposite wall was lined with dance mirrors, the better to reflect, and double, the rain and overcast outside.

At one end of the room was a large square table made from placing four large conference tables at right angles. The entire cast and production staff sat around it, 25 or 30 people.

After the guest star was introduced to every member of the staff, the cast and guest star would read down the script but with little acting or timing. Additionally, the music, technical, props and wardrobe people have the right to jump in, usually in mid-punch line, to ask production questions pertinent to their departments. All the jokes seem to die and the writers died with them.

When this weekly fiasco was over, Don and I would trudge downstairs to our cramped office and try to write. But it was like trying to ski uphill. The weather was bad enough. But since it was Sunday, no one was working except us. The studios, the shops, and the rest of our building had a mausoleumesque atmosphere that was not exactly conducive to writing comedy.

Additionally, since there was no activity in our studio, our television monitor stared blankly at us from the corner of the office. During the week, the fun in the studio was a constant source of inspiration for us. But we soldiered on.

Chapter 36
Nine Guest Stars

The *Muppet Show* was very fortunate to have some of the most famous and talented people as guest stars. Thirty years later, I still have the impressions they left on me. Some were long. Some were short. But, all were memorable. Here are nine of them.

Edgar Bergen

When Edgar Bergen was scheduled for *The Muppet Show*, the usually easy going Jerry Juhl announced in no uncertain terms that he was going to pull rank as Head Writer and write every scene that included the famous ventriloquist and his characters. Jerry had started out as a puppeteer and like the rest of the Muppets, had worshiped Edgar Bergen since childhood.

The thrust of Jerry's story line was that Fozzie, the bear comedian, inspired by Edgar Bergen, had decided to do a ventriloquist act himself. The pay off was that nobody had told Fozzie that the ventriloquist also did the talking for the dummy.

The usual gloomy Sunday morning script read through went well with very few changes. So, Don Hinkley and I left the rehearsal hall and went back to our office to work on our current script.

A short while later, the phone rang. It was Jerry in the rehearsal hall. "You guys better get up here. You don't want to miss this!" Don and I trooped back upstairs to the rehearsal hall and found that Jerry was right.

The Muppet guys, Jim, Frank, Jerry, Dave and Richard were sprawled on the floor like a group of ten-year-old kids watching television.

Seated on a chair in the middle of the room was Edgar Bergen, doing every bit of his "A" material. He had Charley McCarthy out. He used Mortimer Snerd. He did a variety of his lesser known characters and even some blue material.

Our puppeteers sat in rapt attention for almost an hour without moving a muscle, watching their real, live inspiration. It was a private command performance by one puppet genius for another, and one which I shall never forget.

Elton John
I had lunch with Elton John. All he talked about was his soccer team, Watford.

Zero Mostel
One particularly dreary Sunday morning, *The Muppet Show* writing staff, Jerry Juhl, Don Hinkley and I were huddled on one side of the giant table awaiting the arrival of this week's guest star, Zero Mostel.

Zero finally arrived, appearing to be quite elderly and partially crippled. He hobbled in stooped over, and very much dependent on the use of a cane. He slowly and painfully sat down on the other side of the large square rehearsal table, directly across from us.

The live script reading began. And during it, Zero may have delivered his funniest performance for *The Muppet Show*, albeit off camera.

About half way through the script, Zero stopped in the middle of a scene. He politely asked Jerry, as the head writer, to change a line. Jerry made a note and said we, the writers, would look at it later.

Zero asked again, perhaps a little less politely. Jerry repeated that we would look at it back in the writers' office. Zero became even more insistent. He wanted the line changed now and he knew the change he wanted. Jerry hesitated again.

Suddenly, Zero abandoned his crippled old man persona, lunging to his feet, throwing the cane in one direction and the chair in the other, both of them bouncing noisily in opposite directions across the large rehearsal hall. With a great roar, Zero sprinted around the table with the speed of a jack rabbit. He came up behind Jerry Juhl and threw a wrestling hammer lock on him, bending Jerry's arm behind his back.

"I said I wanted that line changed!", Zero hissed menacingly.

Throwing his creative convictions to the winds, Jerry wasted no time in agreeing. After that, the read through went fairly quickly, as all of Zero's suggestions and changes were immediately incorporated into the script.

Bob Hope

In an interview after he performed on *The Muppet Show*, Bob Hope said the success of the show was due, in a large part, to the talent of the writing staff. So, he's okay in my book.

Madeline Kahn

Madeline Kahn was one of those very rare beautiful women who was blessed with a sense of humor and had absolutely no inhibitions about exercising it. It was easy to see why Mel Brooks loved using her in his films.

The night Madeline finished her Muppet appearance, Jerry Nelson had a small party in his flat. In a pensive moment, Madeline said that sometimes in life she wished she were like a New York taxi cab and had a sign on her head that said, *Off Duty*. "You know, as in, 'Don't ask me. I'm off duty."

That reminded me of my days working for the R.A.I. There, the popular expression then was, *Non lo so*, Italian for, *I don't know*. At R.A.I., if you answered a question like, "Where's the camera?", "Where are we shooting tomorrow?", or "Do we have any film?", with *Non lo so*, you were summarily relieved of any further responsibility in the matter.

A few days after Jerry's party, Dave Goelz presented each of the guests with a T-shirt emblazoned with, *Off Duty* in large block letters. One was also sent to Madeline.

The shirt became an instant hit. For about a week the entire staff of *The Muppet Show* was *Off Duty*. When I returned to New York for a visit, my wife immediately confiscated my shirt. Then, alas, she started wearing it to bed.

GEORGE BURNS

The grand old man of the second season of *The Muppet Show* was George Burns, one of the most gracious and charming men I ever met.

The year before, 1976, he had just had a big hit with the movie, *Oh, God!* One of the younger staff members asked him if that was his first movie.

Oh, no.", he responded. "Gracie and I made a bunch of films back in the 30s. Which just goes to show you, kid, you do something well and they ask you to come back."

George also revealed the secret of his acting success. "The director says, 'Stand up.', I stand up. If he says, 'Sit down.', I sit down. That's acting."

"But the most importing thing about acting is sincerity", he told me. "If you can fake that, you've got it made."

Judy Collins

Judy Collins trained as a concert pianist. During an interview, she revealed that when she practiced, she would prop a book up on the piano's music stand and read it while she ran her exercise scales! I've been playing piano on and off for sixty years. If I practice another 60 years, I'll never be able to do that.

Peter Sellers

If you can believe it, Peter Sellers claimed he wasn't funny. He said he was an actor and if there was something funny in the script he could make it work. He said his great fear at parties was that someone would ask him to be funny -- this from the man who invented Inspector Clouseau.

It was during Muppet Show rehearsals that Peter Sellers made his famous remark. When told he had to use his own personality in a Kermit interview piece, he responded, "I once owned personality. But I had it surgically removed."

I was fortunate enough to write a bit for Peter Sellers and Jim Henson. I've often described writing for the Muppets as loading the blunderbuss and pointing them in the general direction of the barn door. They may not always hit it where you expected. But they never missed.

The broad idea of the bit was very simple. A full-bodied Link Hogthrob (Captain of the Swinetrek), would be laying on a massage table. Jim would be under the table with his hand up through it to operate Link's head. The arms and legs would be stuffed like a rag doll.

Peter Sellers is a masseuse. He comes in to give Link a massage and in the course of it bends Link's arms and legs into impossibly painful positions while Link reacts. That's basically all I wrote – a simple exercise in sadism.

The comedy would come from Jim and Peter working out the physical stuff in front of a camera. I had loaded the blunderbuss and led them into the barn.

Jim had worked Link into a wonderful victim. But the real surprise came from Peter Sellers. He decided the masseuse would be played by the most evil, maniacal, sadistic German ever to appear in a "B" Nazi movie.

"Vell, it's time to limber up your nimble little body," he said with an evil grin. He proceeded to drop bar bells on Link, roll his legs up to his waist, rotate his arms 360 degrees, all the while saying, "Yah. I'll bet zat feels good." He finally tied Link completely up in knots and left him bellowing like a sick bull.

Rudolf Nureyev

Somehow, Jim Henson and Rudolf Nureyev got together and decided that when Mister Nureyev guest starred on *The Muppet Show*, he would dance a ballet with a pig. The piece would be called, appropriately, *Swine Lake*.

As the expression goes, this was much easier said than done. The pig ballerina costume had to be big enough to accommodate a real ballet dancer inside. (The job went to the smallest male dancer in the London Ballet.) It had to appear to weigh about 200 pounds more than Mister Nureyev while being as light as possible. Technically, the dancer inside had to breathe (Can't forget about that!). And, for the piece to work, the costume had to bend as flexibly as a real dancer.

Two master Muppet builders, Mari Kaestle and Rollin Krewson spent two weeks on the project. Firstly, they dragged out books on porcine anatomy to make sure that the pig puppet looked convincingly like a pig, with as many of the right porcine muscles in the right places as possible. And, it had to move, as much as possible, like a pig dancing a ballet. Then, they had to figure out what it would finally look like and how to build it. The finished product was truly a work of art.

In the mean time, fifty or sixty gallons of Coca Cola had to be ordered. Rudolf Nureyev's trade secret was Coca-Cola. He had it spread on the studio floor the night before shooting, so it would be nice and sticky when he danced.

While the Muppet workshop and studio crew were hard at work, the writing staff were working on the script. Normally, musical numbers were welcomed by the writers. They were three and a half minutes of the show that we didn't have to write. Usually, we stuck a page in the script that read something as erudite as "Music Number: Rudolf Nureyev dances with a pig.", which is exactly what I did.

Jerry Juhl called me into his office. "We can't send a script to the great Rudolf Nureyev with a page that just says, "Rudolf Nureyev dances with a pig."

"Rudolf pirouettes with a porcine?", I suggested helpfully.

"No," Jerry replied. "You have to give me at least a page or so of something. We have to look like we put *some* thought into it."

I was back at my desk when the realization hit me, *I'm creating choreography for Rudolf Nureyev.* The only thing I knew about dancers I had learned the hard way by dating the female of the species. Female dancers eat like field hands and go home early and alone.

And so I sat and pondered. I knew I was pretty good at writing for pigs. But ballet dancers were another story all together.

And then, like a beacon of hope on a far horizon, the solution came to me in one simple word: *perhaps.*

Perhaps, I wrote, Mr. Nureyev tries unsuccessfully to lift the pig/ballerina. Perhaps, instead, the pig/ballerina lifts Mr. Nureyev. Perhaps Mr. Nureyev can't get his arms around the pig/ballerina. Perhaps we can take the male dancer out of the costume, allowing Mr. Nureyev to spin the pig/ballerina around and throw it up into the air. Perhaps with a tape stop, we can drop the pig/ballerina onto Mr. Nureyev. And, when it comes down, perhaps it knocks Mr. Nureyev on his keister.

This went on for over a page and a half of script, which made Jerry Juhl very happy and, evidently Rudolf Nureyev as well.

The piece worked beautifully and is truly a Muppet Classic. And, perhaps, I even had something to do with it.

Chapter 37
Frank Oz

Frank Oz is probably one of the best known and least seen actors of the 20th Century. If you added up the time of Frank's on-screen appearances, you'd be counting weeks, if not months.

Artistically, Frank has performed a range of characters from the highly sophisticated: Bert on *Sesame Street*; Fozzie and Miss Piggy on *The Muppet Show*; and Yoda in *Star Wars*; to the neurotic Grover on *Sesame Street*; to the sub-human Cookie Monster and Animal the drummer. Being a bit of a revolutionary, I confess to having a special place in my evil heart for the last two.

Caroll Spinney, the Big Bird puppeteer, has been making and performing puppets since childhood. He's also a fine artist and designer. Caroll once told me that one secret of puppet design is controlling how intelligent the character appears. The more forehead and "brain" you give a character, the smarter he looks.

If you look closely at Big Bird, you see he does have a cranium. Granted, his bird "brain" is made of feathers. But, it's sufficient enough to get him into trouble.

My point about Cookie Monster is he has no cranium at all! He is a mouth with two eyes on top of it. He's an eating machine. He's pure id. Yet, over the years Frank has managed to create a gruff, loveable character, with a definite personality.

Cookie even has ethics. I wrote a story line that started when Mr. Hooper had to leave his store on some emergency. But the only one around was Cookie Monster and Mr. Hooper had a giant glass cookie jar, filled to the brim right behind the counter. Mr. Hooper asked Cookie to watch the store but had him promise he wouldn't eat any cookies.

In subsequent scenes he rhapsodizes about the cookies. But he doesn't touch one. However as he fantasizes about the cookies, he eats a frying pan, a stool, the cash register, and most of the counter. Mr. Hooper returns to find an absolutely empty store, except for the cookie jar and an enormously bloated Cookie Monster.

I always thought the Cookie Monster was one of the great secret weapons of *Sesame Street*. Through him, we showed the kids that we're really on their side, and they're not the only ones that have those *I've gotta have it right here, right now, Gimme! Gimme! Gimme! fits.*

Animal, if possible, is even less articulate than Cookie, Frank once told me he pictured Animal at a party over in a corner, making passionate love . . . to a lamp.

Frank, inadvertently, taught me two great lessons about writing for the Muppets. The first was illusionary.

Early in my *Sesame Street* career, I was watching a Bert and Ernie piece. As usual, Ernie had created an enormous mess in their living room. Bert entered and immediately began to complain about how messy the place was, *including the floor.* He pointed out several objects on it and "stumbled" over a few more.

What clicked immediately with me was that Frank Oz was completing the illusion. There is no "floor" in Muppet Land. But Frank was subconsciously creating one in the viewer's mind. Since then, I've carried a "floor" around in my bag of Muppet writing tricks. I used it in Kermit's "chewing gum" introduction, and Piggy's aerobic sketch. We also used it in the Helen Reddy show.

It also inspired one of my favorite backstage episodes, when Fozzie decided he was going to do his act on roller skates. The mechanics were simple: We'd stand Frank on a dolly while he manipulated Fozzie overhead. Another puppeteer, below the camera frame, would roll him around according to script direction. Roller skate sound effects were added later. We got four or five scenes out of it.

In the first few, Fozzie crashed quite badly, But, later on, he gets better. I envisioned him skating on one foot while holding his other leg straight up in the air. All that was required was the shop building a Fozzie leg with a roller skate attached to the foot.

Fozzie could even spin just by rotating the dolly beneath him. I also suggested in the script that a close-up of the foot spinning on its toe could be inter-cut as Fozzie's foot on the ground.

It worked beautifully. Another example of Muppet limitations turned into creative positives.

The other lesson came from Frank's personal approach to performing.

One afternoon, Don Hinkley and I were staring at the ceiling desperately searching for comedy. And, in walks Frank Oz. Frank is carrying two sheets of paper. They are typewritten, single-spaced, top to bottom, with very narrow margins.

On them, Frank has worked out Piggy's back story, e.g., what was Piggy's life before she joined *The Muppet Show*. Like any good actor, Frank was building substance into his character.

It's been more than three decades but I can still remember the main points in Piggy's back story. She grew up in show business. Her parents had a vaudeville act of some kind. So, show business is in her blood. Her parents divorced when Piggy was very young and she had an unhappy childhood. Now all she wanted was her career and her frog.

Ironically, a favorite Frank Oz story does not include puppetry. Although, it started with a puppet character. I saw Frank's name on the assignment sheet for a particular episode of *Sesame Street* that I was writing. Among Frank's lesser known characters was a wall eyed Muppet Keystone Kop. His name was Officer Krupky, a tip of the hat to *West Side Story*.

(Actually, there were many hat tips to the Broadway musical and movie. Jon Stone was a big Sondheim fan. If you look at the original *Sesame Street* set and the opening of the movie musical, it's pretty obvious *Sesame Street* is a West Side cul-de-sac, in the pre-Lincoln Center days of the late 1950s. We also had a young Puerto Rican girl named, "Maria," in our cast of characters.)

One of *Sesame Street*'s Instruction Goals was an area called, *Reasoning and Problem Solving*: Given a set of progressively revealed clues, the child can use those clues to arrive at the correct answer. It occurred to me that it might be fun to have Officer Krupky bumbling around Sesame Street looking for Maria to demonstrate it.

He starts in Hooper's Store. He has a picture of Maria and asks to speak to Mr. Hooper on *official business*.

"I'm looking for a Puerto Rican girl with black curly hair and dark eyes.", says Krupky.

He shows Hooper the picture. "Do you recognize this individual?"

Hooper identifies the picture as Maria. "Is there some kind of trouble?", he asks.

"Sorry, official business. Can't discuss it."

Outside the store, Krupky encounters Gordon and asks him the same questions with the same attitude, *in the line of duty*.

Gordon tells Krupky that Maria lives at 123 Sesame Street.

Maria exits 123. Krupky I.D.'s her from the photo.

"Are you Maria?"

"Yes, I am."

"Are you Puerto Rican?"

"That's right."

Krupky holds up a card with the word, "BESO" on it. (BESO, is another *Sesame Street* Instruction Goals: Spanish Language and Culture.)

"The guys down at the station house want to know what, *beso* means.", he asks.

Maria takes off his hat and kisses him on his bald head. "Beso": A nice big kiss."

"Aw, why do I get all the mushy assignments?", Krupky laments.

MUSIC BUTTON: Whaa-Whaa-Whaa.

When I got to the studio, the piece was already in rehearsal. I was stunned to see that Officer Krupky was being played by real, live Frank Oz, dressed in a New York City Police uniform. I learned very early in television that lowly writers don't interrupt production. And since Frank had the wardrobe, I knew that Jon Stone had okayed it and I wasn't going to win that argument.

Even odder, I had written the dialogue for a none too bright Muppet cop. But Frank, who has a police officer brother, was playing it with that unemotional monotone that state troopers use just before they ask you to get out of the car, *Sir!*

If you read the piece down from the top to just before Krupky produces the "BESO" card, the effect of a white cop (did I mention Frank is very white), with that attitude in an obviously minority neighborhood* was chilling.

The dialogue that sounded so harmless from the puppet took on a sinister ring with Frank's monotone as he asked the minority residents about a Puerto Rican girl with long hair named, "Maria."

But Sonya and Frank played the end beautifully for laughs. And the piece was a solid success.

When the piece was in the can, Bob Myhrum, who directed the episode, told me my writing was, "Pinteresque," the first and last time I was ever accused of whatever that is. I was so stunned I never asked who suggested substituting Frank for the Krupky puppet.

I've seen Frank do cameo parts and, not surprising, he's a solid actor. Catch him in *The Blues Brothers*. But I'll always remember that little piece of drama he brought to one episode of *Sesame Street*.

---

*Mr. Hooper is Jewish. He has counted to ten in Yiddish and been wished, "Happy Hanukkah" on a Christmas special.

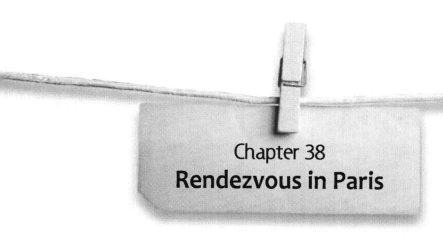

Chapter 38
Rendezvous in Paris

While I was writing *The Muppet Show*, my wife, Gail, was a producer/director for an international children's television show called, *Big Blue Marble*. So, while I was working in England, she was traveling the world, making documentaries with and about children in different cultures. The show took its name from a description and photograph of the Planet Earth taken by an Apollo 17 astronaut in outer space.

One night in the fall of 1977, I called Gail in New York as she was packing to go on the road again. As we spoke, she told me her travel itinerary. First, she was going to Spain to shoot an orphanage where the kids trained for and actually produced a circus. After that, she was going to Paris to film a kids' roller skating club that played basketball on skates to raise money for charities. After that, she was going to Casablanca to do a piece with Berber kids, and then on to Egypt.

During the conversation, she asked if she could take my camera equipment with her since the production company wanted still photographs of each segment. I had a fairly expensive 35 millimeter camera with a good selection of lenses. But, I wasn't thrilled about having it bounced around the world with my wife's film crew. I told her that my camera equipment rented for $50.00 dollars a day, a pig-headed move I would regret later on. Of course, she refused.

Later in the conversation, her travel dates came up and I realized that *The Muppet Show* would have a week-long hiatus during the same week that Gail would be shooting in Paris. Because of the strain and pressure of producing television, it's not unusual for shows to take a week off every six weeks or so. I decided right then that since I had the week off, we could rendez-vous in Paris. *Quelle Romantique!*

Originally, I decided to get to Paris by taking the Boat Train from London and then the ferry across the Channel, as they did in all those old 1940s movies. I had just bought a new trench coat at Burberry's and was feeling pretty Bogartesque. The Boat Train to Paris, *Quelle Romantique!*

But the English strike fever had crossed the Channel to France.

The French had their own unique strike tradition called, *faire le pont*, which means, "to make the bridge". The idea is to start a strike on a Wednesday or Thursday. The strike is usually over by Thursday night. But, what the hell, since we're out of work, let's *make the bridge* over Friday to le weekend.

Since I was 34 years old, and hadn't touched anything soft in six or eight weeks, I thought about how many unions were between me and Paris – and my wife: British Rail Union, British Steamship union, French rail unions, not to mention British and French emigration, immigration and custom inspectors' unions. So, I threw romance to the winds and booked myself First Class to Paris on Air France.

The last time I had flown from London to Paris, I had flown Air France Tourist Class. And just as French women are wont to show you a little leg or a little cleavage, Air France left the dividing curtain open just enough for me to see the champagne, caviar and fresh strawberries served in First Class. So, I vowed the next time I flew to Paris, I was going First Class.

The flight was wonderful. The champagne was cold and dry. The caviar and strawberries were fresh. The stewardesses were beautiful. And, we landed in Aeroport Charles de Gaulle, then the newest, most advanced and most beautiful airport in the world.

De Gaulle was a masterpiece of modern air transportation. People were shunted quickly from one locale to another on moving sidewalks that snaked through transparent tubes. There were signs in about a dozen languages. It was the model of mid-20th century airport efficiency. I was whisked efficiently from my plane to the baggage claim.

However, when I arrived at the baggage claim, I realized I was in the middle of a mid-20th Century airport strike. All that modern efficiency had been replaced with a hand written sign on a piece of old cardboard: *GREVE! STRIKE!* So, the unions had gotten me anyway. After a quick hour or so of investigation, I discovered my bag unceremoniously dumped on the sidewalk near the taxi stand.

Okay, it was still a rendez-vous in Paris. And now, it had a funny side story to go with it. Who knew it would be the first of many? I grabbed my bag and took a taxi to the hotel where Gail's production team had reservations. There I met Franca Tasso. Franca had worked for years at the Cinecittà, the premier film studio in Rome. Franca was Roman. Her father was Italian. But her mother was French. She grew up bouncing from one language to another. And Franca had studied English in university. She was one of the very few real people who could, as they only do in James Bond movies, jump effortlessly between three languages.

Once at dinner in Paris, I was seated next to Franca, who was deep in discussion in English with my wife. The waiter asked what I wanted for dessert and I ordered strawberries in French. The waiter corrected my mispronunciation of the French word for, "strawberries." I apologized to him in French and explained I had learned that word from an Italian. Immediately, Franca let me have it with both barrels in English for blaming my bad French on her.

Franca and Gail had previously worked together on a feature film in Europe. So, Franca was to be the translator on Gail's Paris production.

At our hotel bar, Franca's beautiful linguistic ability had gleaned the following information: When Gail flew to Madrid, Spain, the airline had thoughtfully sent her luggage to Denver, Colorado. So, Gail had been living in the same clothes for at least a week – *Quelle Romantique!*

Also, that same airline was now on strike. So, instead of flying to Paris, Gail would come from Madrid to Paris by train, a trip that couldn't take more than 12 or 14 hours. So, my wife arrived in Paris a half day late, still in her only outfit -- *Quelle Romantique!*

We retreat to our hotel room. But, even by French hotel standards, the room was so small that I couldn't resist doing Chet O'Brien's small hotel room jokes.

The up side of this is that since my wife's luggage had been sent to Denver, and she had no clothes, she was forced to go shopping in Paris. *Quelle domage!* Since production wasn't scheduled to start until the next day, Gail had a whole day to shop in Paris. I would say she was pretty successful. One pair of brown cord jeans she had bought in Paris fit her so well that a friend of mine remembered them fondly 30 years later.

Since serious production wasn't scheduled until the next day, we changed hotels for one with *slightly* larger rooms. So, I got to sleep with my wife in a room and a bed that would finally accommodate my 6'2" frame. At 7:30 the next morning, there was a knock on the door and Franca and five or six strangers streamed into the room. I pull the covers up to my neck like some bashful virgin. "Who are these people?!" I demanded.

Of course I had been in television long enough to know that every morning, a production meeting is held to determine what has to be shot that day, and how to go about it. And, since Gail was the producer, the meeting would be held in her room. However, when the production meeting is held in your bedroom with your wife, it gets a little personal.

So, to avoid future confrontations and to sleep a little later, after the crew left, I went down to the desk and asked the clerk for another room.

Typically French, he asked, "Don't you like the woman you're sleeping with?" It did occur to me that, this being Paris, he might have had a replacement in mind.

I replied that I liked her fine. It was her friends that were the problem. He gave me the room, but I don't think he believed me. He probably figured I had a second wife. This rendez-vous was beginning to feel like an episode of *The Muppet Show.* Gail was reduced to running up and down the hotel halls, much to the amusement of the chamber maids. *Quelle scandal!*

Most days while Gail and her crew were out shooting, I spent my time wandering aimlessly around the beautiful city of Paris. Then one night Gail asked me to go on the next day's shoot. The weather report looked good so she was planning on shooting all the scenic outdoor footage for her show. Since it was going to be a complicated day and the crew would be very busy, she asked me to go along as the still photographer.

The segment was scheduled to open with the basketball team roller skating in front of the Sacre' Coeur Cathedral at the top of Montmartre, then follow them down the ancient, narrow streets, past the markets and shops, along the Seine, ending up at the Trocadero.

There, they would meet up with another roller skating basketball team and play a game with the Eiffel Tower in the background. It was a photography buff's dream, to be driven through the most famous and beautiful sections of Paris with nothing to do but take pictures.

However, if you remember a certain pig-headed conversation I had on the phone with my wife back in London, you know that although I was in Paris, my camera equipment was safely stowed in New York. Instead, I was working with the production's camera, a fixed lens, snapshot Kodak with a fixed focal length of 10 feet. It probably retailed for all of $19.95.

I did the best I could. But most of the time I was framing up a very fast moving basketball game, while trying to hit the shutter when it was exactly 10 feet away. I did the best I could. But in my mind, I was composing the shots I could have taken with my own 35mm SLR Pentax. I did get one decent shot of the two basketball teams' centers on roller skates, facing off for the ball in front of the Eiffel Tower. But I know it could have been so much better.

And so went our Parisian rendez-vous: the bad pictures; the separate rooms; those intimate, candle-lit dinners for seven – not exactly the script I had imagined in London. It was all summed up very nicely in a postcard Gail sent me from Casablanca. Quoting Humphrey Bogart in the movie of the same name, it simply said, *We'll always have Paris.*

Chapter 39
Milton Berle

Milton Berle was such a seminal force of comedy, I had to give him his own chapter.

One usual rainy Sunday morning, I was suffering with a terrible cold and wondering how the hell I was going to be funny that day. Suddenly, the door to my office flew open and in marched Milton Berle.

Like many of the great old comedians who appeared on *The Muppet Show*, instead of waiting for the script meeting to meet the writing staff, Milton Berle made the writer's offices his first stop in the studio. As I would find out later, comedy was serious business with him.

There are showbiz legends about guest stars who abused or aggravated writing staffs. Don Hinkley told me that the old time writers would put their heads together and write a sketch that required the guest star to wear a chicken suit. The bit would always be very funny. But there's no way not to feel like an idiot in a chicken suit. And, they're hotter that Hades under the studio lights. But, Milton Berle was serious about his comedy.

"Here, kid. Have a heater.", he said, jamming an enormous Cuban cigar at me. I was so surprised, I opened it up and lit it. Now, I wish I had had it cast in Lucite.

"You think you're looking at an old Jew?", Berle asked. "Wait until George Burns gets here next week."

I damn near choked on the cigar.

Working with Milton Berle was an education in comedy. At the time I met him, he had already been in show business for more than 60 years. He started as a child actor in silent movies, moved on to vaudeville, night clubs and finally one of the first hit shows on television, *The Texaco Star Theater*. The show ran from 1948 to 1956, and earned Milton Berle the sobriquet, *Mr. Television*.

His show was so popular, a half million American families went out and bought television sets just to see it. *The Texaco Star Theater* regularly garnered 80% of the television viewing audience. It's been reported that the New York City Water Department could tell when the show cut to commercials – so many people went to the bathroom during the commercials that the water pressure dropped dramatically in New York City.

In 1951, NBC signed Milton Berle to an exclusive *30 year contract*, at $100,000 a year, just so he wouldn't work for anyone else. Most of that time was spent hanging out at the Hillcrest Country Club in Beverly Hills.

One day, I had lunch with Milton Berle in the studio canteen and explained my chagrin with television comedy: You write a skit, and then you wait weeks until production to see if it works. And then, it's weeks or months until it runs on the air and, finally, somebody laughs (or not). I was looking for some wisdom from someone who had done live comedy for most of his life. At the time, Milton was teaching a course in comedy at UCLA. I asked him what he was teaching his students.

"Say I'm playing Vegas. I tell the class that I always open with the same three jokes, or variations on them. I'll tell a middle of the road joke, something about my wife or my mother-in-law. Then, I'll do a mild political joke and then one that's slightly off color. Judging by the laugh I get from each joke, I know exactly which monolog to use."

"You've got three "A" monologs?", I asked him.

"Sure," he answered. "First you test the crowd. You don't want to do blue material to a room full of Methodist ministers. But you don't do kiddy jokes to a truckers' convention."

I've told that story to dozens of comedians. Most of them responded, "I do my "A" material, and if the audience isn't hip enough to get it, screw 'em." Those are the comedians whose names you've never heard, and never will.

In the writers' meeting, Milton announced that he wanted to work with the two old hecklers in the box, Statler and Waldorf. (named, by the way after hotel salads.) Milton Berle was famous for his heckler routines.

True to his reputation, Mister Television showed up with a pile of heckler jokes several inches high. Then he started working his way through it in rapid fire progression, one right after another. He continued for more than 20 minutes. Fortunately, Jerry Juhl got most of it down on tape. Here's a sample:

HECKLER

Berle!

BERLE

What is it?

HECKLER

When you were a kid, did you want to be a comedian?

BERLE

Yes, I did.

HECKLER

Well, what happened?

BERLE

I've got a good mind to punch you in the nose.

HECKLER

Please, not while I'm holding it.

BERLE

That's pretty funny.

HECKLER

Then you can use it.

BERLE

I don't need your material. I have a million good lines in the back of my head.

HECKLER

How come they never get to your mouth?

BERLE

If you don't stop heckling me, I'll have the usher take you out.

HECKLER

I don't go out with ushers.

BERLE

Will you stop putting me down?, I've been a successful comedian half my life.

HECKLER

How come we got this half?

BERLE

I'm not going to put up with you guys any more. I have a show to do and if I have to, I'm calling the police.

HECKLER

I don't blame you. You need all the protection you can get.

HECKLER

Hey, Berle!

BERLE

Now what?

HECKLER

Berle, I just figured out your style. You work like Gregory Peck.

BERLE

Gregory Peck is no comedian.

HECKLER

Well?

BERLE

Do you have anything else to say about me?

HECKLER

Only one thing, that you stand too close to the camera.

BERLE

How far away would you like me to be?

HECKLER

How about Cleveland?

BERLE

Since I came on, you have insulted me 25 times.

HECKLER

Oh, yeah? What's the record? ...

BERLE

You have the mind of a three-year-old.

HECKLER

Why? Do you want it back?

BERLE

Did you come in here to be entertained or not?

HECKLER

That's right.

BERLE

What's right?

HECKLER

I came here to be entertained . . . And I'm not.

BERLE
Oh, I'd like to see you get up here and be funny.

HECKLER
You first.

BERLE
I dare you wise guy. Why don't you come down here on the stage and entertain?

HECKLER
I should.

BERLE
Can you sing?

HECKLER
No.

BERLE
Can you dance?

HECKLER
No.

BERLE
Can you get laughs?

HECKLER
No.

BERLE
Then what can you do?

HECKLER
Just what you're doing.

> BERLE

You should be ashamed of yourself.

> HECKLER

I know. But I'm hoping nobody saw me come in.

> BERLE

Well, if you don't keep quiet, I'll have you thrown out and I won't let you see the rest of the show.

> HECKLER

Don't do me any favors.

> BERLE

Wait a minute. Are you trying to tell me I'm not funny, is that it?

> HECKLER

That's it!

> BERLE

I'll have you know I have a ready wit.

> HECKLER

Let me know when it's ready.

> HECKLER

Berle! Do I have time to go out and grab a bite to eat?

> BERLE

Yes. Why?

> HECKLER

You're pretty hard to take on an empty stomach.

> BERLE

I'll teach you to make a fool of me.

HECKLER

Who needs lessons?

BERLE

Does anybody want to buy my interest in this conversation?

The second sketch we had written for Milton Berle involved his being interviewed at the stage door by a gang of Muppet reporters. Basically, each reporter's question would be a set up line and Berle's answer would be the punch line. This instigated a lecture on the comedian's sense of laughter and the timing of a comedy routine.

Since vaudeville, when you had a comedy duo, straight man and a comic, the straight man was always the boss. He owned the act and he always got top billing. Think of Abbot and Costello, Martin and Lewis, Burns and Allen, Rowan and Martin.

In fact, the straight man would often change comics. The thought was that anyone could do the punch lines. After all the punch lines were funny. All the comic had to do was look silly in baggy pants and deliver them.

The straight man also controlled the timing of the act. That is the time between the punch line of one joke and the set up of the next one. It's difficult enough to come up with a good joke. But as good as it might be, a bad straight man could kill it simply by delivering the straight line to the next joke *before* the audience had finished laughing at the previous joke.

Conversely, if a joke bombed, the straight man had the option to move more quickly to the next joke, or skip it all together. So, the straight man had to constantly be aware of the audience's reaction.

Of course, many of the great comics who worked alone, like Milton Berle, Bob Hope and Jack Benny, still had complete control over the timing of their acts. Hope's "But I want to tell you . . .", for example, was a handy segue.

The problem arose when a solo stand up comic had to work live in an ensemble, say on a television or a radio show. Now, whoever delivered the straight line, usually an actor, had control over the timing of a laugh, not the comedian.

Berle contended that a good comedian knew the value of a joke and how long the audience would laugh at it. As Berle explained it, "They can only laugh for four and a half seconds. I timed it."

His fear was that the Muppet reporter would feed the next straight line too soon and kill the laughter. Even though *The Muppet Show* was taped and "sweetened" later, the laugh track could only go as long as the time between the joke and the next straight line. Berle was asking us to give him a "handle" on the joke, or control the laugh track until he thought the joke was laughed out. For example, a routine without a handle goes like this:

1st REPORTER

First straight line.

BERLE

First punch line.

(LAUGH TRACK)

2nd REPORTER

Second straight line.

BERLE

Second punch line.

The first joke laugh track can only run until the 2nd reporter's straight line for the second joke. So, he has the control of the sketch's timing, not the comedian.

Here's the same routine with a "handle."

1st REPORTER

First straight line.

BERLE

First punch line.

(LAUGH TRACK)

                              BERLE
Next question?

                          2nd REPORTER
Second straight line.

                              BERLE
Second punch line.

The "Next Question" line is the "handle". It allows Berle to control the length of the laughter and the pace of the bit.

Milton went on to explain that in the early days when he worked live without a studio audience, the laugh track was laid in as the show was broadcast. Berle had a little flicker light installed on the front of the camera. When the laugh track ran, the light flickered. When Berle thought the joke had run its course, he threw in a "handle", and the laugh track was faded out.

He then went on to explain how the great comedians were even more insistent when they worked with an inexperienced straight man.

"That's what Bob does. You work for Hope, he says, "Will you wait?" And Bob always has the next line. Did you ever work for Jack Benny? Did you ever see a Benny script? Benny has the next line and he will never trust anybody else".

Berle went on to map out Jack Benny's greatest joke. For those too young to remember, for 35 years, first on radio and then on television, Jack Benny had created a comedic persona for himself as the cheapest man on the planet. Thousands of jokes and sketches had been written around how Jack Benny hated to part with money, and how far he would go not to spend it.

The joke was first done in front of a live radio audience. It goes like this:

Jack Benny is walking down a deserted street. Suddenly, a robber with a gun jumps out at him and says, "Your money or your life!"

The joke has no verbal punch line. Benny just stood there with his arms folded and a frown on his face. Finally, someone in the audience catches on that the cheapest man in the world is on the horns of the greatest dilemma he has ever faced: His *money* or his *life?* Once the laughter started it never stopped. Milton Berle claimed the laughter went on for 35 seconds, an eternity in comedy.

There's a "topper" to the joke. After the laughter dies, the robber says, "Well? Well?" And Benny says, "I'm thinking. I'm thinking!" More laughter.

The danger with the joke, of course is that it depends on the audience catching on to Benny's dilemma. If the robber gets nervous, he might deliver the second line, "Well? Well?", before the audience catches on, in effect, killing the joke.

So, as Milton explained it, after the robber delivered the, "Your money or your life!", line, he was instructed not to deliver, "Well, well?", until Benny cued him by stroking his chin and saying, "Hmmmm." And that's how Jack Benny got a handle on the joke, and had full command of its timing.

We got one more lesson in comedy from Milton Berle on *The Muppet Show*. On Milton's television show, Texaco Star Theater, they had a running gag. Whenever Milton said, "make up", as in, "Why don't you two kids kiss and make up?", a weird character would run out of the wings, shout, "Make-up!" and hit Milton Berle with a giant powder puff. Sometimes it happened once a show, sometimes two or three.

We decided to resuscitate it for *The Muppet Show*, but with our own Muppet twist. When Berle said, "make up", a full sized Muppet monster would run out and hit him with a gigantic powder puff. Dave Goelz got appointed to play the monster.

We went into rehearsal. Milton Berle is standing at the center of the stage. Dave is standing next to him in a full sized rubber monster suit without the head. His tail is about four feet long and he can hardly move.

The cue is given. Berle says, "make up." Dave yells. "Make-up!" in his monster voice, waddles toward Berle and swipes at him with the gigantic powder puff. Dave hits Milton in the shoulder.

"Wait a minute!", says Berle. You're gonna hit me here?" He points to his shoulder. "Here isn't funny." He points to his face. "Here is funny. Here is funny. Here is funny. There isn't funny. You got that, kid? Let's try it again."

The cue is given again. Poor Dave stumbles toward Berle in the monster suit, and swats him on the chest with the gigantic power puff.

"Listen to me kid. I've been in show business for 60 years. (Pointing) Here is funny. Here is funny! Here is not funny! Let's try it again!"

This went on again and again until finally Dave managed to hit the sweet spot with the powder puff.

As I said, working with Milton Berle was a great lesson in the very serious business of comedy.

Chapter 40
The Sunglass Lady

Everyone seems to have a story about how civil the English are. And it's true. Instead of just giving directions, Londoners have been known to walk out-of-towners all the way to their destinations. They queue up automatically at bus stops and cash registers – "queue" being English for "line." Even their traffic signs are polite. The English version of, "Do Not Enter", is "No Entry, Please." So, here's my English civility story.

For some reason, shortly after I arrived in London, I developed a stye on my left eye lid. Never had one before and never have had one since. Maybe it was caused by a change of food or water. Maybe it was something I picked up on the trip over.

There's a plethora of folklore information on what causes styes. And now that I was in England, I had two folklores from which to choose. Whatever the reason, it wouldn't go away. It was irritating and ugly and I was getting tired of dealing with it. And, I hated the way it looked. Although most people probably didn't notice it, I felt like a leper.

Finally, I decide to get a pair of sunglasses to hide it. As you might imagine, sunglasses weren't anywhere near the top of my packing list as I was preparing to leave for London. And now that I was in London, I hadn't the foggiest idea of where to shop for sunglasses.

There was, however, what I referred to as an "all nite deli", close to my flat. It wasn't really a deli and it wasn't really open all nite. But, it was the closest thing in London to that hallowed New York institution. One of only two grocery stores that were open that late in the entire city of London, it did a brisk business all evening with new parents in need of milk for their babies. The taxis were parked two deep outside.

Since the "all nite deli" was also one of the few stores in London, open after 6:00 p.m., I decided to give them a shot for sunglasses. "Maybe", I told myself, "When London jetsetters impulsively decide to fly to the Riviera, this is where they go for a quick pair of sunglasses." I spent a good 20 minutes wandering around its aisles, but there were no sunglasses to be found. I also didn't see any suntan lotion and made a mental note to pass the good news along to Don Hinkley.

I finally gave up and decided to ask at the cash register, knowing how foolish I was going to look, asking for sunglasses with an American accent in the middle of London. It was, as usual, pouring rain outside.

When it was my turn at the cash register, I screwed up my courage and asked for sunglasses. As expected, I got the incredulous look from the girl behind the register. Then I heard a woman's voice from behind me with a very cultured English accent.

"Excuse me.", it said. "But would your need for sunglasses have anything to do with that stye on your eye?"

I turned around to see a compact woman of "a certain age." She was wearing sensible shoes, a classic tweed suit, a no-nonsense bun in her grey hair and carrying the ubiquitous, tightly rolled, black, no-nonsense umbrella. In short, she was a classic British matron right out of Agatha Christie.

I, on the other hand, was dressed in a T-shirt and bellbottom jeans. Since it was the 70s, I was all hair and beard. Looking back now, I was pretty scary looking. I told the woman that my need for sunglasses was indeed connected to my eye problem. But I assured here the need was just cosmetic and not medical.

"Well," she said, "I have a perfectly serviceable pair of sunglasses. And, I'd be more than happy to loan them to you. I don't live far from here."

I thanked her profusely and said it wasn't necessary. But, she insisted. I've always had trouble refusing anything to women old enough to be my mother. In truth, I've always had trouble refusing anything to women of any age. So, we left the deli and walked several blocks to a lovely tree-lined street. We stopped in front of a beautiful old Victorian.

"I'd ask you in.", she said. "But, it just isn't done, you know."

I assured her that I knew. And she entered the front door.

For a moment, my New York paranoia kicked in and I half expected to get sapped from behind and mugged. But she came out a few moments later with a perfectly serviceable pair of sunglasses and an envelope with her name and address on it.

"When you're finished with them, just put them in the envelope and pop them in the mail slot," she told me. Then she said good night and went into the house.

I used the sunglasses for several days until my eye cleared up. During that time I told everybody in the studio my sunglass lady story. The Americans couldn't believe it. The Brits couldn't understand what all the fuss was.

Figuring she must have children or grandchildren, I made sure when I returned the glasses I included every piece of Muppet literature and autographed photos I could get my hands on. And, for many years afterwards, we exchanged Christmas cards. Thank you again, Mrs. Victoria Owens.

Chapter 41
All That Jazz

I f it weren't for Jerry Nelson and Richard Hunt I would not have only starved physically in London, I would have starved culturally, too. Between the hours we worked and the distance between Borehamwood and London, proper, I had very little time to explore the city.

Additionally, until you know them, the Brits are a bit reserved. I had heard stories of people moving to a new neighborhood, dropping in at their local pub, and maybe after five years someone might strike up a conversation. I did meet one Brit who had moved but continued to go to his old neighborhood pub for several years afterward to socialize.

Since Jerry and Richard had been in London for the previous season of *The Muppet Show*, they had a handle on London night life. And, fortunately, like me, they were big jazz fans. So, every so often on a Thursday or Friday night, I'd get a call from them and a few minutes later, Richard's antique Ford Cortina would rumble up to my front door and the three of us would roar off into the London night.

One night we went to Ronnie Scott's, London's world famous jazz club. I forget who was performing that night. Suffice to say it was a jazz legend. But, before we got into the main room, we got to talking with a gang of musicians at the bar who knew Jerry and Richard. They got to telling stories about being on the road with "the Count," "the Duke" and "Diz." The conversation went on so long we never got into the main room to hear whoever was performing. (*How hip is that!?*)

On another night, the guys took me to a pub where there was a jam session between our A.T.V. studio orchestra and the studio orchestra at the BBC. Real musicians' jam sessions are wonderful experiences – musicians playing purely to entertain themselves and other musicians.

Years before, when I first moved back to New York, I tended bar at a formal, for want of a better word, jam session. It was the New York musician's holiday party. It was held on New Year's Day night, since most of them worked every other night during the holidays. Every New York jazz man and every Broadway show musician showed up and played that night. The party went on until about six in the morning. I would have worked for nothing. But not only did we get paid well, we also discovered that musicians are among the world's most generous tippers.

The session in London was exactly the same as that night in New York. Every musician shows up with his instrument. There's somebody at the door with a clipboard. The musicians check in with him and he puts them together into groups based on the instruments they play. The groups then form up and perform one after another.

This night, the pub was really rocking, right up to 11:00 p.m., when they rang the bell to announce closing time. In New York jam sessions, most musicians don't even show up until after eleven. But this was London with its arcane pub hours. But, "Not to worry," as Richard put it. The session would continue at a house party and we were invited. So, we got back in the old Cortina and roared off . . . somewhere.

You could hear the party a block away. And when we got inside, it got even better – live music, an elaborate buffet, a house full of artists, performers, dancers, musicians, all talking a mile a minute. The only thing that was missing, this being England, was cold beer. It broke my heart to see a dozen cases of Heineken stacked up against the kitchen wall -- *warm!*

So, I picked up two six packs, elbowed my way through the kitchen, opened the freezer and threw them inside. "Yank.", I explained to the puzzled crowd by the refrigerator. "I'll be back in 20 minutes. Twenty minutes later, I returned and retrieved my two six packs of cold beer.

I took them back to the living room and opened one. Shortly after a black guy approached me.

"You the Yank with the cold beer?"

"Yeah. Would you like one?"

I use the less P.C. expression, "black," because I could tell by his accent that he wasn't African-*American*. And, since he was asking for a cold beer, I could tell he wasn't African-*English*. I gave him a beer. It turned out he was a drummer. Then I asked, "So, where are you from?"

"Africa.", he replied.

"Wow! An *African-African!* Really!?"

"Yes. Why?"

"All the black guys I know come from Brooklyn.", I replied stupidly. (How *un-hip* is that!?)

"There's a lot of us there, you know.", he replied with a smile, before grabbing another cold beer and disappearing with an African-English chorus girl.

But the zenith of our London music quest had to be the night Jerry and Richard called to say that Stephane Grappelli was appearing at a club called, 100 Oxford Street.

For the uninitiated, Stephane Grappelli was one of the great jazz legends of the 20th Century. A jazz violinist, he first entered the limelight in the 1930s as part of the famous Paris Hot Club Quintet. Another member was the guitarist, Django Reinhardt. Together, they played up-beat, swing versions of the music of Gershwin, Cole Porter and other American composers. After World War II, they came to the States and toured with Duke Ellington.

Django Reinhardt was equally famous. A full-blooded gypsy, he had burned his left hand rescuing his wife from a fire in a caravan wagon. His third and fourth fingers were partially paralyzed. Yet, he re-taught himself the guitar and is still regarded as one of the best jazz guitarists that ever lived.

Reinhardt died prematurely in the 1950s. But Grappelli went on working into the 1990s. There isn't much more I can say about these two musical greats in print, except to urge you to go on-line and seek out them and their music.

As I said before, my father was a saloonkeeper and so I grew up in many of them. As an adult I went on to frequent more than a few more. But, 100

221

Oxford Street was the strangest club I've ever seen. It was located at 100 Oxford Street, downstairs in the cellar. Since it was a private club, there was a membership charge at the door. I still have my membership card somewhere.

The one main room was completely devoid of decor and furnished with the world's most uncomfortable metal tables and chairs. It had all the charm of a prison mess hall. Stranger yet, it seemed to be operated by two separate entities. Along one wall was a bar, where drinks could be purchased. Along the other wall was a counter that sold Chinese food.

Since there was no table service, after securing a table, you first went to the bar for drinks, brought them back to the table, and then went to the other side of the room for Chinese food. Everything was paid for in cash on receipt.

Then, the lights dimmed and the man, himself, appeared. Backed up by a band of impeccable young musicians, Grappelli swung his way through classics like, *I Got Rhythm, Night and Day, Honeysuckle Rose, Lady Be Good, Them There Eyes,* and *St. Louis Blues.* We stayed through two sets. It was a magical evening.

After the last set, I was speechless. Then Richard piped up ebulliently, "Let's go back stage and see him!"

"We can't do that.", I protested.

"Sure we can. We're the Muppets. We can go anywhere!"

Sure enough, Richard talked our way backstage and into Stephane Grappelli's dressing room.

Up close, Stephane Grappelli reminded me of my Italian grandfather. He was, in fact, half French and half Italian. He was most gracious. It turned out he was a big fan of the Muppets and told us how much he loved the show and tried to watch it wherever he was.

Jerry and Richard engaged him in a deep conversation about jazz history. But I was still dumbfounded. Then, I realized that, under my turtleneck, I was wearing a special *Muppet Show* t-shirt that had only been distributed to the staff and cast of the show.

MEMOIRS OF A MUPPETS WRITER

I took off my sweater and then the T-shirt and gave it to Stephane Grappelli. He lit up like a Christmas tree, thanked me profusely and announced he was going to wear it when he performed the following week at the annual Montrose Jazz Festival in Switzerland.

So, thanks to *The Muppet Show*, I got to give the great Stephane Grappelli the shirt off my back.

Chapter 42
Chicken Feed

Once a week, the writing staff was scheduled to have a lunch time meeting with Jim Henson in his office. It seemed like a good idea for the writers to get together with The Boss and kick around creative ideas. That's exactly what we did for the first two or three weeks of the season.

However, at the time, along with producing and performing in *The Muppet Show*, Jim was the sole proprietor of Henson Associates, a fairly large company with all the legal, administrative, and human resources problems that went with it. Besides the London production, the company was supplying puppets, costumes, props and puppeteers for *Sesame Street* from the New York headquarters.

Additionally, Bernie Brillstein, Jim's manager in Los Angeles, was lining up guest stars for the show and negotiating future projects. All together, Jim had about 40 highly professional business and creative people working directly for him. He handled it all with amazing grace and efficiency.

To say that Jim was stretched thin may be the understatement of the 20th Century. Since Henson Associates was operating in three different time zones – London, New York, and Los Angeles - Jim pretty much had to be available for business calls from 3:00 a.m. until 8:00 p.m. London time.

Very often, problems in Los Angeles, New York and other places had to be dealt with face to face. So Jim was a frequent flyer -- on the Concorde. The man had his own personal time zone. One year, Dave Goelz gave him a scuba diver's weight belt as a Christmas gift to slow him down. Jim returned it.

All of this meant that during our weekly meetings with Jim we mostly talked quietly among ourselves and ate grilled cheese sandwiches from the canteen while Jim fielded phone calls from various parts of the world. To get any value from our preciously short time with Jim, we suggested that our weekly meetings take place somewhere outside the studio.

A short way down the main street of Borehamwood was an Italian restaurant called, Bamfi's. And that's where we ended up with our weekly meeting with Jim. Of course, since this was *The Muppet Show*, things didn't work out exactly as planned. Bamfi's was the most disorganized restaurant any of us had ever seen. So, half of our meetings were spent flagging down waiters and straightening out orders. It was still better than meeting in Jim's office, but not much.

I was reminded of playwright George F. Kauffman's famous epitaph for a waiter: *God finally caught his eye.* We renamed the place "Fawlty Towers North," after John Cleese's BBC comedy about a dysfunctional country inn.

One of Jim's methods of dealing with writers was to throw out a subject and give them free rein to see what they could do with it. Usually, this worked out pretty well. It gave the writers a sense of what creative direction Jim was currently headed. After all, our job was to be a creative extension of him. And, as a writer, I thought Jim showed a lot of respect for my ability to just aim me in a direction and give me the freedom to run with it. This was typical Henson *modus operandus*.

A good example of this was a meeting about a Christmas album I wrote while I was working on *Sesame Street*. Jim said he'd like to do something that incorporated the story line from the *Gift of the Magi*. That inspired me to write a scenario where Ernie decided to get Bert a cigar box to keep his paper clip collection together. To do it, he traded his cherished rubber ducky to Mr. Hooper for a cigar box.

Meanwhile Bert decided to get Ernie a soap dish to keep his rubber ducky from falling into the tub. So, he traded his paper clips with Mr. Hooper for a soap dish.

On Christmas Eve, the two friends decide to open their presents.

As soon as Ernie unwraps the soap dish, Bert urges him to put Rubber Ducky in it. Ernie covers by urging Bert to open his present. As expected, Bert is thrilled with the cigar box until Ernie tells him it's for his paper clips.

There is an awkward moment until Mr. Hooper comes in with presents for Bert and Ernie. Of course, Ernie's present is his rubber ducky and Bert's is his paper clip collection.

When Bert apologizes for not having a gift for Mr. Hooper, Mr. Hooper replies that he got the best gift of all: seeing everybody getting exactly what they wanted for Christmas.

It's one of the most satisfying things I've ever written. Eventually, it also became part of the *Sesame Street* special, *Christmas Eve on Sesame Street*.

But, in this particular Bamfi's meeting, Jim said he wanted to try and get some live animals into the show. Immediately, Jerry, Don and I began studying our fingernails, searching for a waiter and evaluating ceiling moldings – anything to avoid Jim's eye. Animals are tough to write into comedy. At best, they stand there and do nothing. At worst, they're highly unpredictable and occasionally leave "deposits" at inopportune moments. Jim said he'd like to start with a cow, and Don Hinkley gallantly volunteered.

Don created a wonderful back stage story line with the cow. Watching Kermit deal with the frustration of having a cow back stage was very funny. The scenario then continued with Scooter making milk money jokes, Gonzo trying to date it and the Swedish Chef painting it up like a butcher's diagram while muttering something about barbeque.

Finally, Scooter tells Kermit that the Flying Zucchini Brothers, our hapless human cannon ball act, has decided to include the cow in its act. Kermit is just glad to get rid of it. But during the "good-byes" at the end of the show, Julie Andrews, the show's guest star turns to Kermit and sweetly asks, "Oh, by the way, Kermit, have you seen my cow?"

At that very moment, we hear a cannon go off back stage and something bovine flying through the air.

The cow episode was so successful that Jim decided he wanted a show with live chickens. Since Don had written the cow show, and Jerry Juhl was the head writer with much more important things to do, the chicken routine fell to yours truly.

My first thought was a story I had heard about Colonel Tom Parker, Elvis Presley's manager. On the occasions when the young Elvis couldn't make a performance at a county fair, he substituted an act called, *Colonel Parker's Dancing Chickens*.

The act consisted of two chickens, a record player and an electric skillet covered with straw. Depending on the tempo of the music, the good Colonel would set the skillet heat higher or lower. You get the picture. I suggested something along similar lines to Jim. But, he was too much of an animal lover to go along with it.

A few days later, I got a call from the production department that an animal trainer was downstairs with his trained chickens. I remember walking downstairs and thinking, "I'm auditioning chickens! This has got to be the nadir of my show business career!"

The chickens had a pretty limited repertoire. When bribed with corn, they could dance on one leg, turn around and move in one direction or the other. I went back to my office and dutifully wrote a sketch called, "Gonzo and His Dancing Chickens," a sort of paean to Colonel Parker, of whom I was now extremely envious.

Several weeks later, the shooting day for, "Gonzo and his Dancing Chickens," arrived. I had been hoping for a root canal or a mild heart attack, but no such luck. Around mid-morning, I got an emergency call from the studio floor manager. The chicken trainer had arrived. But somehow, his trained chickens had gone to that great Kentucky Fried Chicken in the sky! All the trainer had was a chorus of untrained, no talent chickens!

As I walked down the stairs, I thought to myself, "Whatever the career level *below* nadir is, this is it!"

Well, the only solution was to capitalize on Gonzo's unhealthy preoccupation with fowl in general, and give him a few lines while the chickens wandered around the stage. So, after a big fanfare and build up, the sketch reduced itself to Gonzo throwing lines at the chickens like, "Wow! Look at the legs on her!", and "Whatcha doin' later, chickie?"

Dave Goelz, who puppeteers Gonzo, wrung every bit of comedy he could out of it. For the next month, I ate nothing but chicken. And, whenever possible, I've avoided writing for animals ever since.

Chapter 43
Richard Hunt

I met the irrepressible Richard Hunt when I joined *Sesame Street* in 1973 when he was just 22. Coincidentally, my wife, Gail, knew him as a child when he hung out around the Tappan Zee Summer Theater and she was the General Manager. Richard Hunt left us much too soon at age 41. He died of that terrible disease, AIDS. It's public knowledge now that Richard was gay. But he was just one of many gay people who made major contributions to *Sesame Street*.

I had never thought of it before, but after I joined the show I realized that human beings feel an innate responsibility to educate our young. You would expect that of parents. But parent or not, straight or gay, that was the true spirit behind *Sesame Street*. And, Richard was a sterling example of that.

When Richard died, Jon Stone said:

"It's impossible to imagine a world without Richard. He came to us a wide-eyed eighteen year old and grew into a master puppeteer and inspired teacher. No one ever had a more manic love of the outrageous and absurd; no one could ever make me laugh the way Richard could. A generation has grown up absorbing Richard's art, and I have to believe that every one of them is a smarter, funnier, stronger, sillier, more generous person because of him."

Richard really could make Jon laugh like no one else. And that was dangerous because Jon had a rare disease that caused him to lose muscle control when he laughed – talk about your occupational hazards! So, when he directed the Muppets, Jon always kept a wheeled office chair handy in case of collapse.

One of Jon's favorite Richard Hunt stories happened while Richard was playing Gladys the Cow during a *Sesame Street* taping. Between takes, Gladys appeared on camera reading a copy of Variety, the show business newspaper. Gladys stopped, turned to the camera and said, *Nothing in here but cattle calls.*

Along with Gladys, Richard's other *Sesame Street* characters were half of the Two-Headed Monster (with Jerry Nelson), Sully, the silent sidekick of Biff (also Jerry Nelson), Placido Flamingo, Forgetful Jones, and Don Music, the manic composer who had Joe Raposo's picture on his wall. (Little inside *Sesame Street* dope, there.)

Richard also played the back end of the Snuffle-upagus, Big Bird's imaginary friend. Jerry Nelson played the front, of course. In 1973, the Muppets won an Emmy for their performance on *Sesame Street*. At the celebration, we kidded Richard mercilessly about winning an Emmy for playing the arse end of a Snuffle-upagus.

On *The Muppet Show*, Richard performed Scooter, Statler (the old man in the right of the box), Janice, the Electric Mayhem's guitarist, Bunsen Honeydew's assistant, Beaker, and Sweetums, the walk-around monster.

I've told you how much fun Richard was on the Queen Elizabeth II and about his and Jerry's generosity toward me when I first got to London. But there are three more Richard Hunt stories I would like to relate.

Richard was the unofficial tour guide of *The Muppet Show*. Whenever we had visitors, Richard would take them in hand, show them the studio, the shop, and put on his characters and perform for them. One day, a class of blind children were touring the show. I walked into the shop to see Richard performing Scooter for them. Scooter was talking to one pretty little blonde girl of eight or nine.

Here, feel my face. Here's my nose. Cute, isn't it. Be careful of my eye! And, what do you think of my jacket? Pretty cool, huh?

The little girl and her friends were giggling uncontrollably. The memory of that is always the first thing that comes to mind when I think of my dear friend, Richard Hunt.

When Jerry Nelson married his lovely wife, Jan, on the beach in Truro, Massachusetts in the summer of 1984, Richard "officiated" at the ceremony in his persona of Reverend Richie of the Church of the Holy Mackerel. Since Jan and Jerry had really married the day before in the Truro Town Hall, the "showbiz" marriage was all classic Richard, written by Richard and Jerry.

The sham ceremony ended with a champagne toast by the Reverend Richie, which ended up with Richard saying something like, "You will be shelter unto each other and feel no rain."

Just as the toast ended, the skies opened up and it started to pour. A tent had been set up for the reception. You could see dozens of guests, dressed in summer finery, simultaneously realize that the tent was too far to reach, even at a dead run. So, we all just stood on the beach in the pouring rain and continued toasting the bride and groom.

The Muppet Show work week usually ran from Sunday to Thursday. On those Thursday nights, I realized there were two types of reactions to creative exhaustion. Some of us, after a hard week, just went home and collapsed. Others of us were so wound up and full of adrenalin, we had to go out and blow off some steam. I, of course, belonged to the latter group.

One Thursday night, Richard, Jerry, myself, and several others piled into Richard's ancient Ford and went rumbling up to Hampstead Heath. We were on our way to an Italian restaurant which had been highly recommended. Good restaurants that didn't require reservations days in advance were hard to find in 1977 London.

The place was small, dark and extremely cozy. The tables were placed close together. The crowd was very friendly and informal, especially for Brits.

It didn't take long before Richard became an informal master of ceremonies and turned the entire place into a party. Richard, without the encumbrances of a puppet, loved to entertain. And he was really "on" that night.

Richard did his John Travolta, *Saturday Night Fever* disco impression. He did his Robert De Niro *Taxi Driver* (Are you talking to me?). He led a sing-a-long of English music hall songs in a cockney accent. I vaguely remember several patrons dancing on tables at this point.

Throughout the evening a young couple, right out of Hollywood central casting, were seated next to us. He was handsome. She was very pretty. Of course, Richard immediately included them in his lunacy, dancing with her and turning him into a straight man.

At the end of the evening, as we were leaving, the couple took Richard aside. Surprisingly, they told him the reason they had gone out to dinner that night was to discuss the terms of *their divorce*. However, they had had such a wonderful time together with Richard that they had decided to reconcile. It wouldn't surprise me at all if their first born son was called, Richard.

Chapter 44
Christmas Eve on Sesame Street

I n 1978, I returned to New York from London for personal reasons: My father had died in late 1975 and, as an only child, it was difficult to deal with the details and take care of my mother from London. The Muppets were gracious enough to let me continue to write for the show from New York.

One day in July 1978, I ran into Jon Stone on Lexington Avenue. Jon had just gotten the go-ahead to produce a *Sesame Street* Christmas Special, and asked me to co-write it with him. I agreed and a deal was made.

The show was eventually called, *Christmas Eve on Sesame Street.* The premise was beautifully simple, as most good premises are. Question: How does big, fat Santa, *with* his big bag of toys, get down those skinny, little chimneys?

Just to add a little anxiety to the mix, we had Oscar pose the question to Big Bird. When Big Bird replies he doesn't know, Oscar tells him, *Well, you'd better find out. Because if you don't, there'll be no you-know-whats under the tree on Christmas morning. Heh! Heh! Heh!*

Since Jon hated going to the office, we wrote the script in Jon's 42nd floor penthouse on the Upper West Side of Manhattan. It's a little disconcerting going crosstown in the middle of the torrid New York summer and thinking about Santa Claus and Christmas carols. We took our breaks on Jon's terrace, checking out the sunbathing women on the roofs below with Jon's telescope.

I had experienced a little of this in advertising because Christmas advertising is usually finished by Thanksgiving. I came close to missing Easter a couple of times because we had finished Easter advertising weeks before and had moved on to Mother's Day. I knew a set designer who refused to have a

Christmas tree at Christmas. He spent every fall doing nothing but decorating Christmas trees for T.V. commercials.

The first few days of writing, as usual, were spent on generalities. The main story line had to be worked out. We knew the start. And, we knew it would have a happy ending. But, we had no middle. And, because of the *Sesame Street* format and pacing, we needed several other elements.

One thing Jon wanted to include was the three part, Bert and Ernie Gift of the Magi story I had written for the *Sesame Street* Christmas album. And, we knew we had to involve kids. Kids love watching kids on television. We also knew we needed music. We had a list of *Sesame Street* Christmas songs. But, who was going to sing what?

So, much more navel gazing was still required. In the meantime, we started to build the show's outline. We set up a bulletin board and got a stack of 3 X 5 cards. Eventually, we would have a 3 X 5 card for each scene pinned on the board. But to start, we literally had two cards on the board with a lot of space in between. The top one said, *OPENING SCENE*. The bottom one said, *CLOSING CREDITS*.

And so, we started. Looking back, it's difficult to say exactly who wrote what. I do know that Jon was better at writing "heart" while my comedy forte' runs more to explosions. We were a pretty good team.

Since we knew we would be using the Bert and Ernie, *Gift of the Magi* story, we made up three 3 X 5 cards:

B&E "GIFT OF THE MAGI" PLOT I

B&E/HOOPER "GIFT OF THE MAGI" PLOT II

B&E/HOOPER "GIFT OF THE MAGI" PLOT III

But, we put the cards on the side of the bulletin board, since we had no idea, yet, where they would go in the script. We made a card for each of the songs we were going to use and pinned them on the side, too.

Then we started refining the main story line about Big Bird, Santa and the chimneys. After Oscar gets him started, Big Bird teams up with a little girl named, Patty. Patty gave us a child in a major role who could also function as Big Bird's, "Tonto." "Tonto" is writers' slang for the hero's sidekick. Tonto is valuable because, as the hero talks to him, the hero's thoughts are revealed to the audience.

Patty and Big Bird go ask Kermit if he knows how Santa gets down those skinny chimneys. Kermit doesn't know but suggests they go ask some kids since nobody knows more about Christmas than kids. Along the way, they meet Mr. Snuffle-upagus. And, since he's big, like Santa, they talk him into getting into a chimney-sized barrel with predictable results.

That didn't work and the kids weren't any help either. It starts getting dark and cold, so Big Bird sends Patty home. But, it's Christmas Eve and how is Santa going to deliver all those toys?

Then Big Bird has one of his not-so-bright ideas. He decides to go up on the roof, wait for Santa and see how he gets down the chimney.

But it's a long wait for Santa, and Big Bird falls asleep. Down on Sesame Street, the gang discovers Big Bird is missing and they panic. While the rest of the cast is frantically searching for Big Bird, he's asleep on the roof and in very real danger of freezing.

But, he's having a wonderful dream about sleighs and reindeer landing, and a big, jolly man in a red suit walking right up to him and touching him on the nose. Big Bird wakes up. There's nobody there. Was it real? Or, was it a dream. What is real is how cold it is. *I think I froze my giblets!*, Big Bird says as he goes downstairs to warm up.

Everyone is glad to see Big Bird safe and sound. But, he still doesn't know how Santa gets down the chimney. Then Gordon takes Big Bird over to their tree, which is carpeted with presents. Gordon explains it's not important how the presents got there. What's important is that they did and that Big Bird is back safe and sound for Christmas.

Then, Oscar walks in. *Listen, you big canary. How do you think the Easter Bunny can hide all those eggs in one night?*

As the story line solidified into scenes, we wrote up a 3 X 5 card for each scene. We added the cards to the others on the side of the board.

I do remember having an idea about Cookie Monster trying to write to Santa Claus for some Christmas cookies. He starts with a pencil. But as he rhapsodizes about what kinds of cookies he wants, he unconsciously eats the pencil. His next try, with a typewriter, isn't any better. He eats the typewriter. Finally, he calls Santa and actually gets him on the phone. But then he eats the phone. Finally, Gordon tells Cookie that he doesn't have to write to Santa. Santa knows to bring him cookies. But, it's traditional to leave a gift for Santa.

Cookie suggests leaving a neck tie for Santa, or maybe some shaving cream. When Gordon tells him the traditional gift for Santa is milk and *cookies*, Cookie Monster faints away.

So, we made a card for each of those scenes and added it to the board. So far, we've worked for a week or ten days and haven't written a word of script. It's all structure.

But now we had five musical numbers, three Bert and Ernie/*Magi* scenes, four scenes of Cookie writing to Santa, and 13 scenes from the major story line, we could start building the show.

We laid out the main story scenes and spaced them apart. Then, we inserted our "B" story lines' scenes in between them. This gave the show the pacing and "feel" of *Sesame Street*. Finally, we found places for our musical productions.

Now we could step back and view the show as a whole. We could get a sense of whether or not main story scenes were separated by too much other material. We could test the timing of the "B" stories' scenes. And, because each musical number's 3 X 5 card carried a musical note on its upper left hand corner, we could see how well the music was spaced throughout the show.

Both Jon and I could stand by the board, point to each 3 X 5 card and describe each scene in order of appearance and describe the show in detail from start to finish. As we did, we continued to refine the story. Changes were made. Punch lines improved.

The final outline looked like this:

Christmas Eve on Sesame Street Outline

1. SKATING PARTY
    Intro Cast/Xmas
    B.B. ballet with little girl: "Feliz Navidad"
    (You can do it if you try)
    B&E/COUNT/COOKIE. jump the barrels
    KID out-spins ADULTS
    CRACK THE WHIP/OSCAR'S EXIT

2. OSCAR SETS UP "SANTA/CHIMNEY" PLOT

3. TRAVELING HOME Song: *True Blue Miracle*

4. KERMIT/B.B./PATTY "SANTA/CHIMNEY" PLOT

5. B&E "GIFT OF THE MAGI" PLOT I

6. MUPPETS AND KIDS EXPLAIN SANTA'S ENTRY

7. BOB/LINDA/KIDS Song: *Keep Christmas With You*
(Self-contained story line Bob and kids surprise Linda, who is deaf, by singing the song and accompanying it with a sign language)

8. B&E/HOOPER "GIFT OF THE MAGI" PLOT II

9. GROVER & BILLY

10. COOKIE WRITES TO SANTA I.

11. B.B/KERMIT/PATTY RESULTS OF KIDS' SURVEY

12. COOKIE WRITES TO SANTA II.

13. B.B./PATTY/SNUFF IN CHIMNEY

14. OSCAR Song: *I Hate Christmas!*

15. B&E/HOOPER "GIFT OF THE MAGI" PLOT III.

16. COOKIE WRITES TO SANTA III.

17. B.B./PATTY NEST. B.B sends Patty home. He decides to take action.

18. GORDON/PATTY -- B.B.'s gone!

19. B.B. ON THE ROOF

20. PEOPLE ON THE STREET/B.B. ON THE ROOF

21. PEOPLE ON THE STREET/B.B. ON THE ROOF/MARIA & OSCAR

22. B.B. ON THE ROOF. SANTA WAKES HIM UP

23. B.B. IN HALL AND GORDON'S APT. RESOLVE "SANTA CHIMNEY" PLOT. OSCAR'S "EASTER BUNNY" BUTTON

24. FINALE Keep Christmas With You

25. COOKIE. TREE/CREDIT

Even though I was his writing partner, I always believed that Jon, the ultimate showman, always kept a few ideas to himself and quietly included them into the final production. That meant that even at the first screening for the cast and crew, there would be some surprises. True to form, there were some wonderful surprises in the final version of *Christmas Eve on Sesame Street*.

I knew that we had scheduled a skating rink and human-sized Muppet characters with skaters inside for the opening scene. But, since it had no dialogue, I didn't give it much thought. As I said before, writers love musical numbers. They simply write, OPENING MUSICAL NUMBER, and that's four minutes or so they don't really have to worry about. To be honest, I did give Jon one punch line. More on that later.

Out of curiosity, I went to the skating rink on the day of the shoot. I knew it was going to be a major production. And you can always learn something by watching major productions. The OPENING MUSICAL NUMBER turned into a series of wonderful vignettes.

The opening master shot of the skating rink immediately set the tone and spirit of the show. The rink was decorated for Christmas. Along with some extras, the entire cast of the special, dressed for the holiday, were skating to Jose Feliciano's *Feliz Navidad*. Gordon and Susan, David and Maria Bob and Linda, Mr. Hooper, Bert, Ernie, Count Von Count, Cookie Monster, and Oscar in his trash can, with only his little furry green legs showing underneath, all skated past the camera.

Next, the piece segues into a small ballet where a little girl coaxes Big Bird into overcoming his fear and daring to ice skate.

One of Jon's favorite children's television tricks was to have a child teach something to an adult. He said kids love watching that.

Then we had the Count counting the barrels as Cookie Monster jumped over them.

Next, was a child teaching an adult to spin on skates. (See two paragraphs above.)

The final, *Crack-the-Whip* segment with the skating Muppets was pure Jon Stone. I'm sure you've seen it dozens of times. Skaters form a line from the center of the rink toward the outside and skate around the rink. As more and more skaters join the line, those at the outside end have to skate faster and faster. The line continued to extend. The last to join it was Oscar in his can.

Around and around the line spun. Usually what happens is the last skater on the line breaks off. But not this time. Oscar was spun around and around until he let go and flew into the air and through an exit door.

Then came the Stone touch. Oscar's can banged, clanged, bounced and ricocheted its way down what seemed like a never-ending stair case. It seemed like the fall lasted forever until Oscar, *en can*, came crashing out onto the street.

As Oscar struggles to his feet, Big Bird enters and asks if he's okay.

Inside Skinny: My original line to Jon for Oscar, which was recorded, was, *Sure. I've been thrown out of better places than that!*

During post-production editing, someone found the line too adult. So, Caroll Spinney came in and over-dubbed, *Sure! Let's go back and do it again!* (You be the judge.)

The other wonderful surprise was a series of interviews between Grover and several very vocal three-year-olds.

First of all, Frank Oz, Grover's puppeteer has, among his many, many talents, the ability to mystically engage children. Kids totally believed in Grover and ignored Frank, who was only a foot or two away.

Of course, the question was also intriguing: *How does big, fat, Santa Claus, with his big, fat bag of toys, get down those skinny, little chimneys?*

No kid ever thinks about this problem. Nor, has any kid ever wanted to think about this problem. The kids' rationalizations were wonderful! Everything from, *He squishes!*, through, *He ties the reindeer's antlers with tape*, to, *He comes through the door with his Santa Claus keys!*, was delivered with amazing sincerity.

Of all the projects Jon Stone and I worked on together, *Christmas Eve on Sesame Street*, is, hands down, my favorite.

Shortly after the special was finished, I re-joined the *Sesame Street* writing staff and remained for another three seasons.

Over the next 15 years, Jon and I worked together on many scripts, including two other Sesame Street specials: *Big Bird in China*; and *Big Bird in Ireland*, which, because of Jon's fatal illness, was never produced. We also wrote *Sesame Street Live!* road shows, as well as other *Sesame Street* and Muppet projects.

Chapter 45
Sesame Street Live!

During the early 1980s, Jon Stone and I wrote several *Sesame Street* traveling road shows. These were live performances with dancers in full sized *Sesame Street* Muppet costumes and pre-recorded audio tracks. The casts consisted of the most popular *Sesame Street* Muppets: Big Bird; Oscar; Bert and Ernie; Grover; Cookie Monster; backed up with some lesser known characters and new ones created especially for the shows.

There were two creative problems associated with these scripts. Firstly, it's almost impossible for two- and three-year-olds to sit still in a theater seat for over an hour. And secondly, like all good children's theatre, the parents also had to be entertained. Word-of-mouth is crucial to the success of any theatrical production. And in our case, word-of-mouth is spread by the parents.

(There was a third problem initially: In the first script, we created a ten minute. energetic, Keystone Kops opening number with characters dancing frantically all over the stage and up and down the aisles. Then, the producers told us, in no uncertain terms, that the costumes were made mostly of styrofoam and rubber and didn't breathe very well. So, if you make the cast members dance in them for that long a time, they die. So, we didn't do that anymore.)

To solve the first problem, we wrote the scripts with as much audience participation as possible. So, we peppered the scripts with urges to sing-a-long with familiar songs from the show, as well as songs with physical participation: clap your hands; stomp your feet; point your fingers; pat your head. We also encouraged the kids to count to ten and recite the alphabet (especially if a character couldn't) and included "pretending" bits like playing an imaginary instrument, or flying.

Additionally, we would write audience participation directly into the script. One show we wrote, *Big Bird's Super Spectacular Totally Amateur Show,* opened with the cast staring directly at the audience. They talk among themselves about how there was supposed to be a show here today. Then someone suggests maybe the kids are going to do the show for them. So, they ask the kids, forcing the audience to tell them that they are supposed to do a show for *them.* Big surprise!

We also did a lot of one character searching for another. The searcher would ask the audience if they had seen the "searchee," who would cross behind the searcher and duck out of sight just before the searcher turns around. With multiple costumes and hand puppets, we could make the "searchee" pop up all over the theater. "There he is! There he is!", the kids would scream.

"Oh, no he isn't!", the searcher would respond. This, of course would start the call and response, "Oh yes he is!" "Oh, no he isn't!" "Oh, yes he is!" It never failed.

To keep the parents interested, we always included some grown-up material for them. The pieces were visual and noisy enough to keep the kids interested. But, we were never sure how much they really understood.

Puns were and are a great part of the Muppet repertoire. We all loved them. Of course, they're corn ball. But, the kids get some of them, and if you jam 20 or 30 of them together, most adults have to laugh, too. Think of the *At the Dance* sketches on *The Muppet Show.*

In its early years, *Sesame Street* had a series of segments called, *People in Your Neighborhood.* It was basically designed to help kids recognize the tradesmen and professionals around them and explain their raisons d'etre. (Bear with me. You don't get to use raisons d'etre very often writing for children.)

Muppets done up as various members of the community would enter and sing about their jobs. We had a song called, *People in Your Neighborhood,* and each character got a verse of his own. In between the verses, the Muppets would do outrageous puns about their jobs. So, in one of the shows, for the edification of the parents, we wrote the following:

This is a big production number with a MUPPET EMCEE, FEMALE LETTER CARRIER, DOCTOR, FIREMAN, FEMALE STUDENT, HOUSE PAINTER, GROCER, BAKER and CARPENTER.

After the opening chorus:

EMCEE

Say, you must be the letter carrier.

FEMALE LETTER CARRIER

Yes, do you know the difference between a donkey and a postage stamp?

EMCEE

No. What's the difference between a donkey and a postage stamp?

FEMALE LETTER CARRIER

One you *stick* with a *lick* and the other you *lick* with a *stick*!

EMCEE

That's really a *third* class joke.

DOCTOR

Oh, *letter* alone.

FEMALE LETTER CARRIER
(SINGS)

EMCEE

Aren't you a doctor?

DOCTOR

I used to be a doctor but I lost my *patience*!

EMCEE

That's too bad.

DOCTOR

Oh, I didn't mind, they were all *pills*!

DOCTOR
(SINGS)

SESAME STREET LIVE!

                    EMCEE
And what kind of person are you?

                    FIREMAN
Does fireman ring a *bell*?

                    EMCEE
Fireman - bell. That's a *hot* one!

                    FIREMAN
Axe me that question again.

                    EMCEE
Okay. What kind of person are you?

                    FIREMAN
That question really *burns* me up!

                    EMCEE
So, you're a student. What are you studying in school?

                    STUDENT
Porpoises and mackerel.

                    EMCEE
Porpoises and mackerel?

                    STUDENT
Yes. It's a *school of fish!*

                    EMCEE
That joke gave me a *haddock!*

                    STUDENT
                    (SINGS)

EMCEE

You must be a house painter.

HOUSE PAINTER

Overall, I'd say, "yes." And, do you know what we say when we've finished painting?

EMCEE

No.

HOUSE PAINTER

Now, that is a *house* of a different color!

EMCEE

Ouch! I'll see you *ladder*!

FIREMAN

I'll do the ladder jokes if you don't mind!

HOUSE PAINTER
(SINGS)

EMCEE

Oh, you're the grocer. I know all about that.

GROCER

I'll bet you don't know *beans* about it.

EMCEE

You just mind your *peas* and Qs.

GROCER

Lettuce not get into a *pickle* over this.

EMCEE

Enough with the *corny* jokes. Sing.

GROCER
(SINGS)

EMCEE

Say, you must be the baker.

BAKER

Yes. But I *donut* want to *loaf* around here all day. I *knead* to get *rolling* back to the bakery.

EMCEE

You seem to work very hard.

BAKER

It keeps me in the *dough*.

EMCEE

You really take the *cake*!

BAKER
(SINGS)

EMCEE

You're a happy looking carpenter. You must like your work.

CARPENTER

I give it my *awl*.

EMCEE

I *saw* that one coming.

CARPENTER

I hope you weren't *board* by it.

EMCEE

It was pretty *tacky*.

CARPENTER

Well, I'd better be *lumbering* along.

CARPENTER
(SINGS)

The entire company sings the finale.

Go ahead and groan..

My favorite child/adult road show sketch involves one of my favorite Sesame Street characters, Grover Monster. Grover is the skinny, blue monster, performed by Frank Oz, with the high pitch voice, who wants only to be loved. Grover is probably the most neurotic character ever to appear on children's television.

Occasionally, Grover appears as one of his alter egos such as Super Grover, the useless super hero. He also appears as Marshall Grover, complete with over sized ten gallon hat and fuzzy chaps. Of course, no great western hero is complete without a faithful steed. Grover's is Fred the Wonder Horse, played by Jerry Nelson. Fred is as laconic and laid back as Grover is frenetic. They roam the deserts and plains of the Old West, accomplishing absolutely nothing.

This piece takes place on a proscenium stage. As Big Bird makes his introduction, Fred gallops back and forth across the stage and into the wings with a dummy Grover hanging on for dear life.

BIG BIRD

From out of the west, with the speed of light, comes the thundering hoof beats of the great horse, Fred!

MARSHALL GROVER

Aaaaaaaaaaaaaaaaaaaaaaaaaaaaaaaaaaaaaaaaaaaaaaaaa-ahhhhhhhhhhhhhhhhhhhhhhhh!

BIG BIRD

. . . And, the daring and resourceful blue rider of the plains, who led the fight for . . .

MARSHALL GROVER

Fredeeeeeeeeeeeeeeeeeeeeeeeeeeeeeeeeeeeeeeeee!

BIG BIRD

. . . law and order in the Old West. Return with us now to those thrilling days of yesteryear . . .

FRED AND GROVER RACE OFF STAGE.

MARSHALL GROVER

Whoooooooooooooooooooa! Freeeeeeedeeeeeeeee!

OFF STAGE CRASH!

BIG BIRD

Marshall Grover rides again!!!

BIG BIRD EXITS

ENTER FRED WITH A LIMPING GROVER BEHIND HIM.

MARSHALL GROVER

Oh, Freddy, watch those sudden stops. (TO AUDIENCE) Well, howdy, buckaroos! It's your old side kick, Marshall Grover! How are you today? . . . Good, because we're going to have a real rooting-tooting time!

FRED BUTTS GROVER FROM BEHIND

MARSHALL GROVER

Oh, yes! And this is Fred, the Wonder Horse. Take a bow, Fred.

FRED CURTSIES.

MARSHALL GROVER

Now, do you know what we're going to do for our part in Big Bird's Amateur show?

FRED THE WONDER HORSE

No, I don't, Marshall.

MARSHALL GROVER

Of course you don't. That is why I am the Marshall and you are the horse. We are going to do a dog act.

FRED THE WONDER HORSE

Marshall, do yuh really think yuh can pass yuhself off as a dog?

MARSHALL GROVER

Not me, Fred! You! I will give the commands, and you, Fred the Wonder Horse, er, Dog, will do what I tell you.

FRED THE WONDER HORSE

Oh, for Pete's sake . . .

MARSHALL GROVER

Here we go. On my command . . . SIT!

FRED THE WONDER HORSE

Horses don't sit.

MARSHALL GROVER

SIT! SIT!

FRED THE WONDER HORSE

Okay. Okay. (TO THE WINGS) Anybody got a chair back there?

SOMEONE CARRIES OUT A CHAIR.

FRED THE WONDER HORSE

Thanks. I hate sitting on a cold floor.

FRED'S BACK HALF SITS ON THE CHAIR. THE FRONT HALF SITS ON THE BACK HALF'S LAP AND CROSSES ITS LEGS CASUALLY.

MARSHALL GROVER

Very good, Fred, the Wonder Dog. Now, for his next trick, Fred, the Wonder Dog, will speak. Ready, Fred? SPEAK!

FRED THE WONDER HORSE

What do yuh want me to say, Marshall?

MARSHALL GROVER

Sometimes I wonder why they call you Fred, the Wonder Horse. We are doing a dog act. You are playing the part of the dog. When I say, "speak", you go, "bow-wow."

FRED THE WONDER HORSE

Aw, Marshall Grover, couldn't I just whinny or recite an Emily Dickenson poem or something?

MARSHALL GROVER

SPEAK!

FRED THE WONDER HORSE

All right! All right! (UNDER HIS BREATH) bow-wow.

MARSHALL GROVER
(SINGING)

I did not hear you!!!

FRED THE WONDER HORSE

Bow-wow!

MARSHALL GROVER

Now, Fred will beg for us. Beg, Fred. BEG!

FRED THE WONDER HORSE

That one's easy, Marshall. I'm begging yuh. Let me out of this corn ball act. Look, I'm down on my knees to yuh. And, I'm beggin' yuh to let me off this here stage.

MARSHALL GROVER

Very good, Fred.

FRED THE WONDER HORSE

I take it the answer is no.

MARSHALL GROVER

Correct! Now, for the big finish, Fred the Wonder Dog is going to fetch!

FRED THE WONDER HORSE

What's that?

MARSHALL GROVER

You know, fetch. I take a stick like this one (HE PICKS UP A STICK). And, I throw it. And, I say, "Fetch, Fred." And then you chase it and bring it back to me.

FRED THE WONDER HORSE

Let me get this straight. You're gonna throw that stick and I gotta go chase it and bring it back to yuh?

MARSHALL GROVER

Right! Oh, Fred, you are so intelligent!

FRED THE WONDER HORSE

If you want to wind up with the stick, why are you gonna throw it away in the first place?

MARSHALL GROVER

So, you can fetch it!

FRED THE WONDER HORSE

But, I don't want to fetch it.

MARSHALL GROVER

Fred! If I do not throw it and you do not fetch it, then there is no trick!

FRED THE WONDER HORSE

Yes, there is. You hide your eyes and I'll show yuh a real trick.

SESAME STREET LIVE!

MARSHALL GROVER

Oh, goody! A real trick (HE COVERS HIS EYES) I covered my eyes, Fred.

FRED THE WONDER HORSE

Okay. No peeking now, Marshall.

FRED TIPTOES TO THE WINGS AND EXITS. GLADYS, THE NO-TALENT COW, COMES ON, CLANKING HER COWBELL, REPLACING FRED.

MARSHALL GROVER

Can I look yet, Fred?

GLADYS
(FLATLY)

Whinny, whinny! That's horse talk for, "yes."

MARSHALL GROVER
(LOOKING HER OVER)

Fred! That's the best trick I ever saw! You made yourself a cow!

GLADYS

I do frogs, too. Ahem, (FLATLY) Hi ho, Kermit the Frog here.

MARSHALL GROVER

Come, Fred, we will show everyone our new trick!

GLADYS
(AS THEY EXIT)

I also do a kangaroo. Watch.

GLADYS HOPS

MARSHALL GROVER

Oh, Fred, you truly are a wonder horse!

LIGHTS FADE TO DARK.

Chapter 46
Aspen, Colorado

In 1982, Jim Henson and John Denver decided to do a one-hour television special on location in Aspen, Colorado. The premise was that John and the Muppet gang would go camping in the mountains outside of Aspen. It was called, *Rocky Mountain Holiday*, starring John Denver and the Muppets. It ran on ABC in prime time.

Jon Stone and I had just finished a special called *Big Bird in China*. Jim liked the script so much that he asked us to write the Aspen special. The original concept specified that the special would highlight Aspen during all four seasons of the year. But financial constraints held the show to summer and fall.

The special turned out beautifully. But, I'm including the following for all of the people who have contacted me over the years, thinking that puppets are a cheap solution to television production. "It's just a guy with a sock on his hand. How tough can it be?" How often have I heard that?

Jon and I flew out to Aspen in the spring of '82. As usual, Jon was air sick most of the way, especially in the puddle jumper from Denver to Aspen.

He was pretty rocky when we landed. But instead of going to our hotel, a car took us directly to the private hanger at the Aspen Airport. Outside the hanger, Jim, John Denver and the production crew were gathered around John's experimental open cockpit bi-plane. He and Jim were discussing a sequence where John would take Rowlf the Dog, one of Jim's characters, flying. Jim was planning on scrunching down in the front cockpit and operate Rowlf from below *while the plane was in flight!*

The problem was Jim's seatbelt, or lack of it. Nobody could figure out how to rig one on the floor of the cockpit. Ever adventurous, Jim said he could probably hang on without one. Jon and I immediately pictured the plane rolling over, Jim falling out and plummeting to the ground, taking our careers along with him.

Later on, John Denver wanted to show Jim exactly where he thought we should shoot the flying sequence. He suggested flying his bi-plane over the scenery and Jim, who was directing, could follow in the camera/chase plane and plan his shots. Just as he was getting into the camera plane, Jim turned to the crowd and said there was another seat if anybody wanted to come along. Jon, who hated flying, blanched. But I jumped at the chance.

The camera plane was a small Piper Cub with the right-hand door removed. Since there was no camera yet, the view was spectacular if a little bit scary.

John Denver, in his bi-plane, led us over some of the most beautiful mountain scenery I've ever seen. We flew over snow-covered peaks and lush valleys. When we were finished, we flew over the next valley and there a balloon race was just starting. It was an incredible sight as these colorful monsters rose below us.

Back on the ground, we toured all over Aspen looking for the most picturesque locations to shoot. It was a difficult decision. Aspen scenery is, in a word, spectacular.

Finally a lakeside location was decided on as the main campsite. So far, so good. Remember, it's just a guy with a sock on his hand. But now, it starts getting a little complicated.

The first small problem was a house that was clearly visible from the campsite. The solution? Move a 40-foot tree in front of the house to hide it.

Now, in order to show just the "sock" and the spectacular Aspen scenery, you have to hide the puppeteer someplace. So, plans were made to build 6' x 6' x 6' boxes to be buried in the campsite. The boxes would be covered with ground cloth and hide the puppeteers who would operate the puppets from below. The boxes also had to be water proofed and heated.

The boxes were built and polyurethaned. The backhoe showed up, holes were dug, the boxes were sunk into the ground and we all went home.

Next morning, we discovered the box holes had been dug below the lake's water line. During the night, water had seeped into the holes and now the water tight boxes were floating on it.

The solution? We'll build a hill. Then we'll sink the boxes into the hill above the water line. Now, dump trucks and a bulldozer show up. Remember, this is just a guy with a sock on his hand.

Finally, the campsite was ready. The boxes were covered, tents were pitched, a fire was created. It was fall in the mountains. We were about two days into the shoot when the snow started. It came up from the valley below us like a great white cloud, blocking out the sunshine. In a matter of minutes, we were wrapped in a blizzard.

I took shelter in the production camper along with John Denver, Jim and Frank Oz. To kill time, we started a nickel and dime poker game. I remember chasing John and Jim out of a pot with a twenty-five-cent bet. "Too rich for my blood," Jim said while he and Denver were paying about 45 people who were sitting around doing nothing.

The storm lasted several hours. At the end, I was up $37.00 and God only knows how many tens of thousands Jim and John had lost while the crew waited for the storm to abate.

Now, it really got complicated. We had only shot half of the Fall campsite scenes. And now, the surrounding countryside and mountains were covered with snow. Nothing would match. A decision was made to reproduce the campsite in a studio, finish the shooting and electronically lay in the scenery later, something that could easily be achieved in a New York studio. But, here we were in Aspen.

Of course, there are no television studios in Aspen, Colorado. The only building that was big and high enough to meet our needs was the lone hangar at the Aspen Airport.

So, we rented the hangar. Arrangements were made to have the locals move their Lear jets out onto the field. (One had a map` on its cockpit wall with a thick red straight line. One end was Aspen, Colorado. The other end was the Caribbean Island of Antigua. *What do you feel like today? Skiing or Scuba?*)

The campsite was duplicated exactly in the hangar on staging seven feet in the air, so the puppeteers could work standing from beneath. The problem was that in order to lay in the scenery electronically later, the campsite had to be shot against black velour.

I was privy to a conversation where the set designer was asking his assistant where they could find about 2,000 square yards of black velour in Aspen, Colorado. They checked with the Denver Opera House who couldn't help them. So, the velour had to be flow in from Los Angeles.

One of the music numbers at the campsite required a full moon in the background. In fact the shoot had been scheduled so we would be in Aspen for the full moon on October 4. So, on the night of October 4, a film crew was dispatched to the campsite location to shoot the full moon.

When the crew returned from the shoot, I asked the lighting designer how the shoot had gone. "Not too badly", he told me, "Considering nobody told me I was going to have to light a lake."

Have I reminded you, lately, of the guy with the sock on his hand?

Meanwhile, back at the hangar production resumed. Of course, the conditions were less than ideal. Sound is always a problem when you shoot outside a sound-proofed studio. But in an airplane hangar next to the only runway in a working airport?

The solution was to station people with walkie talkies at each end of the runway. When a plane was about to take off or land, they radioed in to the hangar, and we stopped production.

Then there was the gas problem. At 12,000 feet, the air is very thin, so engines guzzle gas. Mileage is nil, especially in heavy duty production trucks and oversized RVs. We regularly rendez-voused with a tanker truck to keep our 14 production vehicles in gas. One day, in the middle of shooting, the tanker was gassing us up. He gassed up 13 vehicles and ran dry before he got to number 14.

Number 14, of course, was our electrical generator, which promptly ran out of gas. It's a little known fact that when a generator runs out of gas, the current surges and ebbs at a terrific rate which makes the cameras go haywire. So even after the gas arrives and the generator is up and running, the cameras still have to be locked on a test pattern for a certain amount of time to recuperate.

During the break, I found myself walking the length of the runway to the control tower with Jim. Trying to console him I said, "Well, this is a lot better than selling insurance."

"No", Jim replied knowingly. "It's a lot better than selling luggage door to door".

Because of the *Sesame Street* shooting schedule, Jon had to return to New York before the shoot was finished. I had to stay on in Aspen to make whatever script changes were necessary until the shoot wrapped up.

One night, I was having trouble sleeping. I'm usually a little jittery on location. You never know what kind of problem is going to pop up next. So, I thought that a combination of a couple of beers and Aspen's 12,000 foot altitude might induce some badly needed sleep.

I left the ski condo where I was staying and walked over to the Jerome Hotel bar. This was before the Jerome had renovated itself into *Architectural Digest*. The bar decor was pretty much cowboy/ski bum and included several deer heads, a large bi-plane model made entirely of Budweiser beer cans and a poster extolling *the virtues of Hunter Thompson for Sheriff*.

It was fairly late in the in the evening and the bar was empty except for one other guy around my age – late thirties or early forties. Since this was the West, where people are generally casual and friendly, we exchanged pleasantries and struck up a conversation.

The conversation turned to his girl friend, who was in her early twenties, much younger that he was. He told me she wanted to move in with him and he was sitting there trying to decide whether or not it was a good idea.

I told him I couldn't see any problem. "Let her move in and it will either work out or not in the long run", I said.

That's when he told me that he didn't have much of a long run ahead of him. He was a Vietnam veteran and had been doused with enough Agent Orange to give him multiple medical problems. And he didn't want to put his young girl friend through what looked like a pretty grim future.

I was dumbfounded. Even after spending the first 20 years of my life in my father's saloons, I am still amazed at what perfect strangers will say to each other in a bar.

Now quite knowing what to say, I blurted out that I thought Vietnam vets had gotten a really raw deal. When he asked me what I meant, I explained that there used to be a covenant between the United States and it's citizens. That when the country asked its young men to take up arms there was always a good reason. That had been true in the First and Second World Wars, as well as Korea.

I thought it was a disgrace that 18- and 19-year-olds were drafted into the quagmire of Vietnam, a kind of Dodge City where it was impossible to determine friend from foe. And then, when they returned, they were spat upon and called baby killers. I didn't even realize I felt that way until I vocalized it. At this point, the Vietnam war had been over for seven years.

He was silent for a long moment. Then his eyes welled up and tears started running down his face. "Nobody has ever said that to me. Thank you so much!"

It was just one of those poignant moments in life that you never forget. Whenever I think of my time in Aspen, I always think of the Vietnam vet. I hope things worked out for him in the long run.

Chapter 47
Big Bird in Ireland

Big Bird in Ireland was a wonderful *Sesame Street* travel special that was researched, and written, but, unfortunately never produced. The main reason was that Jon Stone was diagnosed with Lou Gehrig's disease shortly after we finished the script.

The show had several plot lines including some wonderful musical production numbers with master tap dancer, Savion Glover, then a *Sesame Street* cast member, and troops of step dancing Irish children. (Watching the step dances actually made me nostalgic for South Boston. So many Irish immigrants ended up in Southie that Boston is known as the 33rd county of Ireland.)

Another story line had Big Bird captured by Irish fairies with Elmo running around the country trying to save him. The third plot involved an Irish family that ran a horse farm. Jon imagined the matriarch of the family played by Maureen O'Hara. (Jon had a crush on her.) And, since at the time, Ireland had it's first woman President, Mary Robinson, we included her in the show as well.

When Jon first asked me to write *Ireland* with him, I insisted that I go on the *recky*, the research trip. And, I told him that, *If I don't get to kiss the rock, it's a deal breaker.* Jon guaranteed I could kiss the Blarney Stone and so the deal was made.

Jon, Jon's daughter Polly, our still photographer, and I flew to Ireland on June 28th, 1992. There, we teamed up with Blake Norton, the sound man on *Sesame Street* who lived part time in Ireland, and Isabelle Healy who, with her husband, owned the Irish production company that would be co-producing *Big Bird in Ireland*.

Basically, we told Blake and Isabelle to show us everything that was pretty and everything that was fun. And so they did. At the end of ten days, we had put 1,800 miles on the odometer – this in a country that's 275 miles long and 175 miles wide.

Even though I had been in television production for 20 years, watching Jon on the recky was still an education. Any location that we wanted to use was photographed from every angle by Polly at Jon's direction. And, since we were going to shoot almost exactly a year later, Jon had his compass out and made copious notes and diagrams of the sun's location and movement. Now we could tailor the scripts for the best locations. And, we'd have a jump on lighting and camera position when we shot the following year.

I, on the other hand, was trying to soak up some local atmosphere. In the name of disclosure, my father's parents immigrated to New York from Belfast in the late 19th Century. There's always been a generous supply of Irish Blarney on my father's side of the family.

So, when I arrived in Ireland, I expected the occasional, jocular bon mot. But what I discovered was an entire country of stand-up comics. Laughter is in the Irish soul and in the air. Here are a few examples.

We had arrived in Ireland in late June. As the Fourth of July approached, an Irishman asked me if we were going to do anything special to celebrate American Independence Day.

"Yes, we are.", I told him, fatuously. "We're planning to go over to the east coast and moon England across the Irish Sea."

"Well", came the dead panned response. "I understand several hotels on the coast have set up grandstands and offer free bus service for just such activities."

While we were traveling through County Cork along Ireland's south coast, the talk was all about the computerization of the Irish lighthouse system. Ireland is surrounded by some of the roughest seas in the world. So every harbor has it's own lighthouse and rescue boat.

In the past, the lighthouses were manned by crews of lighthouse keepers. Stories abound about the keepers saving boats from running aground, or worse, during storms. Now, the lighthouses had been automated and their schedule would be run by a centralized computer.

The subject came up again while we were having lunch in a pub overlooking Bantry Bay. "For all we know," the female publican lamented. "Boat loads of neurotics could be waiting to come ashore and who's to warn us?"

I immediately pictured a flotilla of ocean liners, just over the horizon, filled to the gunnels with characters from Woody Allen movies. All were chain-smoking furiously while talking to their analysts on their cell phones, and waiting for dark so they could invade the Emerald Isle.

In Ireland, in late June, the sun rises around 4:00 am and sets around 11:00 p.m. It's a great misconception in the United States, but England, Ireland and Scotland are not due east of New York. Rather, they're on a geographical par with Alaska. Their summer days are much longer and their winter days are much shorter. So, if you drive around Ireland in mid-summer with a northeastern American sensibility, you expect the sun to set around 8:00 p.m. But, because you're so much farther north, the sun is fully risen at 5:00 am and doesn't set until around 10:30 at night.

So, our work days were a lot longer than we had anticipated. Your inner clock tells you when the sun starts to set, you quit work and get hungry. So, our work day ended around 10:00 p.m., even though it felt like 8:00 p.m. in New York.

One night, after a very long day on the road, we checked into a Fitzpatrick hotel. Jon and I went into the bar. We found a couple of bar stools and ordered two pints of Guinness. It was only my ten day exposure to the Irish that gave me the courage to throw out a verbal hand grenade.

I turned to Jon and said, in my loudest voice, in my worst New York accent, *Well, Jon, I, guess it's true.*

What's true?, Jon responded in an equally loud voice and American accent.

I guess it's true all the charming Irish are in New York!

By the time I counted to five under my breath, a head popped up half way down the bar.

What do you mean, all the @#**#@& charming Irish are in New York!?, he demanded.

Well, I replied. *We're been in here for ten minutes and nobody's charmed us yet. If you'd like to come down here, have a pint and give it a shot, be our guest.*

That was all it took. By the time we left that bar, 'way too late that night, we had met the high school principal, the dog catcher, both of the town cops, the Ford dealer, the undertaker and everybody else in town.

Since the Irish President, Mary Robinson, was the country's first woman president, Jon and I had planned to write a cameo role in *Big Bird in Ireland* for her. So, we immediately contacted Mrs. Robinson's office as soon as we arrived in the country. But it was at least a week later before one of her staff invited us to tea at Anis House, the Irish Presidential residence. Thanks to my association with the Muppets, the Irish White House was the second presidential residence to which I've been invited.

Over tea, the staff member apologized for the delay in contacting us, and told us the following story:

The week before our arrival, Mrs. Robinson was reviewing the troops at an Irish Army base. She was wearing a bright yellow suit. Some trooper in the ranks murmured, "Oh, look! It's Big Bird!", causing the entire troop to collapse with laughter.

Knowing their own people as well as they do, the President's staff figured that any message they received, at all associated with *Sesame Street*, was going to be one, monumental Irish put-on. Now, it was too late to change the President's schedule to include us. Apologies all around. But it was still an interesting experience.

Though almost in the center of Dublin, Anis House is located in an idyllic spot surrounded by meadow and parkland. A herd of dairy cows grazed placidly across the road. At that time, 1992, a lamp burned continuously, day and night, in one window of the residence.

The reason? Mrs. Robinson literally kept a lamp in the nation's window for all the expatriate Irish who were force abroad because of their lack of opportunity at home. As a descendent of Irish emigrants, I found the gesture quite touching.

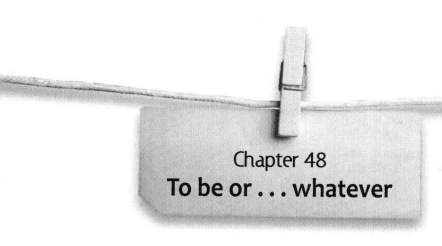

Chapter 48
To be or . . . whatever

It's no secret that film and television are two of the most heavily unionized industries in the country. The actors, directors, writers, set designers, stage hands, electricians, camera men, sound men, prop men, wardrobe people, make-up and hair people, and musicians all have their own, individual unions with their own arcane contracts.

Joining any of these unions is a true exercise in Catch-22. No production company with union contracts will hire anyone who is not a union member. But, most of these unions won't let you join unless you have a job at a union production company. Don't ask. My membership in the Writers Guild came about when I joined *The Muppet Show*. The show insisted on having me so the union accepted me.

But, the first thing I learned about film and TV studios was *DON'T TOUCH ANYTHING!* Every item in the studio, camera, light, prop, is covered by a specific union. Their members, and only their members are allowed to touch it. Cross union touching is a no-no. In 25 years in television I never touched anything in a studio but the floor.

By and large we all get along pretty well. But some union members (including my own) are a little more gung-ho than the rest of us, which is why I got a call from the Screen Actors Guild sometime in the mid-1980s.

When I answered the phone, a pleasant sounding woman informed me that SAG was holding a residual check for me. I explained that it must be a mistake. I was not a member of SAG. I was a member of the WGA. The check was probably a Writers Guild residual that had been sent to SAG by mistake. I asked her to mail it to me.

However, she insisted that I pick the check up in person. I couldn't understand why. But a few days later I was near the Screen Actors Guild office on West 57th Street, so I stopped by to retrieve my check.

I introduced myself to the receptionist and was told that a Mister So-and-so wanted to see me. I couldn't understand why since this was some kind of clerical mix-up. I killed some time wandering around the reception room. Since actors constantly travel, the walls are filled with notices advertising and seeking apartment sublets.

Eventually, Mister So-and-so's secretary fetched me. I was ushered into a nondescript office and invited to sit down. Mister So-and-so (I really don't remember his name) started rifling through a thick file on his desk.

"Did you", he asked me, "Play Itchy the Prospector on *Sesame Street* in 1975?"

I thought back and it came to me. I had written a *Sesame Street* episode where Big Bird imagines what it was like back in the Old West, back in Sesame Gulch. The set was re-dressed with hay bales and hitching posts. I think they put swinging doors on Hooper's Store. All the cast wore western costumes.

In a "Sorting" segment (*Which of these things is not like the others?*) I called for three men with beards and one without. Just for fun, I indicated that one of the beards would be my boss, Jon Stone. Jon simply crossed his name out of the script and inserted mine. So, I showed up for wardrobe and became Itchy the Prospector.

I was used as an extra in several other scenes, as Big Bird first imagines himself first as the bad guy, Bad Bird, fastest wing in the west, and then as the good guy, Marshall Matt Bird. I even had a line. I got to run down *Sesame Street* yelling, *Bad Bird's back in town!*

I told Mister So-and-so that his records were correct. I had played Itchy the Prospector on *Sesame Street*. I still had no idea of where this was going.

"And, Mister Bailey, did you play a pizza delivery boy on, *Hot Hero Sandwich*, in 1979??"

Hot Hero Sandwich was a Saturday morning, pre-teen show on NBC. I was one of the writers. For the final show, the producers thought it would be fun to include the production staff on camera, including the writers. There was a skit about a bunch of girls having a pajama party and ordering a pizza. I was cast as the pizza delivery boy.

I believe my line was, "Pizza." Short, economical and to the point. And, I delivered it with a depth and nuance never seen before or since on television.

So, I told old So-and-so that, yes, I had played a pizza delivery boy, to the hilt, on *Hot Hero Sandwich.*

"All right", he told me. "That's twice. The next time you do it, you have to join the Screen Actor's Guild."

It took a full minute to dawn on me. Entertainment law is not part of a writer's job description. But somewhere in the back of my head I knew that anyone could make two screen appearances without joining SAG. But the third appearance required joining the Actors Guild and paying a hefty enrollment fee.

I couldn't believe this guy had gone back over ten years of records to check my status with the Actor's Guild because of an errant Writer's Guild residual check! And then, call me into his office like a misbehaving school boy to let me know the Screen Actors Guild had their eye on me. Wow! And I thought the teamsters were tough!

All I could think to say to him was, "Well, if I join the Guild, does than mean I can deduct my haircuts from my income tax?"

Before he could answer, I grabbed my check and ran.

In the elevator I remembered thinking that it was a good thing he didn't know about my "playing" Buffy Saint Marie on *Sesame Street* episodes in Taos, New Mexico.

Chapter 49
Carnegie Hall

At the height of the 1984 New York social season, the New York Zoological Society decided to throw a benefit for the Bronx Zoo. For non-New Yorkers, the Bronx Zoo is one of the best in the world. It was founded by Theodore Roosevelt at the turn of the last century on 265 acres of rolling woodland in the Bronx. The Society was formed at the same time to operate the Zoo.

Because of its lofty beginnings, the Bronx Zoological Society is one of the most venerated charities in New York City. The name, Astor, appears rather frequently in their membership rolls. So, these guys really know how to throw a fund raiser!

Get me Carnegie Hall! Get me Bob Hope! And, that's exactly what they did.

The show was billed as, *Bob Hope at Carnegie Hall*, starring, of course, Bob Hope with his wife, Dolores. The rest of the guests included then Secretary of Agriculture, John R. Block, Ex-New York Governor Hugh Carey, Comedienne Imogene Coca, writers and lyricists, Betty Comden and Adolph Green, Composer Jule Styne, The Dance Theatre of Harlem, then Mayor Ed Koch, singer Liliane Montevecchi, Broadway legends Donald Saddler and Helen Gallagher, and Alex Spanos, owner of the San Diego Chargers.

What, you're probably asking yourself, are these super stars doing with the likes of me? Well, somebody, probably one of the Astors, had the idea of getting Big Bird to emcee the show. Calls were made to the Muppets and Caroll Spinney graciously agreed to do the benefit with one stipulation: he insisted on having his own writer, me.

At first, I thought it was a nice gesture on Caroll's part, including me in this star studded event and the black tie reception afterwards. The required writing was only a few opening jokes and introductions, known colloquially in the trade as *gazintas* and *gazatas*.

I was flattered. But I also knew that Caroll is a very shrewd performer who was not about to trust his signature character, Big Bird, to a writer with no real knowledge of the character or *Sesame Street*. He wanted to avoid the "bird brain" and "bird seed" jokes that many, inexperienced writers usually came up with for him.

Additionally, Caroll wanted someone who understood how the puppet actually worked. I didn't realize how important that was until the first production meeting for the fund raiser, which was held about a week before the event.

The first idea that was suggested was for Big Bird to enter through the curtains, greet the audience, introduce Bob Hope, do some business with him, then segue into a song with another guest star and then . . .

That's when I stopped it and carefully explained that Big Bird actually had a man inside him with his right hand extended through the neck and into the head, where he operated the jaw with his thumb. And, when you hold a human arm straight up in the air, very shortly all the blood runs out of it and all feeling and control are lost. So the maximum amount of time that Caroll can operate the puppet is about ten minutes.

"But," they protested, "We've seen Big Bird do extensive musical numbers and comedy skits on television." "That's because," I explained, "Those pieces are broken down into much shorter shots so Caroll can rest between them. When they're edited together in post-production they appear to be one scene." Since all these big name stars have very expensive representation, who regularly have big ideas, it was an up-hill battle all week long.

Then came the rehearsal days in Carnegie Hall. As soon as I saw the stage, I realized we had another problem. I had to explain how in a television studio, Caroll watched himself on the 1½ inch monitor inside the bird costume. Since there was no TV on the night of the benefit, the monitor would be useless. There is a one-eye peek hole in the costume, but Caroll can barely see out of it. And, of course, he has no depth of field or peripheral vision.

So, my great fear was that Caroll could accidentally walk off the stage and fall into the orchestra pit, seriously injuring Caroll, not to mention causing major production headaches on *Sesame Street*. Since Caroll was taping *Sesame Street*, he wouldn't be available until the dress rehearsal on the day of the show. So, I was fighting the good fight alone.

One day at the end of rehearsals, Imogene Coca asked if anybody wanted to share a cab to the East Side of Manhattan. I jumped at the chance. I did, and do, live on the East Side of Manhattan, not very far from Ms. Coca's apartment. But I wasn't interested in saving cab fare.

Imogene Coca and her partner, Sid Caesar, were co-stars in a real piece of television history called, *Your Show of Shows*, in the early 1950s. It ran live for 90 minutes on Saturday nights. It was as popular, if not more so, than *Saturday Night Live*. The writing staff included Mel Brooks, Neil Simon, M.A.S.H. creator Larry Gelbart, Carl (father of Rob) Reiner and Woody Allen. So, I had about 1,000 questions I wanted to ask her.

Since West 57th Street, where Carnegie Hall is located, is a major Manhattan crosstown thoroughfare, I had no problem hailing one of New York's 12,187 yellow cabs. Unfortunately, it was piloted by the angriest of New York's 50,000 taxi drivers.

In 1984, there was still quite a residual radical civil rights movement in the country. And our angry driver, whose name on his license was something like Malcolm Triple-X Shabazz, was outfitted in what could only be described as the full Black Panther: a combat jacket; a gigantic afro; and a 50-caliber machine gun bullet pendant hanging around his neck.

Conversation between driver and passengers was impossible because of the rap music blaring out of the cabs multiple stereo speakers. I did get a sense that Mr. Triple-X Shabazz bore some animosity toward the white race, of which Ms. Coca and I are members in good standing. That's because he tore across Central Park at slightly under the speed of sound, ignoring red lights, stop signs and various other traffic indications along the route, while making obscene gestures at other members of our ethnic persuasion.

So, instead of getting first hand answers to dozens of my historic television questions, my dialogue with Ms. Coca consisted entirely of her screaming at me, "I was in a terrible automobile accident! Please tell him to slow down!

Please tell him to slow down!!!! PLEASE TELL HIM TO SLOW DOWN!!!", all the way from Carnegie Hall to her front door.

Meanwhile, back at the Hall, the day of the big event rolled around. The afternoon dress rehearsal was the first time that the *powers-that-were* got to see Big Bird in action and what was required to sustain his performance.

My God!, they exclaimed. *He can't see! He could walk off the stage!*, all as if they had never heard it before.

The event came off beautifully. The two highlights I still remember were Alex Spanos giving Bob Hope quite a run for his money during a buck and wing duet, and Big Bird singing a very poignant rendition of *People* while Jule Styne, the song's composer, accompanied him on the piano.

Mostly though, I spent the evening on the edge of my seat, using every ounce of body English I could muster to keep Big Bird from falling into the orchestra pit.

Chapter 50
The Day the Music Died

This is hard.

At 7:30 a.m., May 16, 1990, my telephone awakened me from a sound sleep. It was Bill Prady, another writer who worked for the Muppets. I couldn't imagine why Bill was calling me at that hour. I was then, and still am a notorious night owl.

For a moment, I thought Bill and Jim were in some strange corner of the world and had lost track of the time change. Because of Jim's hectic travel schedule, that happened occasionally.

"You'd better sit down.", Bill told me. "Jim died last night."

I was absolutely stunned. It must have taken a full minute for the news to sink into my brain. Jim was only 53. And, as far as I knew hadn't been sick a day in his life.

I asked Bill if there was anything I could do. He told me to call anybody I could think of whom I wouldn't want to hear the news through the media. That's why Bill was calling me so early.

So, I went through my Rolodex. I just remember starting a lot of conversations with a tentative, "Have you heard the news?" Some people had heard, others hadn't. In between my outgoing calls people were calling me to see if I had heard. As you might imagine, we were all devastated.

Eventually, the details came out. Jim had been sick for several days but thought he had the flu. He and his daughter, Cheryl, had gone to North

Carolina to celebrate Mother's Day with his father and step-mother. That's when Jim started to feel sick.

When they returned to New York, Jim's symptoms grew progressively worse. Finally, around 4:00 a.m. on May 16, Jim's wife, Jane, convinced him to go to New York Hospital. There, Jim was diagnosed with Group A streptococcus pneumonia, a viral disease that starts out with flu-like symptoms but goes on to destroy major organs.

Group A bacteria is usually contracted through inhalation, so I assume Jim caught it on a plane. Jim flew a lot. He practically commuted between New York, London, Los Angeles and Toronto. And airplanes are really unhealthy. Basically, they're sealed containers where hundreds of people inhale and exhale the same stale air.

If it's caught early enough, streptococcus pneumonia can be treated with penicillin. However, penicillin is processed through the liver. And by the time Jane got Jim got to the hospital, his liver had already been destroyed. Jim lingered on life support until 1:21 a.m. Then he passed away.

Jim was so low key and accessible, it was easy to forget that he was a world famous entertainer. He kept his celebrity deep in the background. It wasn't until the media started reporting his obituary and condolences from presidents, celebrities and artists world wide that I really realized the enormous effect Jim Henson had on the planet.

I also remember getting a call from an old friend who said he had been contacted by an old friend of his. The friend told him that he remembered that my friend knew someone connected with the Muppets. He asked my friend to pass on his condolences to the Muppets through me. Four days later, the enormity of the world's affection for Jim Henson would become immediately evident.

The Cathedral of Saint John the Divine is the world's largest gothic cathedral. It's located at 112th Street and Amsterdam Avenue on Manhattan's Upper West Side. At 601 feet, the nave is as long as two American football fields. Its 162-foot dome can easily accommodate the Statue of Liberty. It was started in 1892 and, in the best tradition of gothic cathedrals, is still under construction and has an apprentice building crafts program for local youths. Saint John's seats 5,000 people. And at a memorial service on

May 21, 1990, every seat was filled to celebrate the life of Jim Henson. The crowd swelled out to the steps and street outside.

Several years earlier, at around age 50, Jim had written instructions for his memorial service. He didn't want anyone wearing black. He thought it would be nice if a few people said something nice. And, he wanted a brass band. He went on to say that his children might not agree with these instructions. But, since he was dead there wasn't much they could do about it.

No one wore black to the memorial. In fact, it was one of the most colorful crowds I've ever seen. I wore my green satin *Muppet Show* jacket, just like the one Scooter wore on the show, a Christmas gift from Jim. My wife, Gail, who had made films for *Sesame Street*, wore an aqua satin jacket with the *Sesame Street* logo on the back. And, there was a brass band – The Dirty Dozen Brass Band, one of the greatest traditional New Orleans brass bands. In traditional New Orleans style they led the procession in with a dirge rendition of *Just a Closer Walk With Thee*. They led the exit with a rousing version of *When the Saints Go Marching In*. The memorial was 2½ hours of incredible testimony and entertainment.

There's a story that Frank Oz told at Jim's memorial that epitomizes Jim Henson's generosity, artistic talent, and sense of humor in one very short anecdote.

Firstly, you have to understand, Jim and Frank were very close. They were as much of a classic comedy team as Laurel and Hardy or Burns and Allen. Frank was Bert to Jim's Ernie and Miss Piggy to Jim's Kermit. Their magic is available on thousands of hours of video.

During rehearsals for an episode of the first season of *Saturday Night Live!*, Jim lured Frank into a dressing room, and convinced him to take his clothes off and pose naked for some photographs. Jim told Frank it was important. So Frank eventually acquiesced, albeit cautiously.

Jim asked Frank to cover his genitals and look into the camera in a state of complete and utter shock. Both of which Frank was more than eager to do. The pictures were taken, Frank got dressed and he and Jim went back to work.

Several months later, Christmas arrived and Jim gave Frank his Christmas present. It was a wall hanging construction that Jim had made for Frank.

275

As Frank described it, the construction was a bust of Bert. He's holding a ledge with a dozen tiny Bert statues the size of toy soldiers. The little Berts were looking in all different directions. And, across the bottom of the ledge were photographs of the Muppet shop people who had constructed Bert. At the edge of the ledge, Jim had painted striations which Frank perceived as layers of Bert's mind.

The eyes of the big Bert were hollow, allowing the viewer to look directly into Bert's brain, as it were. And when you did, you were confronted with a picture of a naked Frank Oz in a state of complete and utter shock.

The time and creativity that went into the construction speak for Jim's generosity and talent. I'll let the humor speak for itself.

I had planned to go into much greater detail about the ceremony, but I've just made a marvelous discovery -- many of the memorial's highlights: remarks by puppeteers, friends and family; musical numbers, including Big Bird singing, *It's Not Easy Being Green*; and many other Muppet performances and testimonies are available on YouTube under Jim Henson's Memorial. Even more amazing, the entire service is available on DVD!

There are a couple things I remember that aren't readily visible on the videos. Along with a memorial program on each seat was a small, hand colored, foam rubber, butterfly puppet, about six inches across, mounted on a short rod. During several of the musical presentations, without cues, the entire audience animated the puppets overhead on the rods. The effect was a sea of butterflies floating over the congregation.

And as I said before, when the ceremony ended, the Dirty Dozen Brass Band played the crowd out with a rousing rendition of *When the Saints Go Marching In*. But, if you listen closely, you can hear the cathedral's organist join in on the cathedral's enormous pipe organ, jamming right along with the brass band.

Jim Henson surrounded himself with extraordinary people. The memorial is some of these extraordinary people talking about just how extraordinary a person was Jim Henson.

Chapter 51
So, what have you done for me lately?

Funny you should ask. A few years ago, I was doing the *New York Sunday Times* crossword puzzle. And, the answer to one of the major clues was, "Don Quixote" . And as I filled it in, a light bulb went off in my head. It said, *Frog of La Mancha!*

The more I played with the idea, the better I liked it. If anyone was born to dream big dreams while tilting at windmills, it's Kermit the Frog. To me, the essence of Kermit's character and appeal is quite simple: Kermit is the universal Everyman. Like all of us, he loves his fellow man, is good to his dog, and plays by the book. And, like all of us, the sky falls in on him with astounding regularity. But, since Kermit is pure of heart, in the end he always triumphs.

And, of course, the bumbling obsequious Fozzie is a natural to play Sancho Panza, La Mancha's dim-witted side kick.

Finally, for the love interest, who else could star as the lovely, sexy, vivacious, captivating, sensuous, and zaftig Dulcinea but the divine Miss P.?

Add to that the possibilities of talking horses, mules and windmills, along with a seriously demented approach to the Cervantes masterpiece and you have the makings of classic Muppet material.

Frog of La Mancha is still a work-in-progress. But there's enough of it here to give you a general idea. And I think it deserves to see the light of day. The following proposal is actually the first draft of the script.

Nobody has snapped up *Frog of La Mancha* - yet. So, if you happen to be a big honcho at Disney, or own a television network or a movie studio, you might want to keep that in mind while you're reading it. If you get my drift.

(By the way, I also have three unproduced feature scripts: a 16th Century Irish pirate adventure; a motorcycle/buddy/road comedy; and a valentine sequel to *Casablanca*. If you get my drift)

Frog of La Mancha
(This material registered with the Writers Guild of America-East)

#1. OPENING

FADE UP ON: SAM THE EAGLE at a DAIS in front of the DRAPES.

SAM
(READING FROM A SCRIPT)
Welcome distinguished ladies and gentlemen! I am proud to announce that the following Muppet performance finally demonstrates the heights of sophistication to which I *always* knew this organization was capable of rising. It is a production of deep nuance, of complex interpretation, of major social commentary! Well, what else can one say about the works of that great 16th Century Spanish essayist, Miguel De Cervantes! So, without further ado, I'm proud to present the Muppets production of . . . *THE FROG OF LA MANCHA???!!!!*

CREDIT UP: *The Frog of La Mancha*

OPENING CREDITS ROLL OVER FOLLOWING SCENE

DISSOLVE TO: INTER: 16th Century Blacksmith Shop.

SAM
(VOICE OVER)
THE FROG OF LA MANCHA!!!!??? (aside) I don't believe this! . . . (AHEM) Once upon a time in a very poor part of Spain called La Mancha, lived a very poor blacksmith named Kermito La Rana.

ENTER FOZZIE, dressed as a 16th Century blacksmith,

ENTER KERMIT behind him. He is struggling mightily to carry a LARGE ANVIL into the shop.

                              FOZZIE
Gangway! Be careful, Master. Don't drop it!

FOZZIE, of course, is doing nothing to help.

                              KERMIT
Some apprentice you are!

                              FOZZIE
Well, you know, Master, my back.

Finally, KERMIT hauls the anvil into frame.

                              FOZZIE
Maybe a little more to the right!

KERMIT reacts

                              FOZZIE
Yessir! Yessir! Yessir!

KERMIT starts to hammer at something on the anvil.

                              KERMIT
                       (GRUMBLING TO HIMSELF)
Sconces. Sconces! The Queen has to have sconces in all the bathrooms! All one hundred and sixteen of them!

As KERMIT hammers, he constantly hits his fingers with the hammer.

                              KERMIT
Ouch! Ouch! Ouch!

                    SAM
                (OFF CAMERA)
Kermito was not only the very poorest blacksmith in La Mancha, he was also
the very worst blacksmith in La Mancha.

KERMIT continues to hammer on his fingers.

                    SAM

But Kermito had a dream. And in this dream, he saw himself not as a lowly
and bungling blacksmith, but as a knight of the round table brave and bold
and true!

DISSOLVE TO:

#2 KERMIT, now dressed in SHINING ARMOR, is making the same flailing
movement. But this time he is holding a SWORD and dueling with another
knight, obviously GONZO, by the cut of his helmet. A CHEERING CROWD can
be heard in the background.

After a series of flashy moves, KERMIT defeats the other knight, but graciously
allows him to walk away. Trumpets blare and the CROWD goes wild! KERMIT
is waving his arms over his head.

                    SAM
                (VOICE OVER)
But, alas! It was only a dream.

THE CHEERING STOPS ABRUPTLY.
CUT TO:

#3. WALDORF and STATLER in a castle turret, dressed appropriately 16th Century.

                  WALDORF
This will be a knight to remember!

                  STATLER
              (CUPPING HIS EAR)
Remember what?

WALDORF

Not what, *who*!

STATLER

Who?

WALDORF

I said "who" first?

STATLER

Who's on first?

WALDORF

Never mind.

DISSOLVE TO:

#4. BLACKSMITH'S SHOP

KERMIT continues to hammer on his fingers.

FOZZIE

Oh, Master? You remember when I told you about my aunt? The one who has ye oldie gout? And you said that was too bad? Well, she's in ye oldie hospital. And, ye oldie visiting hours are almost over. And I was wondering if I could get off a little early . . .

KERMIT

Ouch! Get out of here.

FOZZIE

Yessir! Yessir! Yessir!

EXIT FOZZIE

KERMIT

Well, time to call it a day.

KERMIT stops hammering and struggles to haul the ANVIL over to a CLOSET. He starts painfully pushing it to the top shelf of the closet.

ENTER FOZZIE

> FOZZIE
>
> Oh, Master! My aunt's coming home tomorrow. And I was wondering if I could get the afternoon off to take her to the turnip fair?

FOZZIE distracts KERMIT so that the anvil slips and hits KERMIT on the head. He collapses to the floor.

RIPPLE DISSOLVE TO:

#5. KERMIT comes to. However, now he is dressed in make-shift KNIGHT'S ARMOR created from pipes and pans and other items from around the blacksmith's shop. It "sort of" resembles his armor from his first dream sequence. KERMIT speaks with a SLIGHT REVERB since he's wearing a helmet. The armor squeaks and rattles when he moves.

> FOZZIE
>
> Oh, Master! Master, are you all right?

> KERMIT
>
> Of course I'm all right! T'will take more than a bump in a fencing exercise to defeat Don La Rana de la Mancha, soon to be knighted *Sir* Don La Rana de la Mancha.

> FOZZIE
> (TO CAMERA)
>
> "La Rana" I think that's Spanish for, "frog".

TRUMPET FANFARE

> KERMIT
>
> The Frog of La Mancha! I fence with the best of them!

FOZZIE

But, we're not in the fencing business! Your brother-in-law's in the fencing business. You used to be partners. You hated the fencing business! We're blacksmiths! I'm your apprentice . . .

KERMIT

You, my impudent clod, are my squire, *Tuck*, and would do well to keep your mouth shut.

FOZZIE

Yessir! Yessir! Yessir! (TO CAMERA) Squire Tuck?

KERMIT

But before I can take my rightful place in heraldry as Sir Don de la Rana . . .

TRUMPET FANFARE!

KERMIT

Frog of La Mancha, I must be formally knighted by a proper liege in a proper castle.

FOZZIE

We're going to a castle?

KERMIT

Pack up, squire, for soon we leave this hovel.

FOZZIE

We're leaving the *hovel*? And going to a *castle*!?

KERMIT

Make haste! And don't forget to pack my knight shirt.

FOZZIE EXITS and RETURNS with a NIGHTSHIRT.

KERMIT

Not the nightshirt! The knight-knight shirt!

FOZZIE
Not the nightshirt, the night-night shirt! Yessir! Yessir! Ohhhh!

DISSOLVE TO:

#6. EXT: COUNTRYSIDE.

KERMIT, in his home made armor, is mounted astride an impossibly sway back MUPPET HORSE. FOZZIE is astride a MUPPET MULE. Both mounts are articulated and are Muppet characters. (They will prove to be the most erudite characters in this production, carrying on their own conversation while completely oblivious to the rest of the action.)

CUT TO: KERMIT'S POINT-OF-VIEW through his helmet slot. A beautiful castle appears on the horizon.

KERMIT
What ho! A castle! I'm sure yon liege of yon castle would be happy to knight me.

CUT TO: FOZZIE'S POINT-OF-VIEW. The "CASTLE" is actually an INN.

FOZZIE
A castle? Oh, A castle! I'm sure yon liege in yon castle would be happy to knight you. And maybe even put us up and feed us for a forte-month or two.

KERMIT'S HORSE
(TO MULE)
I think, therefore I am. That's a philosophy?

FOZZIE'S MULE
It was good enough for Rene Descarte.

CUT TO:

#7. STATLER & WALDORF

WALDORF
Finally!

STATLER

What?

WALDORF

Somebody put *Descarte* before the horse!

CUT BACK TO:

#8. COUNTRYSIDE

They approach the "CASTLE"/INN. A sign proclaims it, "Ye Olde Hog Farm." Basically, it's a 16th Century biker bar. Tied up out front are ENORMOUS LIVE HOGS, outfitted with fringed SADDLEBAGS, WINDSHIELDS, TRACER LIGHTS, AND MOTORCYCLE SEATS.

KERMIT

They call these horses? My brave steed could out run them any day!

FOZZIE

I'd say that's a distinct possibility, Sire.

CUT TO:

#9. INTERIOR: HOG FARM.

The inn is crowded with PIGS. They're dressed in 16TH CENTURY GARB, but it's all black leather and festooned with ZIPPERS. There's a pig band playing that ol' country favorite, *In a Pig's Eye!* Several pig couples are dancing on the floor.

CUT TO:

THE KITCHEN FOOD SLOT.

PIGGY, dressed in a GINGHAM 16TH CENTURY WAITRESS'S UNIFORM is yelling into the kitchen.

PIGGY

One Crusader Special! Hold the gruel! Burn the heretics twice! Give me a Saracen on a raft! And Draw two meads! Chop Chop!

The SWEDISH CHEF, muttering to himself in Swedish, brings several dishes over to the counter.

Cut back to the pig band and dancers. The MUSIC SEGUES into a FLAMENCO VERSION of The Muppet Show AT-THE-DANCE THEME.

The couples do three, very droll, 16th Century Spain, At-the-Dance jokes which I don't have time to write right now.

CUT TO:

KERMIT and FOZZIE at a table.

ENTER PIGGY

PIGGY

Hi. I'm Porcenea. I'll be serving thee tonight. What'll it be, boys.

FOZZIE

Forsooth! How dare you address us so! Do you not recognize Sir Don de la Mancha, the Frog of La Mancha.

(TRUMPET FANFARE)

FOZZIE

And, I, his squire, Tuck?

FOZZIE twirls his finger around the side of his head, making the, "He's crazy" motion.

PIGGY
(SARCASTICALLY)

Of course, the Frog of La Mancha! And his Squire, Tuck. And how are vous today?

286

KERMIT looks at PIGGY for the first time. He FREEZES, DUMBSTRUCK WITH LOVE.

MUSIC: HEART SWELLING HARPS AND VIOLINS!!!

KERMIT IS INSTANTLY SMITTEN!

PIGGY DISSOLVES from the common place waitress into a BEAUTIFUL PRINCESS.

                    KERMIT
Oh, Princess Porcinea! Would'st thou be my lady?

                    PIGGY
                  (SWEETLY)
Well, for how long? I have to lock up later tonight.

                    KERMIT
Forever and a day. I want you to be mine and only mine forever. I will take you
to live in my castle in the lap of luxury.

                    PIGGY
Really?! In that case, speaking of laps . . .

PIGGY jumps into KERMIT's lap.

                    KERMIT
But before I propose formally, I must be properly knighted by the liege of this
castle. Do you think your father would do the honors?

                    PIGGY
And then you'll propose, and take me to your castle with its lap of luxury?

                    KERMIT
Yes, dear Princess.

                    PIGGY
Stay right there!

EXIT PIGGY. She returns with the SWEDISH CHEF, He is carrying a LADLE.

PIGGY drags the SWEDISH CHEF over to KERMIT. She whispers in his ear.

PIGGY

. . . And don't foul it up!

KERMIT drops to one knee. The chef lays the ladle over his shoulder and knights him in ragtime Swedish.

KERMIT

Are you sure that's Spanish?

PIGGY

That's *northern* Spanish. Very *northern*.

The Swedish Chef EXITS

KERMIT Still on one knee produces a RING.

KERMIT

Please accept this ring as a symbol of my troth, er, *trooothe*. Fair Princess, will you be my wife and Lady?

PIGGY

I sure will!

The MUSIC swells.

CUT TO: SAM

SAM

And so, the Sir Don La Rana de la Mancha, The Frog of La Mancha (TRUMPET FANFARE) became betrothed to Princess Porcinea de la Clevelando-Ohocho. (*A cocktail waitress?!.*)

CUT BACK TO:

#10. THE INN, which is now the CASTLE. KERMIT and PIGGY are dressed appropriately as knight and princess. FOZZIE is holding KERMIT's CAPE TRAIN. The pig bikers are now all dressed as KNIGHTS AND LADIES. The pigs' armor squeaks as they walk.

PIGGY

And when shall we be wed, *Ranalito?*

KERMIT

As soon as I complete my quest.

PIGGY

And, what are you being tested for?

KERMIT

Not test! Quest. Every self respecting knight has a quest.

PIGGY

And what, pray tell, is your quest, Sir Don?

KERMIT

That's the problem. I haven't come up with one yet. You could say I'm questing after my quest.

PIGGY

Well, snap to it! And, until you do, the wedding is off!

EXIT PIGGY

KERMIT

Yes, dear. Maybe I'll ask some of the other knights. Oh, sir?

All the MALE PIGS turn around and answer in unison.

PIGS

Yes!

KERMIT
(TO THE CLOSEST PIG KNIGHT)
I was wondering, do you know a good quest?

PIG

There is one quest to which every great knight aspires. But none has succeeded yet.

2nd PIG

Aye! All of us have aspired to it.

3rd PIG

But none have succeeded. (SQUEAKING PAST) Most knights wouldst be content just to borrow this quest.

KERMIT

What the heck is it?

4th PIG
(SQUEAKING PAST)
The Quest for the Golden Oil Can!

KERMIT

The Golden Oil Can. I get it. A little knight humor there. Good night! Anything else?

PIG

Well, you might try slaying a dragon.

KERMIT

A dragon? Hmmmm. (TO FOZZIE) How big is a dragon?

FOZZIE

Oh, they come in all sizes. Large, medium, small . . . petite.

PIG

Yeah. But de bomb these days in Madrid is slaying a four-headed dragon.

FOZZIE

Dragons have foreheads?

PIG

Not foreheads. Four heads!

FOZZIE

Well, don't those four heads have foreheads? That's four foreheads on four heads.

KERMIT

Forsooth That will be my quest! I will slay a four headed dragon! (TO PIG) Where do I find a dragon?

PIG

Try the telephone tome.

KERMIT

We're off to slay a dragon!

KERMIT and FOZZIE EXIT

CUT TO:

#11. EXT INN.

KERMIT and FOZZIE do a "We're off to slay a dragon!" MUSICAL NUMBER. ("We're gonna barbeque the gizzard of that lizard!" "We're gonna hit him in the snout and put his fires out!"))

CUT TO:
#12 STATLER & WALDORF

STATLER:

Boy! That dragon's in trouble now!

WALDORF

Yeah! He could get warts.

KERMIT:

(OFF CAMERA)

Frogs don't give you warts! Toads give you warts!

CUT TO:

#13. SAM

SAM

And so, Sir Don La Rava, Frog of La Mancha (TRUMPET FANFARE) and his faithful Squire, Tuck. set off on their quest to slay a dragon.

DISSOLVE TO:

#14. Witch

GUEST STAR CAMEO

DISSOLVE TO: ENCHANTED FOREST (We know it's enchanted because the sign says so).

KERMIT AND FOZZIE, astride their steeds are traveling through the ENCHANTED FOREST. They come upon a WITCH at her caldron.

KERMIT asks the witch if she has seem a dragon.

She replies that a dragon just left after he finished building a shelter for homeless kittens. She reveals a toad has put a curse on her.

WITCH:

You're not a *toad* are you?

KERMIT:

No! I'm a frog.

WITCH:
(POINTING AT A WART ON HER NOSE)
Toads give you warts, you know.

KERMIT

I know!

She was once a striking beauty. Then the toad put a spell on her. Now she has to kiss a frog to break the spell.

KERMIT does not want to kiss her.

FOZZIE
You'd kiss a pig. What's the big deal, sire?

KERMIT

I am betrothed!

KERMIT struggles. But the witch kisses him and turns back into a beauty. She is so happy she kisses him again and turns back into a witch.

Now, the witch want to kiss KERMIT again to get her beauty back. He refuses. She forces KERMIT to kiss her. He turns into a handsome prince. She kisses him again and he turns back into a frog. WITCH FAINTS.

DISSOLVE TO:

#15. Windmill No. 1:

UP ON: SMALL 16th CENTURY SPANISH VILLAGE.

ENTER: KERMIT and FOZZIE, astride their mounts. The HORSE and MULE are deep in debate about the Copernican Theory of the Universe.

KERMIT
(TO A TOWNS PERSON)
What, ho! Good Towns person!

TOWNS PERSON

What ho, yourself, Frog.

KERMIT

We're on a quest for a dragon. Especially a four headed one.

FOZZIE

But, we'd settle for one with two . . . or even one heads.

KERMIT

Have you seen one hereabouts?

TOWNS PERSON

Let's see. Yep. There was a dragon around here about a week ago. He was fixing the roof on the Children's Wing of the town's only hospital. Don't know if he's still around.

KERMIT

What ho! You say!

KERMIT spots a WINDMILL. It"s four arms are rotating slowly.

As we dissolve into KERMIT's dream POINT-OF-VIEW., The WINDMILL DISSOLVES into a FOUR HEADED DRAGON.

KERMIT

Yon standith ye four headed dragon!

THE DRAGON HAS FOUR WORKING HEADS AND A PAIR OF WORKING CLAWS.

The DRAGON, holding a PLATE in one hand and a SPOON in the other is alternately feeding its first TWO HEADS.

1ˢᵗ DRAGON HEAD

You know, when you eat onions, I get gas!

THE THIRD HEAD IS LOOKING AROUND IDLY. THE FOURTH HEAD IS ASLEEP, SNORING.

294

KERMIT

Prepare to meet thy maker!

3rd DRAGON HEAD

Uh, oh!

KERMIT STARTS TO CHARGE THE DRAGON.

CUT TO FOZZIE IN THE REAL WORLD, WHERE THE DRAGON IS ACTUALLY A WINDMILL.

FOZZIE

But, Sire! That's a . . .

KERMIT CHARGES THE WINDMILL.

This particular windmill has a sign up, *La Moulin Rouge Restaurant Francais. French Bread, French Toast, French Fries on the French Cuff.*

FOZZIE

French Restaurant!

KERMIT CRASHES INTO THE WINDMILL. IT COLLAPSES.

AN ANGRY MOB CHASES KERMIT OUT OF THE RUBBLE.

ANGRY MOB

Chevrolay Coupay! Nanette Fabray! Maurice Chavelier! Zut alores! Look at ze legs on zat frog!

ANGRY DINERS CHASE KERMIT AND FOZZIE FOR A RAVE OFF.

DISSOLVE TO:

#16. COWS

UP ON KERMIT and FOZZIE on their mounts. They are trapped in a HERD OF
LOWING COWS.

                              KERMIT
Hey look, a bunch of cows.

                              FOZZIE
Not bunch. Herd.

                              KERMIT
Heard of what?

                              FOZZIE
Herd of cows.

                              KERMIT
Of course I've heard of cows.

                              FOZZIE
No, no, I mean the cow's herd!

                              KERMIT
I don't care if the cow's heard. I haven't said anything to be ashamed of.

(Humor me. Jerry Juhl told me this was Jim favorite piece of corny dialogue.)

DISSOLVE
#17.   Windmill No. 2:

UP ON: ANOTHER SMALL 16th CENTURY SPANISH VILLAGE.

ENTER: KERMIT and FOZZIE, astride their mounts. The HORSE and MULE are
deep in debate about whether or not Bacon wrote Shakespeare's plays.

KERMIT inquires about a dragon. He's told there's a dragon around
somewhere creating a college scholarship fund for orphans..

KERMIT spots another WINDMILL and mistakes it for a DRAGON.

Again, he TILTS at it.

> FOZZIE
> But sire! That windmill's a catapult factory!

SFX: *SPROOONG!   SPROOONG!   SPROOONG!   SPROOONG!   SPROOONG! SPROOONG!*

THE WINDMILL COLLAPSES.

LARGE BOULDERS raining on the village as the TOWNSPEOPLE run KERMIT and FOZZIE out of town.

FADE

#18. GIANT

KERMIT and FOZZIE meet a Giant. Possible Guest Star Cameo.

(TBA)

#19. Pigs In Lace.

KERMIT and FOZZIE have to cross a river. FOZZIE sees a BARGE. But KERMIT sees it as a SPANISH GALLEON, La Titanica, and discovers it's manned by CAPT. HOGTHROB, DR. STRANGEPORK and PIGGY. All three of them are in 16th Century naval officers' uniforms dripping ostentatiously with LACE.

> KERMIT
> Porcinea! What are you doing here?

> PIGGY
> Oh, tee hee! You've mistaken me for my older, *heavier* sister. I'm Baconea. The cute one.

Somehow the three pigs manage to hit a iceberg and sink the Galleon.

DISSOLVE TO:

#20. Windmill No. 3:

UP ON: YET ANOTHER SMALL 16th CENTURY SPANISH VILLAGE.

ENTER: KERMIT and FOZZIE, astride their mounts. The HORSE and MULE are deep in debate about the Metaphysical Aspects of French Existentialism.

KERMIT inquires about a dragon. He's told there's a dragon around somewhere running a soup kitchen for the homeless.

KERMIT spots another WINDMILL and mistakes it for a DRAGON.

Again, he TILTS at it.

                                    FOZZIE
But sire! That windmill's the bee keeper's house!

SFX: Buzzzzzzzzzzzzzz! Buzzzzzzzzzzzzzz! Buzzzzzzzzzzzzzz! Buzzzzzzzzzzzzzz!

THE WINDMILL COLLAPSES.

The TOWNSPEOPLE, chased by an angry swarm of bees run KERMIT and FOZZIE out of town.

FADE

#21. MUPPET ALCHEMISTS

MUSIC: MUPPET LAB THEME

UP ON: 16th CENTURY LAB. A SQUARE GLOBE prominent in the BACKGROUND. In the center is the TRANSITRON, an enclosed booth with a door in front, festooned with 16th Century scientific equipment. Dr. Bunsen Honeydew and his assistant, Beaker, are standing in front.

                                    BUNSEN
Welcome to Muppet Alchemists, where the future was made yesterday.
Today we're going to demonstrate our latest invention, the Transitron. This
little baby right here. The Transitron can transform anything into anything
else. "Oh ho!", you scoff. Allow me to demonstrate. *They say* you cant make
a silk purse out of a sow's ear. Child splay.

Bunsen hands Beaker a SOW'S EAR, with the SOW still attached, kicking and
bellowing. He pushes the protesting Beaker and the cranky SOW into the
Transitron and slams the door.

                                    BUNSEN
Now, I'll just throw the switch . . .

Bunsen throws an enormous SWITCH in the side of the Transitron.

Immediately there is a deafening CRASH OF THUNDER and spectacular FLASH
OF ELECTRICAL CURRENT through the Transitron. After a moment, Bunsen
opens the door.

A frazzled and confused Beaker emerges, followed by a sow who's EARS have
been replaced by SILK PURSES.

                                    BUNSEN
Ta-Daa! Thank you Beaker. But, you say, you're still skeptical. You probably
don't think I can make dross into gold. That got your interest. Well,, nothing
could be simpler. Get the dross, beaker!

Enter Beaker pushing an enormous PILE OF DROSS. (We know it's dross
because it's labeled as such.) Beaker protests loudly. But Bunsen pushes
Beaker and the dross into the Transitron, and closes the door.

                                    BUNSEN
Of course, we'll need a little more power.

BUNSEN throws the switch. A stronger, louder and longer jolt of electricity
bolt through the chamber.

When the charge is over, Bunsen opens the door revealing a fried Beaker holding a very small lump of gold.

BUNSEN

And, finally *they say* you can't make a tiger change his stripes.

Beaker reacts.

BUNSEN

Here, kitty, kitty, kitty.

ENTER FEROCIOUS TIGER

BUNSEN

Okay, Beaker. You know what to do.

Bunsen ushers the TIGER AND A very unwilling Beaker in to the chamber, closes the door and throws the switch.

Even more electricity again surges through the chamber. Then WE HEAR the tiger attacking Beaker. The chamber rocks dramatically back and forth. The door bursts open.

Beaker rushes out, followed by the now MULTI-COLORED, POLKA DOT TIGER. They run across the frame several times for a rave off.

FADE

#22. Windmill No. 4:

UP ON: YET ANOTHER SMALL 16th CENTURY SPANISH VILLAGE.

ENTER: KERMIT and FOZZIE, astride their mounts. The HORSE and MULE are busy declining irregular French verbs.

KERMIT inquires about a dragon. He's told there's a dragon down at the sit-in for clean water. Actually, only two heads were for clean water. The other two wanted to go to the clean air demonstration.

KERMIT spots another WINDMILL and mistakes it for a DRAGON.

Again, he TILTS at it.

FOZZIE
But sire! That windmill's the town fish factory!

THE WINDMILL COLLAPSES.

Thousands of fish rain on the village as the TOWNSPEOPLE run KERMIT and FOZZIE out of town.

FADE

#23. JOUST TBA. But, it will not go well for KERMIT. Possible Guest Cameo Spot.

#24. VET'S HOSPITAL:

UP ON 16TH CENTURY VERSION OF VET'S HOSPITAL

KERMIT is the patient, dressed in his make-shift armor. His horse is in the background.

PIGGY
Oh, Doctor Roberto! We've been waiting hours for this patient!

ROLF
Just what I need! Another late knight!

KERMIT
Porcinea! Or is it Baconea?

PIGGY
Wrong, again. I'm their much younger and cuter sister, Traifinea

KERMIT FAINTS

JANICE

Oh, Doctor Roberto, is this operation going to take all night?

ROLF

Not all knight. Just the damaged parts. But it won't be simple.

PIGGY

Why not?

ROLF

With all that armor, t'wil be a long day's journey into knight. (ASIDE) That just dawned on me.

JANICE

Oh, Doctor Roberto, what shall we do with his horse?

ROLF

You mean that nightmare!?

HORSE

That's knight's mare!

ROLF

I was right the first time!

PIGGY

Why not get him a night cap?

HORSE

I look silly in hats!

ANNR
(VOICE OVER)

Tune in another night for another knight's night on Veterinarian's Hospital!

ROLF

Good night!

302

FADE

#25. KERMIT Meets the Dragon

UP ON: THE DRAGON

All four heads are wearing BOATER STRAW HATS. He is holding a PITCH PIPE in one hand and a STEIN OF BEER in the other. All four heads are drinking from the stein.

The FOUR HEADS argue about who's drinking too much and who's going to drive home..

The FIRST HEAD blows a note on the PITCH PIPE.

The FOUR HEADS break into four part BARBERSHOP QUARTET HARMONY

SONG: *Four Heads are Better Than One.* (TBA)

ENTER KERMIT and FOZZIE.

KERMIT

Aha!!! There you are dragon! Your day of reckoning has come!

1st DRAGON HEAD

Say! Isn't this the clown who's been busting up windmills all over the country?

2nd DRAGON HEAD

Didn't he put a curse on a beautiful maiden, too?

3rd DRAGON HEAD

Yeah! Turned her into a witch!

4th DRAGON HEAD

And then there was that unpleasant business with the giant. Why, he's a menace to the community.

KERMIT

No use trying to talk your self . . . selves out of it. I'm here to slay you!

THE DRAGON HEADS break into UPROARIOUS LAUGHTER.

1st DRAGON HEAD

Keep it up! You've already got us rolling in the aisles already!

KERMIT

It is I, Sir Don La Rava, Frog of La Mancha (TRUMPET FANFARE) and his faithful Squire, Tuck.

FOZZIE

I'm just an innocent bystander.

KERMIT

In accordance with my sacred quest, I am here to slay the dragon, as a demonstration of my loyalty and courage so I may be initiated into the Brotherhood of Knights of the Round table.

1st DRAGON HEAD

I think this guy is serious.

2nd DRAGON HEAD

Maybe he has unresolved anger issues.

3rd DRAGON HEAD

My sister had that.

4th DRAGON HEAD

Mine, too! (TO KERMIT) You should get some counseling for that.

KERMIT

Prepare to defend thyself! I dedicate this dragon to my beloved, the Lady Porcinea. I will lay his ears and his tail at her feet.

1st DRAGON HEAD

Ouch!!!

2nd DRAGON HEAD

What kind of nobleman shows his love for his lady fair by slaying a poor defenseless dragon?

3rd DRAGON HEAD

Yeah. And just when we had a record deal!

KERMIT

But dragons are evil! They do terrible things!

4th DRAGON HEAD

Like building a kitten's shelter?

1st DRAGON HEAD

Or opening a soup kitchen for homeless?

2nd DRAGON HEAD

And re-roofing the children's hospital?

3rd DRAGON HEAD

We even recycle!

4th DRAGON HEAD

On the other hand, who's been running around destroying catapult factories?

1st DRAGON HEAD

And bee hives?

2nd DRAGON HEAD

And fish houses?

4th DRAGON HEAD

And one *excellent* French restaurant?

KERMIT

Well, there were technical difficulties involved. But, I guess I did.

KERMIT AND THE DRAGON segue into a big musical number with a chorus of Muppets about making up and loving thy neighborhood dragon.

At end of song:

1st DRAGON HEAD

Say, frog. Want to take a little tilt at me?

2nd DRAGON HEAD

Just for fun?

3rd DRAGON HEAD

Just be careful with that pointy thing.

KERMIT

I don't know. How do I know you won't turn into another windmill?

4th DRAGON HEAD

Wouldn't think of it!

1st DRAGON HEAD

Heaven forfend!

2nd DRAGON HEAD

Scout's honor!

HORSE

Here we go again.

KERMIT charges the DRAGON.

3rd DRAGON HEAD

Not!!!

The dragon, again, turns into a WINDMILL. KERMIT crashed into it.

DISSOLVE TO:

#26. BLACKSMITH SHOP.

KERMIT IS COMING TO AND STRUGGLING TO HIS FEET.

                          FOZZIE
Master! You were out for a long time!

                          KERMIT
What happened?

                          FOZZIE
The usual windmill complication.

                          KERMIT
It was another dream! I was a knight! I had a lady! I coulda been a contender!
But I'm nothing! I'm just a lowly blacksmith! Now, I'll never have Porcenea!

SFX: KNOCKING ON DOOR.

                          KERMIT
Yes!

                          PIGGY
Is there a blacksmith in the house? I broke my trombone and I can't go another
day without it!

                          KERMIT
Blacksmith on duty!

ENTER PIGGY

KERMIT looks at PIGGY for the first time. He freezes, dumbstruck with love.

MUSIC: HEART SWELLING HARPS AND VIOLINS!!!

KERMIT and PIGGY are instantly smitten with each other!

KERMIT

Oh, Porcenea! I am not a knight of the round or any table. I am but a lowly blacksmith.

PIGGY

And I am but a cocktail waitress. My name is Shirley.

KERMIT

But you're my cocktail waitress.

PIGGY

And, you're my frog!

THE MUSIC SWELLS! KERMIT and PIGGY SEGUE into a live song for the closing number (TBA), cementing their love forever.

THE END

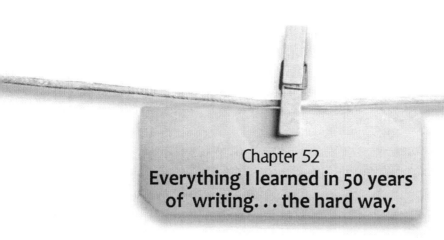

Chapter 52
Everything I learned in 50 years of writing... the hard way.

've always considered myself to be a lunch pail writer. I've written print and broadcast advertising, public relations, stage, screen, record albums and radio. I've done just about everything to make a living as a writer except journalist and novelist, and I'm not finished yet. But, there are similarities that run through most writing jobs. .

Outlines: Whether it's a novel, a script or a letter to your mother, do an outline, first. If you're writing fact, it will force you to present your material as logically as possible.

If you're writing fiction, outlining a story forces you to deal with it in a practical manner. Are the characters interesting enough? Does the story have enough plot points to sustain a novel or a feature film? Do an outline and you'll find out.

If you just start writing with an idea and no outline, you can waste days or even weeks creating characters, writing chapters, or scenes that you may have to throw out later because they didn't fit the final story line when it finally got worked out.

This book started with an outline. So did this chapter.

Deadlines: The job of a professional writer is to produce acceptable results in an expected amount of time. You have to learn to evaluate your given message with the time, money and space available to communicate it.

Imagine you're a newspaper reporter. You're standing on a street corner and you witness a murder. "A" shoots "B" in front of you. You run to your newspaper, tell the editor, and he says, "Give me 1,000 words for the next deadline.", which is an hour away.

That's journalism. Describe a murder in 1,000 words in one hour. You can practice by describing anything you've seen in 1,000 words in one hour -- washing the dog, getting your oil changed, buying fish. But remember: Keep it interesting.

Journalists are the most deadline conscious writers. They face deadlines all day long. So, if you can't turn out large amounts of copy in a very short time, stay away from journalism. Maybe you should get the novel out from the bottom drawer. Novel deadlines are measured in months and years.

But, whether it's advertising, journalism or television, if you have a writing job, you'll be told what to write, how much time or space you have to fill, and when it's due. Not missing deadlines should be a point of honor among professional writers. On the other hand, don't make promises you can't keep.

There's also a school of thought against turning in a project before the deadline. The belief is that if you turn in an assignment *before* the deadline, the client might think you didn't make your best effort. It also gives him more time to meddle with it.

There is a story about Neil Simon and his brother, Danny, who was also his writing partner. The two were working on a script that was due on a Thursday. But they turned in on Tuesday. The producer immediately gave them a load of rewrites.

On Thursday, they handed in the same script they had given the producer on Tuesday.

"I rejected this script on Tuesday! What makes you think I'll accept it now!?"

"Because", the brothers replied, "It's Thursday."

Of course, it helps if your last name is Simon.

All Nighters: There's an old writing cliche that the best writing happens when you're really up against a deadline. The prescribed method is to don a black turtleneck, get two packs of Camels and a bottle of vodka, and sit at the keyboard until 3:00 a.m. Then, when you're half in the bag and have coughed yourself raw, the project will magically write itself.

This belief became popular in English Comp. classes. The people who practice it are known as "D" Students. As soon as you decide on a project or get an assignment, do an outline and get started on a draft as soon as possible. That's how the grown-ups do it.

Re-writing: If you think every word in your first draft is golden and unchangeable, you're in the wrong business. You're not finished until it's in the can, on the screen or on the press. As I've said before, all writing is re-writing. You might as well get used to it.

For example, if you write a feature script, it goes to your agent, then it goes to the producer, then it goes to the director and then it goes to the star. All of these people can and will ask for re-writes. The diplomacy and salesmanship I learned in advertising really comes in handy in these situations.

When I first started writing for *Sesame Street* there was a writer who would argue with Jon Stone when he said a sketch wasn't funny. Comedy is simple. If they laugh, it's funny. If they don't, it's not. How do you argue somebody into laughing? I was going to suggest to her that it was easier to write another sketch than it was to argue Jon into laughing. But, she had already been fired.

Indentured Servitude: Many inexperienced writers find themselves in a situation where they've settled on a flat fee for the job. But, they're working for someone who doesn't know what he wants, but he or she will know it when they see it. DON'T DO IT!!! If you're a writer in this situation, you've just sold yourself into indentured servitude. You could write for decades before the producer sees what he thinks he wants.

Take a tip from Jon Stone. Jon had a sampler over his desk that read, *Make the Deal First!* And the deal should include a limit on how much time you spend writing for the fee. (Jon also had another sampler that said, *Sue the Bastards!*)

Recently, I wrote an animation pilot for a half hour T.V. show with a friend of mine. Since it was animation, it wasn't covered by the Writers Guild of America, the writers' union that sets minimum fees for movies and television.

But, we based our deal on the Writers Guild rules. For the fee, we agreed to give the client an outline, two drafts and a polish. After that, if he still wasn't satisfied, it was time to re-negotiate, or get another writing team.

And, we included a payment schedule: One third at the beginning; one third after the second draft; and a third upon completion. We also guaranteed ourselves First Refusal of Producer and Head Writer jobs should the pilot go to series. (It didn't)

Spec Work: Sooner or later, every writer gets asks to write something on the come. In other words do a script for free for a producer who will pay you if and when he sells it. These things usually turn out badly. You don't see producers with spec dry cleaning, or a spec cell phone do you?

My usual response is that I've got all the spec work I can handle. And that should be true of every writer. If you're going to write for nothing, why not work on your own novel or screenplay or any other project that you will own completely?

I will make an exception if the producer will give me a one-page, simply-worded deal memo (they do exist) that doesn't require my hiring a lawyer, and gives me complete ownership of an acceptable (to me) percentage of the project. But, I'm not holding my breath.

Speech Writing: There are two well-known rules of speech or any presentation writing: "KISS!"; and the Three T's.

KISS: *Keep It Simple, Stupid!*

The Three T's: 1., Tell'em what you're gonna tell 'em; 2., Tell'em; 3., Then Tell'em what you just told'em.

Grammar: Learn it. It's hard enough to attract and keep a reader's attention without breaking their concentration with bad grammar. Bad grammar is like a piece of spinach in your teeth. It's distracting and not particularly attractive.

Paragraphs: (1) Try to avoid starting a paragraph with the word, "the." (2) Try to avoid starting consecutive paragraphs with the same word or letter.

Pet Peeves: (1) Everything isn't a challenge. There are real problems in the world. (2) Major events affect people's lives and sometimes leave them with grave *effects*. *Impact* is what happens when you walk into a door.

Jargon: Use it sparingly to make a point or add realism to a character. Otherwise, try to avoid it. Nothing ages faster than jargon. It goes from cool to corny in about a nanosecond.

Books: Several books are indispensable to writers. The first, of course, is the most comprehensive dictionary you can find. The next is, Roget's *Thesaurus*. Then John Bartlett's *Familiar Quotations*, but don't over use it. *The New York Times Manual of Style and Usage* is probably the most practical grammar book ever written. And, in case of dispute, remember, nobody can argue with *The New York Times*. Finally, if you're going to write a lot of fiction, a copy of, *What to Name the Baby*, is probably a good idea for finding character names.

Bad Days: You will have them. Everybody does.

Consistency: If you're serious about writing, you have to make it and reading a habitual part of your daily life. You should also have two or three original ideas that you turn over daily.

Getting Started: It seems like I spend 90 percent of my writing time trying to get started. If you're a real eager beaver, you can skip the next couple of paragraphs. But, if you're like me, there are a few things you can do to make starting to write easier.

Firstly, make a place to write. A place that when you're there you're all about the business of writing. An architect friend suggests that if you have a view of distance or sky from your work place it aids creativity. I suspect he's right. I write close to a window with an excellent view of my neighborhood.

Secondly, find the time of day when you're most creative. Some people are early morning writers. I, myself, am an afternoon/early evening writer.

Then, make sure you're at your writing spot at your most creative time of day. On those days when you're not on fire with creativity and bursting with ideas, go over what you've previously written. There's always something that needs a little tightening up. And sometimes, that will ease you into your writing mode.

Crossword Puzzles: Many writers, myself included, warm up to write by doing a crossword puzzle. It's a bit like hitting the driving range before you start on the course. You're playing with language. Is this clue a noun or a verb? Is it a pun? Is there a theme running through the puzzle? All of this gets your brain working in the right direction to write.

Now, here are a few serious things I learned about writing comedy.

Truth in Comedy: As I've said before, the secret of comedy is telling the truth. The trick is to tell it just before the audience realizes it.

Carl Reiner once told of emceeing a benefit in Hollywood. On the bill was a well-known mentalist. He came on stage and did 20 minutes of wonderful tricks. Then he continued for another half hour, at which point people were nodding off or going to the bar.

Finally, he finished and left the stage. At that moment, Mr. Reiner took the microphone and said, "Ladies and Gentlemen, wouldn't you think that someone who bills himself as the World's Greatest Mind Reader would realize he was boring 12 hundred people to death?"

Timing in Comedy: Equally important to truth in comedy is timing. To paraphrase that great choreographer, Twyla Tharp: In comedy, as in bank robbery, timing is everything.

Don Hinkley had an anecdote that summed it up beautifully:

Don was working late one night at CBS Television City in Los Angeles. Walking through the parking lot on the way to his car, he passed Red Skelton's limousine. At the time, Red Shelton had the hottest comedy/variety show on television. Skelton and his head writer were having a script meeting in the car, probably because the limo had a bar in the back.

As Don passed the car, he heard Red Skelton say, "There's too many words before chopped liver."

Here's an example of what he meant:

An "insult" comedian named Fat Jack E. Leonard had a heckler line, *Why don't you walk into a parking meter and violate yourself?*

Not a bad joke. But if he had said, *Why don't you go outside, wander around for a while and have a collision with a parking meter, the result of which would be violation?*, it doesn't quite work. Does it? Too many words before chopped liver.

Acting: Although I've written for dozens of actors. The only acting advice I've heard that ever made any sense was the answer the great Spencer Tracy gave a young actor. When asked what the secret of acting was, Tracy replied. "Just don't let 'em catch you doing it.."

Blue Material and the Cheap Laugh: Funny is funny, even if it's off color. But, bad blue material can lead you into the realm of the Cheap Laugh. Here's how it works:

If an X-rated joke or line of dialogue is truly funny, women will laugh as much as men will. But, many women are offended by dirty jokes that are just crude and not funny, and rightly so. In a one-on-one situation these women would tell you off (or maybe slap your face).

But in a broad social situation like a nightclub or theater, woman will smooth it over with a lifeless titter. And that's the Cheap Laugh, the sign of a bad comic or lazy comedy writer.

Know the Show: If you're lucky enough to get a job writing on a television show, your job is to be a part of a team. Write the show you're working on. Write in its style and sensitivity.

For a while, I was responsible for finding new writing talent for *Sesame Street*. I interviewed applicants with many advanced English degrees. I told them to watch the show and get the feel of it. I told them about the three and a half-minute time limit. Then I asked them to write some audition material.

What I got back was no less than amazing. One sketch was more than ten minutes long. Another was a full Muppet opera. But the one that won (or lost), hands down, was a piece in which Ernie's pal, Bert, contemplated suicide. Needless to say, none of these people got hired.

Autobiographic Material: I've just discovered it's the most difficult thing in the world to write.

Viva Rameau!